Guillermo Cabrera Infante

Assays, Essays, and Other Arts

Barco de Aire, 1995, from the series *Ships of the Elements*, oil on wood, 48″ diameter
Lydia Rubio

Guillermo Cabrera Infante
ASSAYS, ESSAYS, AND OTHER ARTS

edited by
ARDIS L. NELSON
East Tennessee State University

Twayne Publishers
New York

Guillermo Cabrera Infante: Assays, Essays, and Other Arts
Ardis L. Nelson

Twayne Publishers
1633 Broadway
New York, NY 10019

Library of Congress Cataloging-in-Publication Data

Guillermo Cabrera Infante : assays, essays and other arts / edited by Ardis L. Nelson.
p. cm.
Includes bibliographical references and index.
Contents: The years at Bohemia and Carteles / Raymond D. Souza — Lunes de Revolución : literature and culture in the first years of the Cuban Revolution / William Luis —Icosaedros : the English letters / Carlos Cuadra — The cinematic imagination / Raymond D. Souza — Movies and mock encomia / Kenneth Hall — Life with the silver screen : cine o sardina / Kenneth Hall — Literary friends at the movies : Guillermo Cabrera Infante and Manuel Puig / Suzanne Jill Levine — On Borges / Carlos Cuadra — The translator within : a conversation with Guillermo Cabrera Infante / Suzanne Jill Levine — Mea Cuba : critical readings from exile / Justo C. Ulloa and Leonor A. Ulloa — On Buñuel and surrealism : the art of audacity / Ardis L. Nelson — Up in smoke / Regina Janes — Mea Cuba : the "Proust -Valía" of history / Nedda G. de Anhalt.
ISBN 0-8057-1644-0 (alk. paper)
1. Cabrera Infante, G. (Guillermo), 1929- —Criticism and interpretation. I. Nelson, Ardis L.
PQ7389.C233Z66 1999
863—dc21 98-49188
CIP

This paper meets the requirements of ANSI/NISO Z3948-1992 (Permanence of Paper).

10 9 8 7 6 5 4 3 2 1

Printed in the United States of America

For my parents

Hazel Adale

and

Louis Orvil Nelson

and their pioneering spirit.

Contents

◆

Foreword

◆

Guillermo Cabrera Infante is—despite the best efforts of political thugs on and off the island—the quintessential Cuban writer. But, as his idol Lewis Carroll undoubtedly would have quipped: Is he a Cuban who is a writer or a writer who is Cuban? Now that Spain has bestowed the Cervantes Prize on him—the highest honor an author in the Spanish-speaking world can receive—the answer might be: he is a writer who happens to be Cuban. His cultural patrimony is absolutely Cuban, but his true tradition embraces both the Old and the New Worlds. *Habanero* ("habanidad de habanidades, todo es habanidad" as he has often said) in his fiction, Guillermo Cabrera Infante is a citizen of the world in his nonfiction, which is as important as his novels and stories, though, unfortunately, not as widely known or studied.

Jorge Luis Borges once said that more than just a writer, the Spanish baroque poet Francisco de Quevedo was an entire literature. The same idea defines Cabrera Infante, whose writing is in every instance a verbal adventure in which the question of style—consubstantial in his case with that of content—is of paramount importance. For that reason, his impact on the Spanish language has been, is, and will be immense. He inherited a Cuban literary language for his fiction, one he could love and simultaneously parody, as the section on the death of Trotsky in *Tres tristes tigres* deftly reveals. But to develop his own style in nonfiction writing, he had to scour the pan-Hispanic tradition and look beyond it into the French and Anglo-American worlds. Like all Latin American writers, he evolves by assimilating and modifying his readings until he makes them his own.

The problem is that his critics, until now, have been unable to recognize the organic unity of his writing, the fact that, as with Jorge Luis Borges, we cannot read his fiction without taking into account his nonfiction. The truth of this statement is clear to anyone who has tried to read his 1963 volume *Un oficio del siglo veinte*, the collected film criticism of G. Caín, Cabrera Infante's alter ego during the Fulgencio Batista era, when, forbidden to publish under his own name, he amalgamated the Ca of Cabrera with the In of Infante to create a cursed film critic. Caín dies, but his writing and life are commemorated by Cabrera Infante in an introduction that threatens to transform critical essays into chapters in a novel by transforming Caín into a character in the way Machado de Assis's Brás Cubas posthumously turns himself into the hero of a novel.

All too often in Spanish America, the essayistic or journalistic writings of authors celebrated for their fiction are lost until some pious editor resurrects them. And all too often in Spanish America, that resurrection is posthumous, so what is frequently a considerable portion of a given writer's total output remains unseen and unstudied during his or her lifetime. Borges is the most obvious Spanish American example, and his affinities with Cabrera Infante are elucidated here. Until recently, Borges's early writings, the books of essays he published during the twenties, were all but inaccessible. Only now, more than a decade after Borges's death, are they being republished, though without annotation they are impenetrable to most readers.

Assays, Essays, and Other Arts is, therefore, an important document in the history of Spanish American literary criticism, a tribute both to Cabrera Infante and to his critic Ardis L. Nelson. Only someone with her extensive knowledge of Cabrera Infante's writings could see why this volume is so urgently needed, but it is Nelson's love of Cabrera Infante's writing that has impelled her to gather these essays. These attempts to come to grips with Cabrera Infante's nonfiction writing now while he is still producing it at a prodigious rate are of paramount importance both for understanding his total literary production and for understanding the growth of a Cuban imagination as it has evolved in the crucible of exile.

These studies are important precisely because they contain the opinions of living critics about the living author, opinions future readers will need in order to understand Cabrera Infante in context, to trace the patterns in a sensibility that develops on the interface between the verbal and the visual, between experience and nostalgia, and between autobiography and fiction. Like all essays since Michel de Montaigne gave them their definitive form, Cabrera Infante's begin with a personal point of view—whether he is meditating on a painting by Pieter Breughel or a film by Howard Hawks. That point of view is Cuban because that is what Cabrera Infante is, but it is how that point of view teases out meanings and nuances in the subject that fascinates me, because we see the fusion of the observer with the object under scrutiny. Cabrera Infante's *écriture* is a seamless web in that it is his personality we see wherever we look, but what these examinations of his nonfiction reveal is the fertility of his imagination and the extraordinary power of his intellect.

ALFRED MAC ADAM
Barnard College–Columbia University

Preface

◆

This book is a celebration of Guillermo Cabrera Infante's essays and film scripts. The original plan was to publish an annotated bibliography of his vast body of essays that are not well known outside of Spain and England. In my search for Cabrera Infante's essays I came to realize that to find them all would be a monumental task and one that Richard Cacchione had already begun. A more useful contribution at this time would be to bring Cabrera Infante's essays and film writing to light for the reading public.

The contributors to this book are distinguished scholars and critics who know and appreciate Cabrera Infante's life and work. To each of them I am most grateful.

On two occasions I worked directly with Miriam Gómez and Cabrera Infante at 53 Gloucester Road in London, where they allowed me access to their personal archives. I am indebted to Miriam and Guillermo for their openness, collaboration, and encouragement since we first met in 1980.

My deepest appreciation goes to my life partner Victor Marma for moral support and unconditional assistance with research; to my sister Carol Tuynman for editing suggestions and assistance in the preparation of the manuscript, whether from Beaufort, New York, Johnson City, or Haines; and to Mingkwan Pongrakthai for organizing and retyping revisions of the chapters. Their commitment has been essential to the completion of this project.

I also extend my gratitude to my colleague Eduardo Zayas-Bazán for reading the manuscript and for offering insights into

Cuban history, to Kathy Martin for efficient secretarial support, and to Marsha Beeler, Margaret Day, Julie Umanova, Anupama Prasad, Alberto Ceffalo, Micah Holloway, Anna Johnson, Diana Poister, and Jacob Chávez for fact checking and proofreading at different stages of the project.

A special thanks goes to my graduate research assistant Marsha Beeler, my dear friend Brian Hedges, and to Kelly Hensley at East Tennessee State University's Sherrod Library interlibrary loan department for crucial assistance in tracking down bibliographic materials.

Chronology

◆

1929	Born April 22 in Gibara, Cuba, to Guillermo Cabrera, a journalist and typographer, and Zoila Infante, a local communist beauty.
1932	Gibara is bombed from the air on orders of General Machado. Begins to look at the funnies in the paper.
1933	Enters kindergarten, but becomes ill and is unable to go to school for the next two years.
1934	Teaches himself to read from comic strips.
1935	Enters Primary School at Los Amigos, a Quaker school.
1936	Parents are imprisoned for several months by the rural police for clandestine Communist Party meetings.
1937	Parents are freed; father unable to find work.
1939	Parents campaign for Batista.
1941	Family moves to Havana.
1943	Begins *bachillerato* (high school and college).
1946	Inspired by a professor, develops great interest in literature.
1947	First story published in *Bohemia,* a leading literary magazine in Latin America.
1948	Quits school to work as secretary to *Bohemia*'s managing editor.
1949	Founds literary magazine *Nueva Generación.* Works as part-time proofreader for U.S.-sponsored *Havana Herald* and is literary ghost editor for *Bohemia.*
1950	Enters National School of Journalism.

1951 Cofounds literary society *Nuestro Tiempo* and quits when he realizes it is turning into a communist organization. Cocreates *Cinemateca,* patterned after the Cinémateque Française.

1952 Publishes short story in *Bohemia,* resulting in a jail term. Forced to quit the School of Journalism for two years.

1953 Writes under the pseudonym Caín. Marries Marta Calvo.

1954 Publishes a weekly movie column in *Carteles* as G. Caín. First daughter, Ana, is born.

1955 Visits the United States for the first time.

1956 *Cinemateca* ends.

1957 Writes for underground press. Visits Mexico for the first time. Visits New York for the second time. Several of his friends are imprisoned and/or killed by Batista.

1958 Political content of his column is censored. Writes short stories and vignettes, later collected in *Así en la paz como en la guerra.* Second daughter, Carola, is born.

1959 Founds and edits *Lunes de Revolución.* Travels with Fidel Castro to United States, Canada, and South America.

1960 Visits Europe, including the Soviet Union. Is divorced from first wife. Stops writing movie criticism. *Lunes* is now also on TV. *Así en la paz como en la guerra* published.

1961 Serves as correspondent for the invasion of Bay of Pigs. The film *P.M.* is confiscated. *Lunes* is banned. Marries Miriam Gómez, a successful actress.

1962 Sent to Brussels as cultural attaché.

1963 *Un oficio del siglo veinte* published. *Así en la paz como en la guerra* published in France, Italy, and Poland. Nominated for the Prix International de Littérature.

1964 First novel (later titled *Tres tristes tigres*) receives Premio Seix Barral, top prize for a novel in Spanish. Appointed chargé d'affaires in Belgium and Luxembourg.

1965 *Tres tristes tigres* is nominated for Prix Formentor. Visits Cuba for his mother's funeral. Leaves Cuba definitively with his daughters Ana and Carola to live in Madrid.

1966 Denied a resident's visa in Spain. Moves to London.

1967 Collaborates in *Mundo Nuevo. Tres tristes tigres* published.

1968 Denounces Castro and is considered a traitor in Cuba.

1969 Begins writing screenplay *Vanishing Point.*

1970 Visits Southwestern United States and Hollywood. Recipient of Guggenheim Fellowship.

1971 *Three Trapped Tigers* published. French translation earns Prix du Meilleur Livre Étranger. *Vanishing Point* opens in London.

1972 Writes screenplay *Under the Volcano,* based on the book by Malcolm Lowry. Suffers a nervous breakdown.
1974 *Vista del amanecer en el trópico* published.
1975 *O* published.
1976 *Exorcismos de esti(l)o* published. First granddaughter, Florence Robertson, is born.
1978 Lectures at Yale. *Arcadia todas las noches* and *View of Dawn in the Tropics* published.
1979 *La Habana para un Infante difunto* published.
1980 Conducts lecture tours in the United States. Conducts book promotions in Mexico, Colombia, and Venezuela for *La Habana.* Holds a reunion with several exiled Cuban friends.
1981 Presents a paper "Parodio no por odio" [An American in Parody] in Washington, D.C., protested by the Cuban Embassy.
1982 Teaches one semester at University of Virginia, guest lectures at universities of Chicago, Kansas, Wisconsin, Yale, and New York.
1984 *Infante's Inferno* published.
1985 *Holy Smoke* published in English. Teaches at Wellesley College.
1986 Lectures at West Point Military Academy. Visits Australia. Begins and abandons translating *Holy Smoke* into Spanish.
1987 Lectures at the University of Oklahoma, where he is featured guest at the Eleventh Puterbaugh Conference on World Literature. Grandson, Joshua Morris, is born.
1988 Lectures in Germany, Italy, Brazil, and at the Barcelona and Miami film festivals. Grandson, Jacob Morris, is born.
1990 Writes film script "The Lost City" for Paramount and Andy García.
1991 *A Twentieth Century Job* published.
1992 *Mea Cuba* published. Receives honorary doctorate from Florida International University and the Carlos IV medallion from the Universidad Complutense in Madrid. Granddaughter, Hannah Morris, is born.
1993 *Writes of Passage* published. Granddaughter, Jessica Morris, is born.
1994 English version of *Mea Cuba* published in New York and London. *La Habana* published in Italian.
1995 *Delito por bailar el chachachá* published. Lectures in Madrid and Paris on José Martí, commemorating the 100th anniversary of his death. Awarded the biannual prize for

La Habana para un Infante difunto by the Instituto Latinoamericano de Roma.

1996 *Ella cantaba boleros* published. La Semana del Autor [Week of the author] dedicated to Guillermo Cabrera Infante in Madrid in November.

1997 *Cine o sardina* published. Summer course dedicated to Guillermo Cabrera Infante offered by the Universidad Menéndez y Pelayo at El Escorial in Spain in July. Granddaughter, Isabela Ash, is born.

1998 1997 Cervantes Award conferred by King Juan Carlos of Spain, April 23, at Alcalá de Henares. Acceptance speech *Cervantes, mi contemporáneo* published.

1999 *Todo está hecho con espejos* and *La ventana pineal* published.

Introduction

Ardis L. Nelson

◆

Guillermo Cabrera Infante, winner of the 1997 Premio Cervantes de Literatura [Cervantes Literary Award], has achieved international status primarily as a writer of fiction. His novels *Tres tristes tigres* (1967) [*Three Trapped Tigers* (1971)] and *La Habana para un Infante difunto* (1979) [*Infante's Inferno* (1984)] have seen many editions and translations. Notwithstanding the fame guaranteed by his fiction, Cabrera Infante is a screenwriter and a prolific essayist. This aspect of his writing has only recently come to light in the Americas with the publication of *Mea Cuba* (1992) [*Mea Cuba* (1994)] and *Cine o sardina* (1997) [Movies or meals]. As a youth in Havana, Cabrera Infante was a journalist and film critic and wrote short stories collected in *Así en la paz como en la guerra* (1960) [*Writes of Passage* (1993)] and historical vignettes published in *Vista del amanecer en el trópico* (1974) [*View of Dawn in the Tropics* (1978)]. Most of his reviews were published in *Un oficio del siglo veinte* (1963) [*A Twentieth Century Job* (1991)] and his lectures on movie directors in *Arcadia todas las noches* (1978) [Arcadia every night]; other essays can be found in *O* (1975), *Exorcismos de esti(l)o* (1976) [Style exorcisms], and *Holy Smoke* (1985).

For the student of genre studies, Cabrera Infante is a chameleon. His writing is modern Menippean satire, with topics that range from political to poetic and a style that leaves us amused and bemused. His essays, the focus of this book, are not essays in the traditional sense of a soliloquy on topics such as friendship, virtues, society, and justice, as in Michel de Montaigne's *Essais* (1580), although they do share some of the qualities of the originators of the genre. For

Montaigne the essay is a means of self-expression characterized by the free association of ideas. For Ralph Waldo Emerson the essay is "essaying to be," and for Martin Heidegger it is "thought thinking about itself." The British subject Francis Bacon described his *Essays* (1597) as "grains of salt which will rather give an appetite than offend with satiety." Bacon's later essays (1612, 1625) were characterized by quotation, figures of speech, sentence rhythm, and imagination, all of which can be seen in Cabrera Infante's writing, from his early days as a journalist to his latest book of essays. Cabrera Infante's film writing, including reviews, obituaries, and scripts, is an integral part of his *oeuvre* and, as such, shares the stylistic characteristics of his other writing.

I. The Writer as Journalist

In "The Years at *Bohemia* and *Carteles*," Raymond D. Souza chronicles Cabrera Infante's first experiences as a writer, which began with a story written on a dare. When he took his short story to *Bohemia,* he met the literary editor Antonio Ortega, a Spanish exile who was to become his mentor for the next 13 years. Ortega introduced the young man to the writing of his Spanish and American contemporaries during Cabrera Infante's six years at *Bohemia* as his personal secretary. When Ortega became director of the magazine *Carteles* in 1953, Cabrera Infante went with him and became a film critic, writing a weekly column under the pseudonym G. Caín. While most of his film reviews were collected and published in *Un oficio del siglo veinte,* some were not included, undoubtedly for political reasons. Souza discusses one such review that appeared in *Carteles,* as well as several capricious photo essays, for instance "La belleza de la bomba" [The beauty of the bomb] and "Las 10 fotografías más bellas transmitidas por teléfono" [The 10 most beautiful photographs transmitted by wire], published under different pseudonyms.

Cabrera Infante's activities at *Bohemia* and *Carteles* between 1947 and 1960 provided him with a training ground where he developed skills that allowed him to become the editor of *Lunes de Revolución* (from March 1959 to November 1961) and led to his later achievements as a creative writer. *Lunes* was a literary supplement begun by Cabrera Infante and Carlos Franqui in the early days of the revolution that served as a cultural forum and grew to a circulation of a quarter of a million. In "*Lunes de Revolución*: Literature and Culture in the First Years of the Cuban Revolution," William Luis presents a detailed history of the exuberant birth of *Lunes,* its successful role in promoting Cuban culture in Cuba and throughout Latin America, and its painful demise following the censure of *P.M.* (1961), a film by Cabrera Infante's brother, Sabá, that was sponsored by *Lunes* on Cuban television. This turbulent epoch and the subsequent disillusion and exodus of many writers is closely paralleled by the rise and fall of *Lunes.* On 30 June 1961 Castro pronounced the famous "Palabras a los intelectuales" [Words to the intellectuals]: "Within the Revolution everything. Outside the Revolution, nothing."

Cabrera Infante eventually chose to live outside the revolution. He left Cuba in October 1965, marking the beginning of his life as an exile. After a difficult period of transition and several moves, he settled in London with his wife Miriam and wrote for the daily newspaper *El País,* beginning a relationship with a Spanish readership that continues to this day. In 1977 and 1978 a series of his essays under the rubric "Icosaedros" record his pun-laden reflections on any number of events and customs, past and present, that take place in London. In "'Icosaedros': The English Letters," Carlos Cuadra finds the "Icosaedros" to be a coherent work of social and political satire that reflects the angst of the recently exiled Cuban in a world and a time where it was taboo to criticize Castro. Rather than making direct reference to Cuba, however, Cabrera Infante's essays in *El País* comment by inference and are in some ways analogous to Voltaire's *Letters on England* (1734) written while he was in forced exile from France (1726–1729). The "Icosaedros" essays represent Cabrera Infante's reflections during his transition from a severe depression suffered in the early 1970s to a period of renewed literary activity. Three collections of essays were published: *O*, *Exorcismos de esti(l)o*, and *Arcadia todas las noches*. In 1978 he delivered his first lecture in 16 years at Yale University, and the next year his second novel, *La Habana para un Infante difunto,* was published in Spain.

II. The Writer as Cineaste

Cabrera Infante's lifelong love for the cinema began at the tender age of 29 days, when his mother took him to see *The Four Horsemen of the Apocalypse* (1921). In "The Cinematic Imagination," Raymond D.

Souza explores the influence of film on Cabrera Infante by drawing a parallel between that film and events in his life. The difficult phases of Cabrera Infante's literary career are chronicled as encounters with apocalyptical horsemen, including the failed negotiations surrounding his film script based on *Under the Volcano* (1947) by Malcolm Lowry. His successful film script for *Vanishing Point* (1971) is analyzed and compared with a more recent script "The Lost City," which has not yet been produced. Souza weaves into his essay the complementary threads of film and literature in Cabrera Infante's life and works.

In "Movies and Mock Encomia," Kenneth Hall provides a unique approach to Cabrera Infante's essays on film stars and directors by writing on his obituaries for movie personalities. Indeed, this chapter represents the first critical attention these essays have received, since until the publication of *Cine o sardina*, they did not enjoy a readership beyond newspapers and magazines in England and Spain. Hall analyzes the obituaries of such notables as Ava Gardner, Barbara Stanwyck, and Rita Hayworth as mock encomia, an ironic form of the funereal eulogy, suggested by Cabrera Infante's affinity for the Spanish classical, baroque, and Renaissance writers. This original study shows how Cabrera Infante brilliantly employs the techniques of conceit, ironic reversal, circumlocution, anatomy, picaresque strategies, and conceptista wordplays in the service of antonomasia.

Cine o sardina represents the culmination of a lifetime of movie fanaticism, with an eclectic collection of essays on topics ranging from the history of the cinema to film theory, and from fan mail of the stars to directors. In "Life with the Silver Screen," Kenneth Hall focuses on just a few of the essays, to wit, "Latinos y ladinos en Hollywood" [Latinos and Ladinos in Hollywood], a valuable contribution to the literature on Hispanics in U.S. cinema; "Por quién doblan las películas" [For whom the films toll], a series of now humorous, now critical anecdotes on the art of dubbing films; and "La caza del facsímil" [Fax hunt], an essay on the cult film *Blade Runner* (1982).

In "Literary Friends at the Movies," Suzanne Jill Levine discusses Cabrera Infante and Argentine Manuel Puig, two movie-going youths who were to become the first Latin American writers to incorporate popular culture into their novels. Cabrera Infante and Puig became friends in 1967, when they met through the Cuban cinematographer Néstor Almendros, and their friendship was strengthened by a shared belief in the importance of the actor/actress in creating the magic in movies. Levine's essay is based in part on their correspondence over the years until Puig's death in 1990.

III. The Writer as Critic

Another significant relationship in Cabrera Infante's life is the acquaintance he had with Jorge Luis Borges, whom he greatly admired for his humor. Cabrera Infante learned a lot from Borges, as have all Latin American writers, and he believes that Borges will be the only writer of this century who will still be read in 100 years. In "The Man Who Knew Too Much," Carlos Cuadra discusses the anxiety of influence Cabrera Infante experienced in his meetings with Borges, as recorded in several essays on this mythical figure. The issue of the classical versus the romantic writer is broached, along with that of the disciple's attempts to free himself from his master. In Cabrera Infante's dinner meetings with Borges in various settings over the years, he gets to know the human side of Borges as well as the heroic. Cuadra examines the dynamics of their relationship.

In an interview with Suzanne Jill Levine, "The Translator Within," Cabrera Infante reminisces about his first reading of William Faulkner's *The Wild Palms* (1939) in a Spanish translation by Borges, a version he considers better than the original in English. In this seemingly casual interchange, both Cabrera Infante's and Levine's words are peppered with puns and profundities. Cabrera Infante ponders, for example, the influence of Lino Novás Calvo on his writing and reveals his thoughts on this great translator of Ernest Hemingway and Faulkner. He also compares his infamous short story "Balada de plomo y yerro" ["Ballad of Bullets and Bull's-Eyes"] (1952) with similar stories by Hemingway and Novás Calvo. He talks about how he writes and rewrites and muses on the suggestivity of words in both English and Spanish.

In "*Mea Cuba:* Critical Readings from Exile," Justo and Leonor Ulloa present Cabrera Infante not as a literary critic but rather as a curious reader who weaves fiction and reality, poetry and history to create a tantalizing portrait of Cuban writers and intellectuals in *Mea Cuba*, a compilation of more than 60 essays written between 1968 and 1992. His blurring of the boundaries between criticism and biography plays tricks with exposition, shakes up expectations, and undermines the belief that we can know a writer solely through the analysis of his writing. The Ulloas address the integration of politics, literature, and lifestyle in Cabrera Infante's essays on the Cuban writers José Lezama Lima, Virgilio Piñera, Reinaldo Arenas, Nicolás Guillén, and Alejo Carpentier.

IV. The Writer as Commentator: Arts, Leisure, and Memoirs

While the emphasis in this volume is on Cabrera Infante's essays on film and literature, his writing on the arts is significant, if not extensive. He has written exquisite essays on painters from Edouard Manet to Ramón Alejandro, on music from rock to rhumba and on culture from pop to punk. Until now many of these essays have been unknown except to those who read certain magazines and newspapers in Spain and England. As an audacious writer and person, his tenaciously held beliefs on life, liberty, and language show some striking similarities to the surrealist worldview as expressed in the films and life of the surrealist filmmaker Luis Buñuel. Ardis L. Nelson's "On Buñuel and Surrealism: The Art of Audacity" illustrates Cabrera Infante's connectedness to art and culture of the twentieth century through an examination of Cabrera Infante's references to surrealism and his writings on Buñuel.

As in *Tres tristes tigres,* Cabrera Infante continues to be fascinated by "what the flame of a candle looks like after the candle is blown out" and seeks to preserve in print that which is about to disappear. In order to do so he goes against the grain of accepted norms and casts a favorable light on the outcast, giving voice to the subdued, the unacknowledged, the silenced. In *Holy Smoke* he comes to the rescue of an age-old vice, fallen of late into disrepute during a health-conscious epoch. He writes of the virtues of tobacco and all of its glory, mostly past. True to his tendency toward the apocalyptic, Cabrera Infante immortalizes the dressed-up weed before its extinction becomes a reality. "Up in Smoke" is Regina Janes's poetic interpretation of this seriocomic essayistic treatise in two parts. For Janes the first part is a movie evoked in writing, with Pretorius from *The Bride of Frankenstein* (1935) presiding; the second part is about a writer who is smoking, with literary excerpts on the topic. She relates the images of smoke and smoke rings to the experience of exile, interprets the cigar as character, and considers Cabrera Infante's multilingualism in her analysis of his use of a poem by Stéphane Mallarmé.

The final chapter in this volume is an intuitive and comprehensive overview of *Mea Cuba* as a literary-political-historical memoir of Cuba. In "*Mea Cuba*: The 'Proust-Valía' of History," Nedda G. de Anhalt compares the life patterns and literary themes of Cabrera Infante and Marcel Proust. Her analysis is in musical terminology, as if the work were an operatic cantata complete with an overture and three acts, ever mindful of the Proustian focus on time and nostalgia. Anhalt captures the essence of Cabrera Infante's instinct for historical veracity, good political judgment, and penetrating wit.

The purpose of this volume on Cabrera Infante is to provide a more rounded picture of an important writer for the twentieth century. Cabrera Infante's essays and film scripts offer a wealth of humorous and historical reading and are as rich a contribution to literature as his fiction. While I do not suggest that this volume is the definitive critical statement on the lesser-known writings of Cabrera Infante, it is nonetheless a first attempt to introduce the English-speaking reader to the study of Cabrera Infante as journalist, cineaste, critic, and commentator. I can only hope that it will prove to be an enjoyable read and a useful compendium for the friends and followers of Guillermo Cabrera Infante's works.

THE WRITER AS JOURNALIST

The Years at *Bohemia* and *Carteles*

RAYMOND D. SOUZA

When the newly created company Publicaciones Unidas (United Publications) acquired control of *Carteles* and *Vanidades* in December 1953, Antonio Ortega was transferred from his position as news and literary editor at *Bohemia* to that of director of *Carteles.* All three magazines were now under the wing of one consolidated entity managed by Miguel Angel Quevedo, the editor of *Bohemia,* and Francisco Saralegui, former president of the Reciprocity Trading Company.[1] A new editor was also appointed at *Vanidades,* Herminia del Portal, "la periodista que ella sola había revolucionado la prensa femenina cubana como lo haría después con la continental" [the journalist who had single-handedly revolutionized the Cuban women's press as she would do later with the continental women's magazine].[2] This major reshuffling of responsibilities at three of Cuba's most popular magazines changed the journalistic activities of many individuals. Since Ortega was Guillermo Cabrera Infante's mentor at *Bohemia,* he took the young writer with him to *Carteles,* and that journal played an important role in Cabrera Infante's career until it ceased publication in 1960.

Ortega and Cabrera Infante first crossed paths in 1947. Unimpressed with selections from the novel *El Señor Presidente* (1946) by the Guatemalan Miguel Angel Asturias that had appeared in *Bohemia,* the 18-year-old Cabrera Infante brashly declared to his friend Carlos Franqui that if that was writing, then he was a writer. Intrigued by his companion's claims, Franqui challenged Cabrera Infante to write a story. Cabrera Infante responded to the dare by producing a parody of Asturias's style, "Aguas de recuerdo" [Waters of memory], which Franqui read. He then sent Cabrera Infante on to *Bohemia* to see if the story could be published in that magazine. Luckily for Cabrera Infante, the elegant and aristocratic Ortega was responsible for the magazine's literary contents.

A refugee from Franco's Spain, Ortega was a man of considerable literary sensibility and experience. He won the Alfonso Hernández Catá prize for the short story in 1945 and published the novel *Ready* in Havana in 1946. When the aspiring young writer appeared at his door, Ortega received the manuscript and told the author to return in a week. Several days later Cabrera Infante learned that the story would be published and that his remuneration would be the equivalent of $50, a princely sum at that time in Cuba. It was the beginning of a fruitful and close relationship. Ortega recognized that Cabrera Infante needed to expand his literary background, and he introduced him to a generation of contemporary Spanish authors and writers from the English world including T. S. Eliot and George Orwell. Eventually, Ortega hired Cabrera Infante as his personal secretary, and he began to assign to him different tasks at *Bohemia,* including the evaluation of manuscripts and collecting information for the column "La figura de la semana" [The figure of the week]. When the featured individual was American, Cabrera Infante would research the celebrity's background, at times at the library of the U.S. Embassy, and one of the first columns he wrote was about William Faulkner.

After the move to *Carteles,* Cabrera Infante began to review films and write articles on the movie industry, and in 1957 he was appointed managing editor of the journal. Cabrera Infante's association with Ortega changed his life, and by the time Ortega left Cuba in 1960 to go into exile in Venezuela, Cabrera Infante was the editor of *Lunes de Revolución* (1959–1961), the weekly cultural supplement of the daily newspaper *Revolución* directed by Carlos Franqui.[3] In 12 years Cabrera Infante had gone from an unknown to the prominent editor of an innovative and experimental cultural supplement. Between 1947 and 1960 he also became a promising writer of fiction, Havana's most accomplished film critic, and a controversial journalist.

Bohemia and *Carteles* were eclectic weekly magazines designed to appeal to a wide range of readers, although *Carteles* stressed the news and arts and had more highbrow appeal than *Bohemia.* Everything from lurid crime stories accompanied by shocking photographs to the most accomplished literary works could be found on their pages. According to Cabrera Infante, Miguel Angel Quevedo transformed *Bohemia* "en un semanario popular, crudo y sensacionalista y al mismo tiempo profundamente democrático y sentimental. *Bohemia* fue de cierta manera uno de los creadores del carácter cubano de entonces y no es casualidad que surgiera en Cuba junto con el auge del bolero" [into a popular weekly, crude and sensationalist and at the same time profoundly democratic but sentimental. *Bohemia* was in a way one of the creators of the Cuban character of the time and it is no accident that it arose in Cuba along with the apogee of the *bolero*].[4] Energetic entrepreneurs would hawk the magazine in the streets of Havana as soon as it was available and the issues quickly disappeared into eager hands.

During his approximately six-year association with *Bohemia,* Cabrera Infante published short stories such as "Las puertas se abren a las tres" ["The Doors Open at Three"], "Resaca" ["Remains"], and "Balada de plomo y yerro" ["Ballad of Bullets and Bull's-Eyes"], and all of these were included in his first book *Así en la paz como en la guerra* [*Writes of Passage*].[5] When "Resaca" came out in the 5 October 1952 issue of *Bohemia,* it opened with a quotation from *A Portrait of the Artist as a Young Man* (1916), an indication that Cabrera Infante was absorbing the works of James Joyce, whom he had begun to read in 1947 or 1948. The epigraph later was dropped. Another story that appeared during the same month produced serious consequences and was an early manifestation of Cabrera Infante's tendency to challenge established norms.

When "Balada de plomo y yerro" appeared in the 19 October 1952 issue of *Bohemia,* Cabrera Infante had no inkling that the inclusion of English obscenities in the story would land him in jail and complicate his journalistic activities for several years. The only other time that a literary work had provoked serious trouble for him was back in school. While reading *Les Fleurs du mal* [*The Flowers of Evil*] (1857) by the French symbolist poet Charles Pierre Baudelaire in the library, he offered to share the book with another student. The scandalized girl reported the episode to one of her teachers, Mercedes García Tudurí, without revealing the name of the tempter who had encouraged her to savor the forbidden literary apple. The teacher responded with an emotional lecture in class on the evils of Baudelaire and of those idlers who attempted to corrupt innocent minds with obscene works. It was Cabrera Infante's first encounter with what he has called "bourgeois authority."[6] The authorities who came looking for him after his story appeared in *Bohemia* used morality as a pretext, but their real intent was the intimidation of a magazine they perceived as a threat to the preservation of political power.

There was not much enthusiasm at *Bohemia* for the government after the illegal seizure of power by Fulgencio Batista on 10 March 1952, and governmental officials regarded the people at the magazine as a bunch of potential troublemakers. The author of the story became a pawn in a game of cat and mouse between the director of

Bohemia and the minister of the interior when everyone professed innocence as to the meanings of the English words. Cabrera Infante was arrested on a Friday and hauled off to the headquarters of the secret, rather than regular, police. The timing was auspicious for his tormentors because the court that normally would have heard his case was conveniently closed, which meant that nothing could be done until the following Monday. He was taken to a prison, the Castillo del Príncipe, and thrown in a large cell with common criminals. An infamous bank robber took a liking to the bewildered newcomer, who was obviously out of place in his new surroundings, and provided protection and edible food. Many of Cabrera Infante's fellow prisoners were avid readers of *Bohemia,* and when they discovered he was the author of a piece about an attempted assassination, some freely offered literary advice. One of the inmates who thought the story was a news report rather than a fictional work told Cabrera Infante that the article was full of errors because it exaggerated the difficulty of killing someone. Murder, he explained, is a simple enterprise, and quite easy to accomplish. Cabrera Infante was impressed; it is rumored that he even took notes.

After five days of exchanging social and literary pleasantries with his new associates, family members and friends finally secured his release, but not before an appearance before a "hanging judge."[7] The judge had the case removed to his private chambers, a tactic that piqued the curiosity of everyone awaiting their turn at the bar of justice, including pimps and prostitutes. Once in chambers, the judge lectured Cabrera Infante about the perils of confusing literature and life. The judge, who was noted for his enthusiastic association with the kind of women who were marking time in the courtroom before their own adjudication, conceded that scandalous language was used every day, but he nevertheless felt that the innocent should be protected from such words, an argument still used today by would-be censors. Cabrera Infante was then fined more than he could pay, and two friends, Antonio Ortega and Juan Blanco, helped him cover the amount. The alternative to paying the fine was to spend time in jail at the rate of one dollar per day, which would have taken many months, so the incentive for a monetary solution was very high. Apparently, Cabrera Infante also was no longer interested in the literary opinions of other inmates. As a result of the hearing, Cabrera Infante was unable to continue his studies at the National School of Journalism for two years, and he could no longer publish in *Bohemia.* He emerged from his ordeal badly shaken and soon fell into another trap—an unhappy marriage.

After his brief sojourn as a guest of the Cuban government, he resumed publishing, but frequently under pseudonyms or anonymously. His motto became "out-of-sight, out-of-mind," although he could not resist sticking his head out now and then like a gaudy turkey to see if any governmental sharpshooters were lurking about. His pen names included the now widely known G. Caín and colorful concoctions like Jonás Castro and S. del Pastora Niño. His fictional works, however, proudly and imprudently proclaimed their creator's actual name: "Mar, mar, enemigo" ["The Sea Changes"] by Guillermo C. Infante in the 27 June 1954 issue of *Carteles* and "Un nido de gorriones en un toldo" ["Nest, Door, Neighbours"] by Guillermo Cabrera Infante in the 25 September 1955 issue.[8] Both stories were preceded by an introduction to the author, most likely written by Cabrera Infante. The first gave information about his years in Gibara, the move of the family to Havana when he was 12, and his participation in several Hernández Catá short-story contests. It also announced his intent to publish a volume of stories based on his experiences in Gibara and closed with the following comments: "Cabrera Infante pertenece a la última generación de cuentistas cubanos, gente preocupada por encontrar un acento nacional liberado de pintoresquismos y a la vez exento de influencias exóticas, aunque él confiesa que la literatura inglesa (especialmente la escuela norteamericana) le interesa más que ninguna otra." [Cabrera Infante belongs to the latest generation of Cuban short story writers, a group preoccupied with finding a national voice freed from the picturesque and at the same time devoid of exotic influences, although he confesses that English literature (particularly the North American school) interests him more than any other].[9]

The second story, "Un nido de gorriones en un toldo," appeared nearly three years after his run-in with the law, and like "Mar, mar, enemigo," it had an introduction that placed him within the context of contemporary Cuban writers: "Guillermo Cabrera Infante (1929) ha divulgado su entera producción—muy escasa hasta la fecha—en revistas del patio. Al igual a otros cuentistas de la última generación—Ramón Ferreira, Silvano Suárez, Lisandro Otero, Matías Montes, René Jordán, José Lorenzo Fuentes, Raúl González de Cascorro, Surama Ferrer, etc.—los cuentos de Cabrera Infante aparecen fuertemente influídos por la moderna literatura norteamericana." [Guillermo Cabrera Infante (1929) has published all of his stories—which are very few in number at this writing—in local magazines. Like other young writers of his generation—Ramón Ferreira, Silvano Suárez, Lisandro Otero, Matías Montes, René Jordán, José Lorenzo

Fuentes, Raúl González de Cascorro, Surama Ferrer, etc.—the stories of Cabrera Infante are strongly influenced by modern North American literature].[10] "Un nido de gorriones en un toldo" also contained an epigraph from Nathaniel Hawthorne, but like the quotation from James Joyce in "Resaca," it was removed in subsequent publications.

Since nearly two years had passed between Cabrera Infante's arrest and the publication of "Mar, mar, enemigo," he obviously was testing the waters by using his name. Fortunately for him, dictatorships of the Right in Spanish America are notorious for their indifference to literature, and most of their functionaries would not be caught dead reading a literary work. The Batista gang was no exception to this flight from fancy words. Whoever pointed out the use of inappropriate language in the "Balada de plomo y yerro" affair had the convenient cover of dirty words to preserve his reputation. In 1954 and 1955, the government had more pressing concerns than obscenities.

When Cabrera Infante published stories during his years at *Bohemia* and *Carteles,* he was a young writer experimenting with different narrative modes, in search of his own voice. His development as a movie critic was another matter, however, and he demonstrated a command of that medium very early in his journalistic career. After following Ortega to *Carteles,* Cabrera Infante started to publish articles about the movie industry in 1953, and he was soon writing film reviews. Ortega knew that his young charge loved movies and he decided to make use of that knowledge. Cabrera Infante's reviews started appearing twice a month, and then they became a weekly column, "El Film de la Semana" [The film of the week].

An early example of Cabrera Infante's rapid grasp of the movie scene was "Recuento fílmico de 1953" [A second look at the films of 1953] that appeared in the 17 January 1954 issue of *Carteles* under the name G. Caín. This critical survey concentrated on the quantity and quality of movies produced in several countries and commented particularly on Hollywood's response to the threat of television. In 1953 Hollywood embraced CinemaScope, the projection system that had been developed in France. The mad scramble for gimmicks was in full swing in Hollywood, and Cinerama and 3-D were among the innovations being touted to lure the viewing public back to movie theaters. Cabrera Infante acknowledged that the threat from television was real but nevertheless lamented Hollywood's proclivity to stress technique over substance. He also suggested that European filmmakers were producing just the opposite result (privileging content but neglecting technical innovation) because of their disdain for commercialism. Two other articles that appeared anonymously dealt with trips to New York in 1955 and 1957, and commented on the cinematic highlights of his visits to that city.[11]

Fortunately for contemporary readers, most of the reviews that Cabrera Infante published between 1954 and 1960 in *Carteles* and from 1959 to 1960 in the newspaper *Revolución* are available in book form. Originally published in Havana in 1963 as *Un oficio del siglo veinte* and reprinted in an English version in 1991 as *A Twentieth Century Job,* the reviews are still fresh and timely.[12] The appearance of the original Spanish edition in Havana was a minor miracle because the collection contains fictionalized meditations on the role of the critic in an ideologically committed society. When the work came out, Cabrera Infante was employed at the Cuban Embassy in Brussels and was far removed from the day-to-day process of preparing the manuscript for publication. *Un oficio del siglo veinte* is decidedly subversive because the fictionalized sections contain veiled criticism of Marxist ideology. The book's release was in doubt for some time before Virgilio Piñera, the editor of Ediciones R, decided to go ahead with the publication despite his many misgivings. However, the edition of 4,000 copies was small by Cuban standards at that time, and Cabrera Infante's father, Guillermo senior, did some pruning before the book appeared.

One review from *Carteles* that didn't make it into the collection was Cabrera Infante's assessment of an animated version of the political satire *Animal Farm* (1945) by the English novelist and essayist George Orwell. His review of the British production appeared in the 31 August 1958 edition of *Carteles,* and its political content would have made it a problematic publication in Cuba in 1963.[13] More space was dedicated to a discussion of the significance of Orwell's career and writings than to the film. In 1958, Cabrera Infante was beginning to struggle with the mental fatigue of producing a review every week, and he often employed a tactic of evasion, writing about other matters rather than the movie. More often than not, these other concerns were literary.

For Cabrera Infante, Orwell's hallmarks were his "sincerity, honesty, and courage" (p. 42), and he quoted Orwell's criticisms of some of Stalin's actions during the Spanish Civil War. In his concluding remarks, Cabrera Infante attempted to move away from some of Orwell's more melancholy conclusions about revolutions. He observed:

> *Rebelión en la granja* es una cinta importante . . . y peligrosa. Su mensaje tiene un doble filo, porque parece recomendar lo contrario de lo

> que quería Orwell. Las revoluciones fracasan y terminan por volver todo al punto de partida. Esto no es lo que importa y la lección debe tomarse más como una interpretación de la realidad que como una premonición. En el libro, todo terminaba en el marasmo del gobierno de Napoleón; en la cinta hay otra revolución para acabar con Napoleón. Ese es el camino. No importa cuál sea su destino, el hombre seguirá tratando de ir hacia adelante. Aunque sea por el sangriento medio de prueba y error de las revoluciones.
>
> [*Animal Farm* is an important film . . . and a dangerous one. Its message is double-edged, because it seems to suggest the opposite of what Orwell wanted. Revolutions fail and end up going back to the beginning. That is not what is important, and the warning should be taken more as an interpretation of reality than as a premonition. In the book, everything ended up in the marasmus of Napoleon's government; in the film there is another revolution to put an end to Napoleon. That's the correct course. Whatever his destiny, man will continue to try to move forward. Even if it is by the bloody means of the trial and error of revolutions.] (44)

The optimistic conclusion is due in part to the review's appearing in 1958 during the struggle against Batista, a movement in which Cabrera Infante wholeheartedly participated. Ironically for him, Orwell's work would prove to be both accurate and prophetic. Four months to the day after the publication of the review, Batista abandoned the island to the joy and jubilation of most of the population. Cuba experienced an enormous outburst of energy and optimism, but the promises of democracy soon faded. In time, Cabrera Infante reluctantly found himself resisting the country's slide into a dictatorship.

Like all of his cinematic publications, the review of *Animal Farm* appeared under the pen name G. Caín. Although a 1956 interview with Ernesto Pedro Smith of Columbia Pictures in Cuba followed the same procedure, a photograph of Cabrera Infante with Smith accompanied the article but without a mention of the interviewer's identity.[14] Since Caín was one of Cabrera Infante's more mischievous personas, the calculated risk was not surprising. Also, he may have been trying to impress the literary friends he had made back at the Castillo Príncipe in October 1952. A review of *I'll Cry Tomorrow* (1955) published two weeks earlier in the 15 April 1956 issue of *Carteles* had nearly cost him his job when a major advertiser, Bacardí and Company, objected to a remark that bottles of rum should add a skull and crossbones to their label. However, although Caín was quite capable of intellectual mayhem, he was not necessarily the most accomplished mischief maker during the years at *Carteles.* That honor belongs to Jonás Castro, the most roguish commentator of all. Why that specific surname was chosen is open to speculation, but the superstitious or fatalistic might regard it as an intuitive harbinger of things to come.

Jonás Castro liked to combine pithy commentary with outlandish or compelling photographs. Early examples include "Los espectadores las prefieren rubias" [Spectators prefer them blonde] and "El bikini tiene más de 2,000 años" [The bikini is more than 2,000 years old], which appeared in 1954.[15] After exploring the delights and splendors of cheesecake, Jonás moved on to more intellectual fare in an excursion into popular science: "35 preguntas y respuestas sobre el catarro común" [35 questions and answers about the common cold].[16] This informative piece, supposedly gleaned from the research of an institute in New York City, was accompanied by cartoons and a large photo of a man about to launch a sneeze right at the reader. Another article ventured into the realm of cultural symbols when Jonás reproduced an interview with Salvador Dalí that featured Dalí's facial hair in different guises and shapes.[17] But the "yellow brick road" to real mischief began innocently enough, that is, anonymously, with the appearance of "Las 10 fotografías más bellas transmitidas por teléfono" [The 10 most beautiful photographs transmitted by wire].

The introduction to the photographic essay commented on the power of visual images and how they frequently determine what editors and reporters offer the public. The author even speculated reasonably that photographs influence literary modes. The introduction closed with the observation that modern technical means of reproduction and transmission have produced "fotos de una belleza extraordinaria y de sumo interés periodístico. De entre un cúmulo de ellas, extraemos éstas, que pueden considerarse sin lugar a dudas, las más bellas fotografías transmitidas por teléfono" [photos of extraordinary beauty and compelling journalistic interest. From a stack of them, we have selected these, which can be considered, without a doubt, the most beautiful photographs transmitted by wire].[18]

The first image that catches the reader's eye is a large photograph of the dirigible Hindenburg collapsing into an enormous ball of flames. The caption declares: "Hoy, casi veinte años después, la foto conserva su duro impacto dramático y su tremente belleza plástica" [Today, almost twenty years later, the photo retains its harsh, dramatic impact and its exceptional, plastic appeal]. In another, a woman is plunging to her death from an Atlanta hotel in a futile attempt to escape a consuming fire. Yet another shows a ship moments after it has been fatally torpedoed. These images of disaster frozen in time seem more horrific than aesthetically pleasing, but their morbidity is also compellingly attractive. On the top of the second page of the article, there is a picture of a nuclear explosion at Bikini atoll, which is described as "la más bella de las fotografías escogidas, y la más terrible y la de más resonancia histórica" [the most beautiful and terrible of the selected photographs, and the one with the most historical resonance]. Bucolic palm trees belie the false tranquillity of a fleet of moored ships about to be overwhelmed by an enormous mushroom of exploding power. This image was the link or inspiration to another survey of photographs that Jonás Castro published a few months later.

The appearance of "La belleza de la bomba" [The beauty of the bomb] in the 5 August 1956 issue of *Carteles* scandalized many of the journal's readers. Unlike "Las 10 fotografías más bellas transmitidas por teléfono," which integrated a photograph of a nuclear explosion into a collage of other disasters, "La belleza de la bomba" concentrates exclusively on nuclear images. The top half of the first page offers a spectacular photograph of a brilliant mushroom. The bright explosion occupies the upper part of the scene and appears over a darker foreground that highlights the equally vivid letters of the article's title. A cryptic caption reads: "Una bola de helado letal" [A ball of lethal ice] (58). In the lower left of the same page, a close-up of a swirling and dirtier-looking explosion has the following heading: "Satanás surgiendo del infierno, él mismo creándolo" [Satan springing from and creating hell]. If the viewer returns to the picture after reading the suggestive caption, a sinister image of Satan, horns and all, begins to emerge from the destructive chaos. Like a Rorschach inkblot test, the photograph and accompanying caption exploit the human tendency to project the known onto ambiguous stimuli.

The two photographs on the first page set the stage for 10 others that are also accompanied by provocative comments. The captions focus on a specific characteristic of each photograph and every combination is designed to set the reader's imagination in motion. Some examples: "Un árbol que es algo más y algo menos que un árbol: irreal, hierático, satánico . . ." [A tree that is something more and something less than a tree: surreal, solemn, satanic] (59); "Un crepúsculo fantasmal, una aurora de muerte" [A spectral dawn, an aurora of death] (60); "Un cerebro lunático y su malvada médula espinal" [A crazed cerebrum with its perverse, spinal marrow] (60); and the most repulsive of all: "Un pólipo excreciente, canceroso" [An excrescent, cancerous polyp] (60). The learned language of Jonás Castro's quips and references (the article opens with a quotation from Shakespeare's *Macbeth*) didn't protect him from the wrath of readers who were offended by his categorization of nuclear horrors. The introduction to the article did not help matters either, because in it he suggested that there are sinister relationships between beauty, creativity, and evil in the human imagination.

Reactions to "La belleza de la bomba" confirmed Cabrera Infante's belief that graphics could be an important complement to written works. He had been complaining at *Carteles* for some time that many of his columns were too cluttered, and he had campaigned for a cleaner appearance. His recognition of the power of the visual is related in part to his fondness for film, but another longtime interest also contributed to this awareness. Comic strips had intrigued him since childhood, and he was particularly fascinated by their capacity to create the illusion of motion in a basically static medium. In articles such as "La belleza de la bomba," Cabrera Infante explored combining dynamic words and images. A few years later, his interest in graphics found ample expression during his editorship of *Lunes de Revolución,* and in two particular books: *Un oficio del siglo veinte* and his great experimental novel *Tres tristes tigres* (1967) [*Three Trapped Tigers* (1971)].

In retrospect, the letter *b* seems to have been Cabrera Infante's Achilles' heel during the first two decades of his career. When he offered Baudelaire to a scandalized classmate back in school, he unleashed a swarm of *b*s of biblical proportions. That embarrassing episode was followed by the publication of "Balada de plomo y yerro" in *Bohemia,* which attracted the undesirable attention of Batista's bullies. Then there was the run-in with Bacardí and Company over a review that criticized the deadly potential of booze, and finally the uproar provoked by "La belleza de la bomba." In time, it would take a trinity, *Tres tristes tigres,* and the tiger's surrealist friend Bustrófedon to exorcise the curse: "¿Quién era Bustrófedon? ¿Quién fue quién será quién es Bustrófedon? ¿B?" [Who was Bustrófedon? Who was/is/will be Bustrófedon? Boustrophedon?][19] By the time that novel appeared, the next letter in the alphabet had become Cabrera Infante's nemesis.

During his years at *Bohemia* and *Carteles,* Cabrera Infante experimented with different fictional modes in a variety of short stories, and some of those publications produced serious difficulties. He also developed into Havana's most accomplished film commentator and critic, and these activities set the stage for future accomplishments as a screenwriter. Cabrera Infante acquired considerable editorial experience, particularly at *Carteles,* which eventually made possible the editorship of *Lunes de Revolución.* His mentor at *Bohemia* and *Carteles,* Antonio Ortega, was a decisive influence in his literary and journalistic career and a major contributor to his acquisition of a keen literary sensibility. Ortega sponsored his protégé during good and bad times and provided publishing outlets during Cabrera Infante's difficulties with the Batista government. The two magazines were the launching pads for many of Cabrera Infante's literary and journalistic shenanigans, at times under his own name, but more frequently anonymously or under pseudonyms. Several of Cabrera Infante's personas launched their barbs at an unsuspecting world or at themselves from the pages of *Bohemia* and *Carteles,* paving the way for later mischief in *Un oficio del siglo veinte* and *Tres tristes tigres.*

Cabrera Infante's cultivation of humor, whether comical, satirical, or sardonic, evolved into an effective survival technique, a way of deflecting or overcoming adversity. Over the years, that talent has been sorely tested and has been a major factor in his ability to endure.

Notes

1. "La nueva empresa de *Carteles,*" *Carteles* 35, 1 (3 January 1954): 25.
2. Guillermo Cabrera Infante, "La luna nona de Lino Novás," in *Mea Cuba* (Barcelona: Plaza and Janés, 1992), 360; "The Ninth Moon of Lino Novás," in *Mea Cuba,* trans. Kenneth Hall and Guillermo Cabrera Infante (New York: Farrar, Straus, Giroux, 1994), 372.
3. For a more detailed account of Cabrera Infante's relationship with Antonio Ortega, see Raymond D. Souza, *Guillermo Cabrera Infante: Two Islands, Many Worlds* (Austin: University of Texas Press, 1996), 22–30, and Cabrera Infante, "Antonio Ortega Returns to Asturias—Dead," in *Mea Cuba* (1994), 400–406. For basic information on Ortega's life and a representative short story, see Salvador Bueno, *Antología del cuento en Cuba, 1902–1952* (Havana: Ministerio de Educación, 1953), 201–11. Ortega's other publications include the novel *Ready* (Havana: Editorial Lex, 1946) and the volume of short stories *Yemas de coco y otros cuentos* (Santa Clara, Cuba: Universidad Central de las Villas, 1959).
4. "Entre la historia y la nada (Notas sobre una ideología del suicidio)," in *Mea Cuba* (1992), 177; "Between History and Nothingness, Notes on an Ideology of Suicide," in *Mea Cuba* (1994), 156.
5. *Así en la paz como en la guerra* (Havana: Ediciones R, 1960); *Writes of Passage,* trans. John Brookesmith, Peggy Boyars, and Guillermo Cabrera Infante (London: Faber and Faber, 1993). The English titles are from the latter.
6. Personal interview, 20 June 1990.

7. Personal interview, 21 June 1990. The interview is the source of most of this account, but written versions are available in "Obsceno," in *O* (Barcelona: Editorial Seix Barral, 1975), and in the translation "English Profanities," in *Writes of Passage*.

8. English titles are from *Writes of Passage*.

9. "Mar, mar, enemigo," *Carteles* 35, 26 (27 June 1954): 30. The translations of editorial comments from *Carteles* and *Bohemia* are my own.

10. *Carteles* 36, 39 (25 September 1955): 74.

11. "Cine en Nueva York," *Carteles* 36, 41 (9 October 1955): 42–44. "Cine: Excursiones. Los Estrenos de Nueva York," *Carteles* 38, 47 (24 November 1957): 42–45.

12. *Un oficio del siglo veinte* (Havana: Ediciones R, 1963) and *A Twentieth Century Job*, trans. Kenneth Hall and Guillermo Cabrera Infante (London: Faber and Faber, 1991). Hereafter cited in the text.

13. "El film de la semana: una granja llamada utopía," *Carteles* 39, 35 (31 August 1958): 42–44.

14. "Las bodas de plata de Ernesto P. Smith," *Carteles* 37, 18 (29 April 1956): 103.

15. *Carteles* 35, 33 (15 August 1954): 4–6, 8; *Carteles* 35, 36 (5 September 1954): 51.

16. *Carteles* 36, 31 (31 July 1955): 4–5.

17. "El bigote de Dalí, Fotos y preguntas de Philippe Halsman, Bigote y respuestas de Salvador Dalí, Texto de Jonás Castro," *Carteles* 37, 21 (20 May 1956): 4–5.

18. *Carteles* 37, 12 (18 March 1956): 4.

19. *Tres tristes tigres* (Barcelona: Editorial Seix Barral, 1967), 207. *Three Trapped Tigers*, trans. Donald Gardner and Suzanne Jill Levine with Guillermo Cabrera Infante (New York: Harper and Row, 1971), 213.

Lunes de Revolución: Literature and Culture in the First Years of the Cuban Revolution

William Luis

Be educated to be free.

—José Martí

Of all the arts, for us cinema is the most important.

—Lenin

It is widely known that along with Carlos Fuentes, Mario Vargas Llosa, Gabriel García Márquez, and Julio Cortázar, Guillermo Cabrera Infante is one of the authors of the "boom" period that brought Latin American literature to the attention of a world audience.[1] What is less well known is that at the outset of the Cuban revolution Cabrera Infante helped set the foundation for the "26th of July Movement." He did so in his capacity as editor and movie critic for *Carteles* (1953–1960), but more so as editor of *Lunes de Revolución,* the literary supplement of *Revolución,* the official newspaper of the "26th of July Movement" that brought Fidel Castro to power.

The literary boom that accompanied the triumph of the Cuban revolution was marked by a surge of new publishing ventures. The first and most important was *Lunes de Revolución,* which was sold on Mondays with *Revolución.* The newspaper was edited by one of Castro's advisers, Carlos Franqui, and the supplement was edited by Cabrera Infante with assistant editor Pablo Armando Fernández.

Lunes was the most significant and most widely read literary supplement in the history of Cuban and Latin American literary publications. In the brief period it was published—23 March 1959 to 6 November 1961—*Lunes* became a leading literary supplement. The first issue contained 6 pages and the last one listed 64. *Lunes* was distributed with *Revolución* and grew from a circulation of 100,000 to 250,000, surpassing other comparable publications of larger countries, including the *New York Review of Books.*

Although Cabrera Infante gave *Lunes* its name, the magazine was Franqui's idea. Cabrera Infante considers Franqui to be one of the most important promoters of Cuban culture of this century.[2] Franqui had ample experience in the field of culture. He founded *Mella* in 1941; *Nueva Generación* in 1948; and in 1950 *Nuestro Tiempo*, which was later taken over by members of the Cuban Communist Party. These three cultural publications allowed young writers to openly express their political and literary ideas. In the 1950s Franqui was involved with the clandestine media, including Radio Rebelde. From its founding in February 1958, he wrote the news bulletins and directed Radio Rebelde from the Sierra Maestra. In 1955 Franqui organized the clandestine weekly *Revolución* and with the triumph of the Revolution in January 1959 became its director. Franqui then envisioned a literary supplement for the newspaper and asked his close friend Cabrera Infante, who was fiction editor and movie critic for *Carteles* and movie critic for *Revolución,* to take charge of the magazine. To make the supplement run smoothly, Cabrera Infante wanted to enlist the help of Armando Fernández, who lived in New York. Cabrera Infante recruited Fernández when he, Franqui, and other dignitaries escorted Castro on his first trip to the United States. Shortly after Fernández returned to his native province of Oriente, Cabrera Infante asked him to move to Havana and join the magazine *Lunes* whose mission would be to promote culture in the new Cuba.

The "26th of July Movement" and *Lunes* represented a step toward modernity. If history implies an affirmation of the past, then modernity is a desire to break with the past and start anew.[3] Cuban leaders and writers wanted to distance themselves from previous political and literary trends and promote a new beginning, where ideas of the present were favored over those of the past. *Lunes* was indeed an important part of the revolution. It attempted to be modern and incorporate the latest literary and artistic currents of the time. Jacques Brouté, Tony Evora, and Raúl Martínez were in succession the magazine's three designers, and the style and artistic talent of each would leave an indelible mark on the magazine. At the recommendation of Brouté, *Lunes*'s first artistic designer, the magazine took on the appearance of a newspaper tabloid, similar to *L'Express,* the popular French weekly newspaper. With Martínez, *Lunes* took on the surrealistic qualities that gave the magazine its lasting identity.[4]

As the first magazine of its kind to emerge in the new government, *Lunes* aspired to be inclusive and appeal to the broad base that the "26th of July Movement" represented. The first issue contained *Lunes*'s editorial position:

> The Revolution has done away with all obstacles and has allowed the intellectual, the artist, and the writer to become part of the nation's life from which they were alienated. We believe—and want—this paper to be the vehicle—or rather the road—to a desired return to ourselves. . . . We are not part of a group, neither literary nor artistic. We are simply friends and people more or less of the same age. We do not have a defined political philosophy, although we do not reject certain systems that approach reality—and when we speak of systems we are referring, for example, to dialectical materialism or psychoanalysis, or existentialism. Nevertheless, we believe that literature—and art—of course, should approach reality more and to approach it more is, for us, to also approach the political, social, and economic phenomena of the society in which we live.[5]

From its inception, *Lunes* was an important cultural forum. Many writers and artists living in Cuba and others returning from self-imposed exile found an outlet for their ideas and works in *Lunes.* The magazine attracted the best young writers and artists of the time. Some were friends, and others had even collaborated in previous magazines, such as *Orígenes* (1944–1956), *Ciclón* (1955–1957, 1959), and *Nuestro Tiempo* (1954–1959). *Lunes* was reminiscent of some of the prerevolutionary magazines. Virgilio Piñera, who was one of *Ciclón*'s editors, became an important adviser to *Lunes.* Although it was modeled after the French weekly, in some respects *Lunes* also incorporated ideas from Cabrera Infante's movie review section in *Carteles* published in the 1950s.

There was an apparent connection between the previous publications and *Lunes,* but in particular between *Lunes* and *Revolución.* The early issues of *Revolución* contained the literary page "Nueva Generación," reminiscent of the earlier magazine *Nueva Generación* published by Franqui in 1948. There is indeed a link between one publication and the other, between "R/en el arte/en la literatura/R" [Revolution in art / in literature Revolution] and *Lunes de Revolución,* as stated in an unsigned editorial note and as pointed out by Matías

Montes Huidobro.[6] Some of the writers contributing to the literary section of *Revolución* also wrote for *Lunes de Revolución.*

The Cuban revolution was a centerpiece in the development of the novel of the "boom" period, and *Lunes* was its most important vehicle.[7] *Lunes* rapidly began to influence all aspects of culture in Cuba. The staff of *Lunes* was in control first of channel 2 and then channel 4, which sponsored a weekly television program aired on Monday evenings. It featured a range of programs such as dramas by Tennessee Williams and Anton Chekhov; music of Ignacio Piñeiro and jazz; the staging of Cabrera Infante's "Abril es el mes más cruel" ["April is the Cruellest Month"] and even a showing of *P.M.* (1961), the controversial 16-minute documentary that signaled the radical changes that were to come. Orlando Jiménez Leal, one of the codirectors of *P.M.,* was a cameraman for the television program and in charge of *Lunes*'s film department.[8] The staff also produced a televised theater program that included works such as Virgilio Piñera's *Electra Garrigó* (1943) and Eugène Ionesco's *The Bald Soprano* (1950). In addition, *Lunes* had a record company, Sonido Erre, and a publishing house, Ediciones Erre, which promoted Cuban literature and exposed Cuban readers to new literary currents.[9] *Lunes* reached its high point at the time of the Campaign Against Illiteracy, which focused the nation's attention on reading and writing and created the necessary infrastructure for the development of literature in Cuba and Latin America. A similar idea would be initiated by U.S. President Kennedy's Alliance for Progress, which developed social and cultural programs and ironically attempted to stop the spread of communism in Latin America.

This period was also that of the Bay of Pigs invasion, which brought unity to a nation facing a common enemy, similar to what would take place two years later during the Cuban Missile Crisis. The writers for *Revolución* and *Lunes de Revolución,* like many other Cubans, helped defeat the invading forces. These two historical events served to focus world attention on what was taking place in a remote but strategically important region of the world.

Lunes was responsible for bringing a diverse group of Cuban writers together and also for putting them in contact with others from abroad. The magazine provided the means to participate in and identify with the construction of a new society. But *Lunes* would also figure in the discord among writers who supported the revolution. This discord was highlighted in 1971 by the Padilla affair, which brought this era of the "boom" to an end.[10] Heberto Padilla was an important contributor to *Lunes* and a member of its staff. *Lunes* and its writers contributed to the creation of the "boom" and to its demise.

During its publication, *Lunes* was a new and innovative supplement. The magazine published works of Cuban writers, but it was not limited to them. Unlike previous magazines that were limited to a particular literary current, ideology, genre, or region, *Lunes* provided a home for writers and artists of different ideologies, genres, and generations from Cuba and the rest of the world. The editors included works produced in North America, Eastern Europe, Asia, Africa, and Latin America. *Lunes* published writers from the Spanish-speaking world such as Pablo Neruda, Jorge Luis Borges, Federico García Lorca, and others from Europe such as Jean Paul Sartre, Albert Camus, James Joyce, Franz Kafka, Marcel Proust, and T. S. Eliot. It also gathered political essays written by Fidel Castro, Che Guevara, Mao, Lenin, and Trotsky. *Lunes* even provided space for works and writers unknown to Cuban readers, such as the Polish novelist Bruno Shultz, whose writings first appeared there. *Lunes* gave the same consideration to all metanarratives, a truly postmodern publication.[11]

Lunes was a heterogeneous magazine that offered a wealth of information. There were special issues dedicated to Cuban writers such as Emilio Ballagas (issue 26), Pablo de la Torriente Brau (42), and José Martí (93); Spanish-speaking writers and artists such as Neruda (88), García Lorca (119), and Pablo Picasso (129); and writers from Eastern European and North American countries such as Anton Chekhov (91), Ernest Hemingway (118), and Constantín Stanislavski (125). There were issues about developing countries such as Guatemala (22), the People's Republic of China (108), Laos (115), Vietnam (116), and Korea (117); and others on agrarian reform (10), Castro's speech of 26 July 1961 (19), and blacks in the United States (66). *Lunes* reflected the strong nationalistic and anti-imperialistic sentiment that existed in Cuba during the early stages of the revolution, mirroring the government's political voice. *Lunes* supported the revolution and condemned its past enemies. Castro's denunciation of Jorge Mañach and the alleged capitalist newspaper *Diario de la Marina* on the television program "Ante la Prensa," was followed by similar attacks in *Lunes.* In "Mañach y *la Marina*" Padilla accused Mañach, a former member of the vanguard *Revista de Avance,* of complicity with the conservative policies of the *Diario,* which had aided the Batista dictatorship.[12] In a separate issue, Gregorio Ortega charged the *Diario de la Marina* and its director, José I. Rivero, of formulating editorial policies against the nation's progress and interests.[13] The solidarity between the revolution and *Lunes* was also voiced by José Alvarez Baragaño. In "Una generación: ni dividida ni vencida" he concludes: "Neither divided nor defeated: We should make the words of the revolution our cry."[14]

The magazine's mission was both political and literary. In an attempt to be modern, the writers of *Lunes* rejected literary currents previously popular in Cuba. Some writers, in particular Padilla and Baragaño, wrote articles against established writers and earlier literary circles, such as José Lezama Lima and the *Orígenes* group. Lezama Lima, Cintio Vitier, and Eliseo Diego, who wrote under different historical circumstances, were criticized for their political apathy. Their poetry was classified as hermetic, obscure, and elitist. In "La poesía en su lugar," Padilla described the group in the following manner: "*Orígenes* is an instance of our most pronounced bad taste. It is the proof of our past ignorance, evidence of our literary colonialism and our enslavement to old literary forms. It is not by accident that the words, the vocabulary of these poets make repeated monarchic allusion: Kingdom, crown, prince, princess, heralds."[15]

The sentiments against Lezama Lima and the *Orígenes* group should be understood as part of a younger generation's coming of age, as its members reacted to the anxiety of the influence of an older one.[16] The attacks were not new and were already present in Baragaño's "*Orígenes*: una impostura," in *Nueva Generación*, where he accused Lezama Lima of having obscure ideas. Baragaño wrote: "We, those who compose a new consciousness, and not a new sensibility, abolish the *Orígenes* group, an imposture we will no longer talk about."[17] In fact, Baragaño's words recall those already expressed in the first issue of *Ciclón,* "Borrón y cuenta nueva": "We erase *Orígenes* with one blow. *Orígenes,* which everyone knows, after ten years of useful service to Cuban culture, in the present is only dead weight."[18]

Wanting to separate the present from the past, *Lunes* from *Orígenes,* Padilla assessed the current mission of poetry and *Lunes*'s role in the construction of a new society:

> The poetry that will emerge now in a new country cannot repeat the old Trocadero slogans. The poet who expresses his anguish or happiness for the first time will have a responsibility; the gratuitous song must be opposed by a service voice. To the uncontrollable rhetoric, a breath of fresh air. I believe *Lunes de Revolución* has the obligation to divulge poetry written everywhere. I believe that *Lunes* can guide the voices of those who are still looking for their calling. I believe that it is the youths' duty to correct, research, and analyze our past.[19]

While the younger Baragaño, Padilla, and others attacked Lezama Lima, a symbol of the father figure, *Lunes* did not close its doors to the master poet. Pablo Armando Fernández had published in *Orígenes* and had strong connections to Lezama Lima. According to Cabrera Infante, Fernández was the diplomat of the group and was sent out on delicate missions, including one that involved asking Lezama Lima to write for *Lunes.*[20]

Lunes had gathered many of the best and brightest minds of the period. With writers and artists such as Padilla, Baragaño, César Leante, Rine Leal, and Cabrera Infante, *Lunes* was the cultural vanguard of the revolution. The magazine followed an independent policy and even published controversial works by Roman Polanski, Andrew Bach, Pablo Neruda, Milovan Djilas, and other international figures frowned upon by some of the more conservative Cuban officials. Its writers attacked critics such as Mañach and literary currents such as the one *Orígenes* and Lezama Lima represented, but they also challenged an increasingly powerful voice represented by the members of the old Communist Party.

In the short period that *Lunes* became a major literary phenomenon, it also fell sway to the challenges to that status. Contributors were aware that *Lunes* had the official backing of *Revolución* and Franqui and that they were at the forefront of culture in Cuba. This status made *Lunes* a controversial magazine. As Castro moved away from the "26th of July Movement," other political trends began to emerge. Many of *Lunes*'s writers became entrenched in their positions. They would soon discover that the magazine was swimming against the changing tide. The problems facing *Lunes* began with a simple disagreement over editorial policies and led to the eventual suppression of the magazine.

The changes taking place in Cuba were reflected and recorded in the magazine. Although there were many letters to the editor supporting *Lunes,* others opposed the magazine. In one issue, for example, Marcos Jiménez complained that *Lunes* published too many foreign writers and not enough Cuban ones.[21] In another letter in that issue, Hilda Rodríguez made specific reference to Cabrera Infante's "Abril es el mes más cruel." She wrote: "It's a pity that the refined and intelligent magazine *Lunes de Revolución* insists on publishing offensive short stories, which would make anyone nervous and upset. Why does the bride commit suicide in 'Abril es el mes más cruel?' It's not right. They seemed so happy! I must admit that after reading that story, even if you offer me the crown jewels I will never read another story in *Lunes,* unless you promise to be more considerate with the sensibility of your readers. Can't you do something for the beautiful couple to remain together?"

In the same issue, Odilio González wrote a more polemic letter entitled "Todo al revés (Carta abierta a Guillermo Cabrera Infante)" [Everything backwards: Open letter to Guillermo Cabrera Infante]. In the letter, González complained to the editor that many young writers were excluded from publishing in the magazine. González's letter listed some 50 young writers who should have been eligible to write for *Lunes.* The majority of letters to the editor published in subsequent issues agreed with González's position.[22] The editors were sensitive to the complaint, which may have led to the creation of Piñera's "A partir de cero" [From zero on], a section that featured beginning writers.

Lunes clashed with powerful political and ideological groups that opposed the magazine's broad policies. *Lunes*'s opponents favored a narrow interpretation of culture and wanted to control the publication. One of these groups included the Dirección de Cultura. In one instance, *Lunes*'s editorial board and Baragaño, in particular, criticized the organizers of the National Art and Sculpture exposition for their mediocre selection. Although the editorial board recognized the importance of some of the painters and sculptors represented in the exposition, its members felt that the overall selection was inferior. Even the works of the well-known artist René Portocarrero, whose paintings were often featured on the cover of *Bohemia,* were the object of criticism.[23]

As a liberal supplement with a broad but anti-imperialistic cultural content, *Lunes* held its ground. It remained defiant: the editors of *Lunes* did not see any need to adjust to the changing political climate. Néstor Almendros best summarizes the period:

> A lot of things were happening pretty quickly at that time. One country was an ally and suddenly it wasn't. All of these "mistakes" had the Communist Party and Fidel Castro very irritated. Above all, *Lunes* had committed the sin of publishing stories by Soviet authors, like Isaac Babel. Such authors from the first generation before Stalin had ended up in disgrace in the USSR; some had even been sent to Siberia. *Lunes* had published works by Arthur Koestler. It also had the gall, according to the government, to have produced that previously mentioned issue praising Marilyn Monroe and Brigitte Bardot.[24]

Lunes was frowned upon by members of the Communist Party who occupied key positions not only in the Dirección de Cultura, but also in the Instituto Cubano de Artes e Industrias Cinematográficos (ICAIC) [Cuban Film Industry]. The most serious controversy occurred in 1961 over *P.M.,* a film by Sabá Cabrera Infante, Guillermo Cabrera Infante's brother, and Orlando Jiménez Leal. In this short documentary, the camera-eye moves from one location in Havana to another, from bar to bar, where Afro-Cubans are dancing, drinking, smoking, and having a good time. The film was an inappropriate expression of the revolution at a time when the Cuban government was assuming a more defensive position with regard to the United States. The festive attitude of the Afro-Cubans in the film was considered antithetical to the ideology that "white" leaders of the revolution wanted to impose on the rest of the population.[25] Almendros, at the time a film critic for *Bohemia,* provided the following account of *P.M.*:

> And, what is "Post Meridian"? Simply, it is a short film (of some fifteen minutes), which captures faithfully the atmosphere of the night life of the popular bars of a large city. The camera-scalpel travels like an untiring noctambulist from Regla, in a water taxi to the port of Havana, to the cafes of Cuatro Caminos, and ends in the small bars of the Playa de Marianao, and back to Regla. The process could not have been simpler. It belongs to the spontaneous movie, the "free cinema" which is in vogue in the world. Never impertinent, the hidden camera gathers images without the awareness of those being filmed. Reality is captured as is, without actors, without additional lighting like in the studios, without a director ready to falsify things advising and deciding each of the movements or the dialogues. There is no film script a priori, without the scenes developed in life, without "fixing" them. Essentially, this is a documentary movie, which selects and extracts from reality, surrounding the elements used to compose the film. "Post Meridian" is a visual and musical document, but one in which a poetic transfiguration of common daily events take place. *P.M.* is immensely realistic, but it is also immensely poetical.[26]

In some respects, *P.M.* became a response to Julio García Espinosa's *Cuba baila*, a film portraying Cuban life and dance. Although Almendros's review of *Cuba baila* was cautiously positive, he nevertheless described the film's defects. But there was a major difference between *P.M.* and *Cuba baila*: García Espinosa had the support of the official movie industry (ICAIC), while Sabá Cabrera Infante and Jiménez Leal were young aficionados (Jiménez Leal was 19 years old when *P.M.* was completed) who were associated with *Lunes* and had received a modest sum from the magazine to finish the film. In spite of the monetary and artistic resources available to García Espinosa,

Almendros gave *Cuba baila* three stars and awarded the amateur filmmakers four stars. Almendros's review was reinforced by Luis Orticón who, in *Bohemia,* claimed that *P.M.* accomplished something absent in other Cuban films.[27]

During this period, films became the battleground between *Lunes* and the ICAIC. This was the case with *P.M.,* as well as with Soviet and Czechoslovakian films that were suspected of challenging their respective governments. Almendros worked for the ICAIC, but his political and personal allegiances were with the *Lunes* group. He became involved in another dispute, which sealed his fate as a writer for *Bohemia*. Almendros awarded four stars to Frantisel Vlacil's *La paloma blanca* {The white pigeon}, exhibited during a week of Czechoslovakian films. Almendros ranked *La paloma blanca* as the best film of the series and placed it within the vanguard of neo-expressionistic and experimental film, praising its humanistic and poetic content. He questioned what would have happened 10 or 15 years before, during the Stalinist era. More likely than not, Almendros believed, the film would have been prohibited or classified as formalist like so many others, including Sergei Eisenstein's *Ivan the Terrible* (1945).[28]

Almendros's review was met with a strong backlash. An anonymous article "Cine: Debate en torno a 'La paloma blanca,' " in *Mella,* a publication of the Young Communist Organization, captured the events that followed the review.[29] The Medical Students' Association sponsored a debate on *La paloma blanca*, moderated by Dr. Oldrich Tichy of the Czechoslovakian Embassy. While some commended the film for its cinematography, the sentiment was not unanimous. The film critic for *Mella,* Miguel Ángel Moreno, took issue with Almendros's article and argued against formalism, that is, art for art's sake. Since Cuba was involved in an intense struggle, he preferred less symbolism and a more straightforward message. The anonymous writer sided with Moreno's criticism and took exception to Almendros's use of the term "Stalinism." Contrary to Almendros, he defended Stalin and claimed that his was a period in which Soviets opposed Nazism and constructed socialism. In addition, Stalin fought for the working class and helped to advance Marxist-Leninism. He ended his article with a warning: "We point out to Mr. Almendros that the reaction, which he has pretended to write about, conveys his hatred of socialism and Marxist-Leninism, hidden under the cloak of the XX Congress of the Communist Party of the Soviet Union, regarding the cult of personality. Since he is not a Marxist-Leninist, we advise him not to fall into that trap. In such situations

Mr. Almendros should call a spade a spade." The writer's words were prophetic, as the line was drawn between those who accepted the Marxist-Leninist interpretation of culture promoted by the ICAIC and the communists and those who opposed it. Even though the latter supported the revolution, they now became enemies of the state. Shortly thereafter, Almendros was fired from *Bohemia* and replaced with a more politically sympathetic critic.

The tension that existed between the supporters of each position was already evident and expressed in an issue of *Lunes* dedicated to movies, "*Lunes* va al cine," prepared with the help of Fausto Canel and Almendros, who also contributed an article on Spanish films.[30] The entire issue focused on movies and included material pertinent to the *P.M.* debate that was to follow. Emilio García Riera opens the debate with what could have been interpreted as *Lunes*'s position, in support of the New Wave in filmmaking. For him, movies did not reflect reality, rather they recreated it. He also considered neorealism a thing of the past; the present belongs to the New Wave. He appraised the two as being not only different but complete opposites.

According to García Riera, the New Wave, which is not exclusively French, is open to the ideas and styles of the filmmaker. Neorealism, on the other hand, offers a failed recipe. He claims that Cesare Zavattini is a part of history and orthodox neorealism. Luchino Visconti, Roberto Rossellini, Michelangelo Antonioni, and Federico Fellini were Italian filmmakers who began their careers with neorealism but moved on to give birth to a new cinema.

García Riera's essay takes an interesting turn toward the second half, when he stresses the importance of liberty, especially when commenting on the commercial and decadent movie industry. Though he recognizes the downfall, he also realizes that the talent of a Fritz Lang can be instructive and revealing and therefore creates an appreciation for all films. He also underscores the form, which he believes moviemakers should develop but without giving in to commercial interests. García Riera ends his essay by stating that the problem of creation is one of liberty.

The second article "El neorrealismo y la nueva ola francesa" [Neorealism and the French New Wave] by García Espinosa defends the position associated with the ICAIC. He studies the two most recent currents: the Free Cinema and neorealism. He recalls that prior to 1959 many considered neorealism to be the future of movies. More than a style, it was an attitude toward reality and a weapon against dictatorship and imperialism.

García Espinosa considered the Free Cinema as deriving from the camera-eye of the Russian Dzhiga Vertov. Therefore, the French New Wave, which some claimed to be similar to neorealism in content, differs in cinematic language. New Wave emphasizes style and the artist's point of view, which García Espinosa associates with the petite bourgeoisie. Unlike the New Wave, neorealism takes its subject matter from the popular sectors of society. García Espinosa is not willing to say whether one form of art is better than the other, but for him neorealism deepens an understanding of the masses.

Alfredo Guevara contributed the third article. His "Realidad y deberes de la crítica cinematográfica" [Reality and duty of cinematographic criticism] is overtly political. It starts out by attacking the bourgeois sentiments that have dominated the movies. Guevara claims that criticism has been controlled by opportunism and ignorance but also by financial and political interests of the U.S. Embassy. The revolution represents change and the critic cannot ignore the changes. He should ask for whom is he writing? Why and in which period and society? And, above all, why write? In answer to those questions he should ask other questions, such as how to write, what to write, and when to write. Another article by Tomás Gutiérrez Alea is limited to explaining the use of nonprofessional actors in the film *Rebelde*.

The first section of the "*Lunes* va al cine" issue captures the debate between neorealism and Free Cinema, and contains articles on film in other countries such as Poland, Czechoslovakia, France, and Spain. The second section of this issue looks at another tradition in movies, eroticism. "El erotismo en el cine" [Eroticism in the movies] contains pictures of the sexiest women of the times: Theda Bara, Gloria Swanson, Virginia Bruce, Greta Garbo, Jean Harlow, Carol Lombard, Marlene Dietrich, Rita Hayworth, Sofia Loren, Kim Novak, and Hedy Lamarr. In "Técnica del erotismo" [Techniques of eroticism], Lo Duca explores the commercial movies and their insistence on sex or eroticism, even in films such as *Bernardetti* and *Joan of Arc* that do not call for such scenes, but where mouth, breasts, and pubic area are treated as erogenous zones. The second half also features essays on Marilyn Monroe by Arthur Miller and Brigitte Bardot by Simone de Beauvoir, where innocence and the image of the child woman, but above all her breasts, are the focus of attention.

Cabrera Infante had an open-minded attitude toward film, and he was a connoisseur of Hollywood films. His openness may help to explain the presence of the second section of "*Lunes* va al cine."

As a film critic for *Carteles,* Cabrera Infante had already taken a position regarding Zavattini and Vittorio De Sica in his review of *El oro de Nápoles* [Naples's Gold] dated 15 January 1956. The version that appears in *Un oficio del siglo veinte* [*A Twentieth Century Job*], whose title recalls the Hollywood film giant Twentieth Century Fox, is preceded by an epigraph: "la decadencia de zavattini (y también la de de sica) fue advertida a tiempo por caín" [the decline of zavattini (and also that of de sica) was pointed out ahead of his time by caín].[31] In this review, Caín claims that *El oro de Nápoles,* which attempts to represent Neapolitan reality, is not one of their best pictures and in fact is the worst of the series. Cabrera Infante seizes the opportunity to undermine neorealist ideas that divided Italian criticism and at that time were not important to the organizers of the famous Cannes Festival. He goes to great lengths to point out that in Naples, De Sica, Giuseppe Marotta, and Zavattini tricked the people into believing they were making a glorious film about Naples but instead showed the perennial pizza vendors and prostitutes. Naples's mayor even classified De Sica alongside Curzio Malaparte, Naples's number-one enemy.

Cabrera Infante maintained a consistent position regarding these films. He wrote "El canto del cisne neorrealista" [The neorealist swan's song] about *Two Cents Worth of Hope* (1952) preceded by an ironic epigraph that sets the tone for the review: "creo que caín amaba al neorrealismo más de lo que admitía: era su ossessione" (*Oficio,* 284) ["*i believe that caín loved neorealism more than he admitted: it was his ossessione*" (*Job,* 216)]. Though he praises Renato Castellani's *Two Cents Worth of Hope* as one of the best works of neorealism, he also points out that others attempting to follow his example have failed. Toward the end of the review, however, Cabrera Infante undermines the film's neorealist qualities and considers it an intellectual example of the popular Italian Renaissance comedy. This interpretation makes it seem new though it arrived in Havana ten years after it premiered.

Cabrera Infante had much kinder words for Hollywood films such as *Summertime* (1955), with Katherine Hepburn; *Bus Stop* (1956), with Marilyn Monroe; and *And God Created Woman* (1956), with Brigitte Bardot, which Cabrera Infante considered the best erotic movie ever. Though the film accents Bardot's nude body, an observation Beauvoir would also make in her essay for *Lunes,* Cabrera Infante also sees morality. He concludes by suggesting that this film would contribute to the Bardot myth in a way similar to what *Rebel Without a Cause* (1955) did for James Dean. This praise, however, does not mean that he hailed all Hollywood films. On the contrary, he also criticized them, as is the case with *The Old Man and the Sea* (1958). He gave the film a thumbs down, claimed it was worse than mediocre, and accused it of not being a picture; moreover, he implied that Spencer Tracy was a contributing factor to its failure.[32]

Cabrera Infante's position is best represented in articles published in *Carteles* about the cycle of Soviet movies shown during the month of February 1960, one year before *Lunes* published its film issue and *P.M.* was censored. In the first segment of a two-part article entitled "El cine soviético cabalga de nuevo (I) *Potemkin* versus *Chapaiev*" [The Soviet movie gallops again] he refers to socialist realism, whose most important exponent between 1928 and 1953 was Iosif Vissarionovich Dzhugashvili, alias Stalin. Cabrera Infante agreed with Dwight MacDonald that, thanks to Khrushchev, the Soviet movies had returned to developing the theme of love and its triumph over ideology. The movies under review were those that were best able to resist the lack of creativity imposed by socialist realism. He praises Eisenstein's *The Battleship Potemkin* (1925), which earned the distinction of being one of the 10 best pictures ever, a distinction Cabrera Infante questioned. Many reviewers have referred to famous scenes, but he preferred the simplicity of the arrival of the marine's cadaver.

Cabrera Infante also praised *Chapaiev* (1934), though with less enthusiasm than *Potemkin*. While the film brought Stalin to tears, for Cabrera Infante it contains the primitiveness of an American Western and its poetic ending overshadows its propaganda.

In the second set of reviews published toward the latter part of the month, Cabrera Infante asserted that Soviet films were the ones to watch for during the next five years. This view was attributed, in part, to young film directors such as Mark Donskoi, whose work was of equal caliber to that of Eisenstein or Alexander Dovjenko. Donskoi, who in *La madre* (1956) borrows Hollywood cinematic techniques, remains tied to the academic tone reminiscent of the old Stalinist tradition. Cabrera Infante had less kind words for Greigrij M. Kosintzev, who decided to make a film that is slow and boring based not on the novels of his Soviet compatriots but on Miguel de Cervantes's masterpiece *Don Quixote*.

Cabrera Infante considers Sergei Yutkevich's *Othello* (1956) one of the most beautiful Soviet films of the last 20 years. The film director stays away from social and economic issues and concentrates on the theme of love. The technique, which he considers to be "formalist," is a search for expression appropriate to the content. He also applauds Elia Kazan's adaptation of Fyodor Dostoyevsky's *The Idiot* (1868), but this film was controversial since Dostoyevsky had been accused of writing decadent czarist literature.

Cabrera Infante dedicated more time and space to his review of the Soviet film *The Last Shot*, which shows that the greatest problems of our century are not political but those related to love. Cabrera Infante would develop this theme in *Tres tristes tigres* (1967) [*Three Trapped Tigers* (1971)] and *La Habana para un Infante difunto* (1979) [*Infante's Inferno* (1984)] and repeat it in *Ella cantaba boleros* (1996) [I Heard Her Sing]. In *The Last Shot* the two protagonists, representing two distinct political systems and ideologies, fall in love. But Isolda's shooting of Oleg, before being rescued by his men, indicates that socialism has triumphed over eternal love. Her tears over her lost love suggest the film's ambiguity, that is, the hero is not totally good and the villain is not totally evil. Cabrera Infante considered this motion picture a triumph for the Soviet movie industry.

Cabrera Infante ends his review of *The Last Shot* and the cycle of Soviet films with an allusion to the debate unfolding in Cuba at that time. He takes the opportunity to take a pot shot at the communists. He explains that he does not want to answer questions about the film's double meaning, such as the implication that, like Isolda with her final gunshot, the communists have killed all that was subtle and elegant in Russia.

> [A]dmitir por un momento esto es hacerle un daño irreparable al nuevo cine soviético y confesar que sólo traicionando a la revolución puede en la Unión Soviética hacerse un film que sustituya la trivialidad ampulosa y la pesantez académica de los días de Stalin (además que hay en Cuba la necesidad de hacer un cine que a la vez que revolucionario en su contenido, sea nuevo en su forma como para hacer propia una tesis que es, a primera vista, profundamente reaccionaria). El cronista confiesa que prefiere creer que es el viejo amor consuntivo de los románticos, que regresa ahora en términos actuales: la política puede separar a dos que se aman, como cualquier fuerza divina, sólo que esta vez el destino es probable que haya leído a Carlos Marx. (*Oficio,* 398)

> [To admit this for one moment is to do an irreparable harm to the new Soviet cinema and to confess that only by betraying the revolution can there be made in the Soviet Union a film that may replace the pompous triviality and academic ponderousness of the Stalin days

> (besides the fact that in Cuba there is the need to make a cinema that while being revolutionary in its content will be new in form, that will make for itself a thesis that is even, at first sight, profoundly reactionary). The cronista confesses that he prefers to believe that it is the old consumptive love of the Romantics, that is returning now in present-day terms: politics can separate two people who love each other, like any divine force, only this time fate has probably read Karl Marx.] (*Job,* 305)

From Cabrera Infante's perspective, love was not spontaneous but rather, like other aspects of society, subject to communist control.

While Cabrera Infante did not contribute an article to "*Lunes* va al cine," his opposition to socialist realism and neorealism was evident. His reviews, and in particular the last two described here, constituted Cabrera Infante's position in the debate unfolding in Cuba. Cabrera Infante, the "*Lunes* va al cine" issue, and the film *P.M.* represented a direct affront to communist ideologue leaders such as Guevara, who wanted to control the movie industry.

The differences between the ICAIC and the directors of *P.M.* and Almendros were at the same time political and aesthetic. Members of the ICAIC supported the neorealist ideas of the Italian school that Rossellini and De Sica originated at the end of World War II and that Zavattini, the famous neorealist filmmaker, represented. By the time *P.M.* was filmed and Almendros wrote his review for *Bohemia*, Zavattini had been invited to Cuba as a guest of the ICAIC and was paid handsomely to teach a seminar.[33] The ICAIC was interested in promoting the neorealist tradition, and Zavattini was its supreme spokesperson.

Unlike the members of the ICAIC, the members of *Lunes* rejected the antiquated neorealism and embraced the English Free Cinema or the French cinema verité. This new current did not transform reality to make it what it should be. On the contrary, the eye of the camera captured reality in the making. Almendros himself had put this technique into practice with his film *Cincuenta y ocho cincuenta y nueve* [Fifty-eight fifty-nine] in which his camera recorded the New Year's Eve celebration in New York's Times Square. In the film the happy faces of the celebrants were juxtaposed with that of a man begging for food, invisible to all but the camera.

P.M. was censored for portraying an aspect of Cuban life which officials of the revolution wanted to eliminate. The censorship of *P.M.* was also an attack on *Lunes de Revolución.* In their attempt to give culture a new direction, the creators of *P.M.* and *Lunes* became victims of a transition that was giving the Cuban Communist Party an increasingly powerful voice in the new government.

Although modernity attempts to be new, it also draws on a tradition of rupture. For Octavio Paz, this implies the negation of the tradition and the rupture.[34] But modernity is not totally free from the past; in some strange way modernity depends on tradition, even as it reacts to move away from the past. In Cuba, the revolution was new but the ideas it embodied were not, at least not in the implementation of cultural reforms. The conflicts that erupted around *P.M.*, *Lunes,* and the ICAIC can be traced to ideological differences that had emerged in the Cine Club and the Sociedad Nuestro Tiempo. Almendros explains the origin of these groups and their conflicts:

> The Cine Club of Havana was founded by Germán Puig and Ricardo Vigón. Then Guillermo Cabrera Infante, Tomás Gutiérrez Alea (who at that time still was not a Marxist), and I joined. That was around 1948 and 1949. The Cine Club, which showed classic films, did not have a precise political ideology but rather defended cinematography as an art and nothing else. Later on, our film club was renamed Cinemateca de Cuba. At first, this Cinemateca de Cuba was part of the film department of Nuestro Tiempo. It was a private society in which there were departments of painting, dance and music and which, in the beginning, had backed Carlos Franqui. But elements of the Cuban Communist Party, then known as the Popular Socialist Party, infiltrated this society little by little. It was then that we decided to abandon Nuestro Tiempo and continue our sessions on the side. The Communists wanted to impose their political point of view. We didn't. We were interested in defending cinema and nothing more. We defended a good Russian film as if it were a good film from any other country, including the United States. This Marxist Cine Club, which was originally ours and later Nuestro Tiempo's, then divided. . . . When the Revolution triumphed, in January 1959, Nuestro Tiempo's Marxist film club had the chance to gain control of the ICAIC. That is to say that the rivalry between the group from the Cinemateca of Cuba, consisting of Cabrera Infante, Germán Puig, Ricardo Vigón and me, and the other group, consisting of Alfredo Guevara, García Espinosa and Gutiérrez Alea, which had by that time become Marxist, had been passed on. We of the Cinemateca were almost completely excluded, even though we had been the pioneers, the founders of the first Cine Club of the Cinemateca in Havana, one of the first such societies of this type in Latin America.[35]

History would be repeated. When the ICAIC was first formed in March 1959 there was a sense of openness and Cabrera Infante became its vice president but soon resigned his position when he realized that the ideas of the past also existed in the present. A fundamental rift existed between the ICAIC and *Lunes.* While *Lunes* encouraged dialogue, the ICAIC wanted to control the film industry.

P.M. was filmed outside of the supervision of the ICAIC, and in a style contrary to the neorealist tradition the communists wanted to impose. Cabrera Infante and *Lunes* attempted to champion openness toward culture that included fostering those literary and artistic currents in vogue. *P.M.* became a casualty in a long-standing struggle between opposing political and artistic currents. Its suppression indicated that the ICAIC was in firm control of the film industry in Cuba and would not tolerate any film or criticism not sanctioned by the official industry. "*Lunes* va al cine" was probably considered a daring affront to the ICAIC and the Cuban government. If it was viewed as the editors' attempt to influence the direction of film in Cuba, the magazine was a formidable enemy and had to be eliminated. *P.M.* may have been interpreted as another sign of what was to come from the *Lunes* group. The ICAIC was not willing to share its newfound power. Almendros rightfully attributed the ICAIC's insistence on staging an ideological battle over *P.M.* to the importance Lenin had placed on film as a political weapon. Cubans were movie aficionados and constituted a large block of economic clout, a fact that was recorded in "*Lunes* va al cine."[36] The communists were well aware that whoever controlled the movie industry would have a direct line to the heads, hearts, and pockets of the people.

By the time *P.M.* was completed, the Cuban Communist Party had gained strength within the revolutionary government, and Fidel Castro was in control of the government. He had embraced the members of the well-organized Communist Party, and he had a more definite idea of the government's direction. Castro's 26 July 1961 speech confirmed what had been suspected. He stated that the different revolutionary groups had come together under the Organización Revolución Integrada (ORI) [Integrated Revolutionary Organization], controlled by prominent communist leaders of the old school. K. S. Karol says that "Aníbal Escalante was in charge of organization, his brother César of propaganda, Carlos Rafael Rodríguez of economic matters, Edith García Buchaca of culture—and that they were all Communist leaders of the old school."[37]

On 16 April 1961, the day before the Bay of Pigs invasion, Castro had declared that the Cuban revolution was socialist. The invasion brought unity and strength to the country and, like many others, the writers and artists of *Revolución* and *Lunes de Revolución* went to the Ciénega de Zapata to defend the revolution. The momentum that brought an overwhelming defeat to the counterrevolutionary forces and their U.S. supporters was used to further unify the country by doing away with individuals and groups that did not fit into the new socialist character of the revolution. Karol points out that the Bay of Pigs was followed by a wave of arrests of more than 100,000 people.[38] Among those arrested were Lisandro Otero and Marcia Leiseca. Franqui lobbied for their release.[39]

P.M. had been shown on channel 2 with enormous success; however to have it shown at the Rex Cinema, one of the few privately owned movie houses, required permission from the Comisión Revisadora de Películas [Film Review Commission]. The commissioners responded to the request by confiscating the film. Franqui's informal meeting with Castro to head off a possible confrontation with the ICAIC was converted into a national meeting of writers and artists at the Biblioteca Nacional José Martí. The debate between Alfredo Guevara on one side and Jiménez Leal and Sabá Cabrera Infante on the other was turned into an opportunity for Castro and the old communist guard to disband *Revolución* and *Lunes de Revolución.*

The three June (16, 23, and 30) meetings in 1961 that signaled the end of *Lunes* were presided over by García Buchaca, in charge of culture; Rodríguez, of economics; and Guevara of the ICAIC, all members of the old Communist Party. Also present were Castro, "el comandante"; Osvaldo Dorticós, president; Armando Hart, minister of education; Haydée Santamaría, president of Casa de las Américas; Vicentina Antuña, director of Consejo de Cultura; and Joaquín Ordoqui. Neither Franqui nor Guillermo Cabrera Infante attended the first meeting, but they felt compelled to be present at the second one to defend their publications, actions, and film from the opposition. Franqui did not attend the last meeting and left for Europe.

Guevara accused *Revolución* and *Lunes de Revolución* of being enemies of the Soviet Union and of dividing the revolution from within. Franqui reminded the accusers that the intent of the newspaper and supplement was to combat imperialism. *Lunes* published Marxist texts and its writers participated in the defeat of the Bay of Pigs invaders. Franqui affirmed that contemporary culture was anticapitalist and stood up for *P.M.,* stating that music and dance are an intrinsic part of Cuban culture, inherited from Africa. Franqui's defense received overwhelming support from the writers present who had rejected the official position.[40]

Castro's idea of consolidating the revolution involved a turning away from his rebel friends, such as Franqui, and accepting the help of the better organized members of the Communist Party, even though they had not participated in the revolution. The writers of *Lunes* had worked for the revolution. Nonetheless, the political climate had changed. Castro needed the Soviets in order to fight U.S. imperialism and remain in power. The political and cultural concepts promoted by the *Lunes* staff became incompatible with those advanced by the ORI. In the transformation of Cuban society, culture was perhaps the last and most difficult segment to be altered and controlled.

Lunes was closed because of an alleged shortage of paper. At the last meeting Castro pronounced his famous "Palabras a los intelectuales" [Words to the intellectuals], setting the stage for judging literature and culture in the revolution. According to Castro's speech, *P.M.* was discussed widely. Although he acknowledged that there was a difference of opinion regarding the film, and that some questioned the nature of the process used to judge it, he did not relinquish the government's right to impose its puritanical worldview. Castro's dictum "Within the Revolution everything. Outside the Revolution, nothing" left no room for interpretation. He offered little clarification of the problems facing intellectuals in Cuba. Many would repeat his words but also would interpret them to coincide with their own position regarding the revolution. The problems surrounding *Lunes* did not end when the magazine closed in November 1961. They continued to affect writers and artists alike, in particular those who continued their loyalty to *Lunes* and the ideals for which it stood.

At one of the June 1961 meetings orchestrated to destroy *Lunes*, José Baragaño, a regular contributor to *Lunes*, admitted that he was wrong to criticize the revolution. Baragaño's confession would be echoed by Padilla's staged confession in 1971 before a similar gathering of Cuban writers and artists, also presided over by members of the Communist Party.[41]

The closing of *Lunes* created a literary and cultural void that needed to be filled. The Unión Nacional de Escritores y Artistas de Cuba (UNEAC) [Union of Cuban Writers and Artists] was formed to gather and supervise writers and artists looking for avenues of expression. UNEAC essentially appropriated from *Lunes* the role of promoter of literature and the arts and formalized it under its own umbrella. Three new publications emerged from UNEAC: *Unión, La*

Gaceta de Cuba, and *Hola,* as well as the Editorial House UNEAC, which also produced its own television program.

The last issue of *Lunes* was a defiant protest against the meetings at the Biblioteca Nacional and the attacks on the literary supplement. It was a tribute to Picasso and modern art. As a supporter of the Cuban revolution, Picasso created works that stood in opposition to the more rigid communist interpretations of art. This issue featured an essay by Guillaume Apollinaire, as well as essays by Franqui, Cabrera Infante, Fernández, Edmundo Desnoes, and Lezama Lima.

Lunes was a truly revolutionary magazine due not only to the quality of its content but also to its presentation of literature and culture in what could have been a truly significant revolution. Since the closing of the magazine, most of those who wrote for *Lunes* have left Cuba.

Notes

1. See, for example, introduction to *Modern Latin American Fiction Writers, First Series,* ed. William Luis (Detroit: Gale Research, 1992), xi–xv.

2. William Luis, "Un mes lleno de *Lunes,*" unpublished interview with Guillermo Cabrera Infante, 1978. In this interview Cabrera Infante reacts to Luis's interview with Pablo Armando Fernández and Lisandro Otero and their comments about *Lunes.* See also Luis, "Autopsia de *Lunes de Revolución:* Entrevista a Pablo Armando Fernández," *Plural* 17, 126 (1982): 52–62, and Otero, "Lunes de un frustrado," *Prisma* (October 1983): 41–43.

3. See Paul de Man, "Literary History and Literary Modernity" in *Blindness and Insight: Essays in the Rhetoric of Contemporary Criticism* (New York: Oxford University Press, 1971).

4. "Un mes lleno de *Lunes,*" 4.

5. *Lunes de Revolución* 1 (23 March 1959): 2. Also cited in *Diccionario de literatura cubana* 1 (Havana: Editorial Letras Cubans, 1980), 525. References in the text are to *Lunes de Revolución,* hereafter cited in the text as *Lunes.* Unless otherwise indicated, all translations are by William Luis.

6. "Nueva Generación," *Chasqui* 9, 1 (1979): 39–66. The first issue of "Nueva Generación" of *Revolución* contains the following statement: "De nuevo sale a la luz pública, que es el pueblo, tras once años de su aparición y nueve del último número. Ahora como página de artes, letras y humanidades de 'Revolución,' órgano del Movimiento Revolucionario '26 de Julio.' Antes como revista tirada en papel gaceta tamaño tabloide . . . sus primeros números—hablamos de la etapa precedente—recogía la voz de un grupo de jóvenes artistas. Sus editores fueron: Carlos Franqui, Ithiel León, Guillermo Cabrera Infante, Rine Leal, Matías Montes Huidobro y Jorge Tallet. Pero esto es hacer historia. Mas lo que importa es la obra que ellos nos dejan y la que ellos, hoy, están haciendo . . . colaboraron en 'Nueva Generación,' en aquella época, los pintores Wilfredo Lam, Roberto Diago, José María Mijares y Sabá Cabrera. Y los poetas y escritores Antonio Súarez, Nora Badía, Carilda Oliver Labra, Armando Cruz Cobos, Rafael Enrique Marrero, Queta Farias y otros"

("Nueva Generación," *Revolución* [13 January 1959]: 4. Also cited by Montes Huidobro in "Nueva Generación," 40).

[Once again in the public eye, 11 years after its appearance and 9 years since its last issue. Now, as a page of arts, letters, and humanities of *Revolución*, a branch of the "26 July Revolutionary Movement." Before, as a magazine printed in tabloid form. . . . Their first issues—we are talking about that earlier time when precedents were set—captured the voice of a group of young intellectuals. Their editors were: Carlos Franqui, Ithiel León, Guillermo Cabrera Infante, Rine Leal, Matías Montes Huidobro, and Jorge Tallet. But this is history. What really matters is the works that they have left us and the ones they are producing today. . . . In that period, the painters who contributed to "Nueva Generación" were Wilfredo Lam, Roberto Diago, José María Mijares and Sabá Cabrera. And the poets and writers were Antonio Suárez, Nora Badía, Carilda Oliver Labra, Armando Cruz Cobos, Rafael Enrique Marrero, Queta Farias, and others (Trans. by editor).]

7. See, for example, Emir Rodríguez Monegal's *El boom de la novela latinoamericana* (Caracas: Editorial Tiempo Nuevo, 1975) and Luis, "Culture as Text: The Cuban/Caribbean Connection," in *Translation Perspective: Culture as Text,* eds. Luis and Julio Rodríguez-Luis (Binghamton: SUNY at Binghamton, 1992).

8. Fausto Canel, "Orlando Jiménez Leal y el 'affaire P.M.,' " *Linden Lane Magazine* 6, 2–3 (April/September 1987): 17.

9. "Un mes lleno de *Lunes,*" 8. Also see "Mordidas del caimán barbudo," *Quimera* 39–40 (1984): 72–73.

10. See "Culture as Text."

11. See François Lyotard, *The Post-Modern Condition,* trans. Geoff Bennington and Brian Massumi (Minneapolis: University of Minnesota Press, 1984).

12. *Lunes* 33 (2 November 1959): 15.

13. *Lunes* 39 (14 December 1959): 10.

14. *Lunes* 38 (7 December 1959): 15.

15. *Lunes* 38 (7 December 1959): 5. Cabrera Infante was also critical of Lezama Lima. Many years later he would write: "Desde esta posición de fuerza máxima nos dedicamos a la tarea de aniquilar a respetados escritores del pasado. Como Lezama Lima, tal vez porque tuvo la audacia de combinar en sus poemas las ideologías anacrónicas de Góngora y Mallarmé, articuladas en La Habana de entonces para producir violentos versos de un catolicismo magnífico y obscuro—y reaccionario. Pero lo que hicimos en realidad fue tratar de asesinar la reputación de Lezama." ("Mordidas del caimán barbudo," 72). [From this position we dedicated ourselves with maximum force to the work of annihilating respected writers of the past. Like Lezama Lima, perhaps because he had the audacity to combine in his poems the anachronistic ideologies of Góngora and Mallarmé, articulated in Havana to produce violent verses of a magnificent and obscure, and reactionary, Catholicism. But what we actually did was to try to assassinate the reputation of Lezama (Trans. Mykal Duffy)].

16. Harold Bloom, *Anxiety of Influence: A Theory of Poetry* (New York: Oxford University Press, 1975).

17. *Revolución* (14 March 1959): 2. Also cited by Montes Huidobro in "Nueva Generación," 49.

18. *Ciclón* 1 (1955): 22–23. "Borramos a *Orígenes* de un golpe. A *Orígenes* que como todo el mundo sabe tras diez años de eficaces servicios a la cultura en Cuba, es actualmente sólo peso muerto." Also cited in *Diccionario de la literatura cubana,* 214.

19. *Lunes* 38 (7 December 1959): 6.

20. See "Un mes lleno de *Lunes.*" Also see Luis, "Autopsia de *Lunes de Revolución.*"

21. *Lunes* 31 (19 October 1959): 4.

22. *Lunes* 32 (26 October 1959): 15.

23. "Punto de mira: situación del Salón Nacional," *Lunes* 32 (26 October 1959): 14.

24. "Cinema and Culture in Cuba: Personal interview with Néstor Almendros," trans. Virginia Lawreck, *Review: Latin American Literature and Arts* 37 (January–June 1987): 21.

25. For race relations in Cuba, see Carlos Moore's *Castro, the Blacks, and Africa* (Los Angeles: Center for Afro-American Studies, University of California, Los Angeles, 1988) and my *Literary Bondage: Slavery in Cuban Narrative* (Austin: University of Texas Press, 1990).

26. "Pasado Meridiano," *Bohemia* 53, 21 (21 May 1961).

27. See "Imagen y sonido," *Bohemia* 53, 22 (28 May 1961): 96.

28. "La paloma blanca," *Bohemia* 53, 25 (18 June 1961): 88.

29. "Cine: debate en torno a 'La paloma blanca,' " *Mella* (4 July 1961).

30. *Lunes* 94 (6 February 1961).

31. "No es oro todo," in *Un oficio del siglo veinte: G. Caín 1954–60* (Barcelona: Editorial Seix Barral, 1973), 90–92; hereafter cited in the text as *Oficio;* "All is not gold," in *A Twentieth Century Job,* trans. Kenneth Hall and Guillermo Cabrera Infante (London: Faber and Faber, 1991), 63–65; hereafter cited in the text as *Job.*

32. "Viejo y mareado," in *Oficio,* 337–41; "Old and Seasick," in *Job,* 258–61.

33. "Cinema and Culture in Cuba," 19.

34. See Octavio Paz, "La tradición de la ruptura," in *Los hijos del limo* (Barcelona: Editorial Seix Barral, 1974), 13–35.

35. "Cinema and Culture in Cuba," 17.

36. For the economic importance of the Cuban movie industry, see Francisco Mota's "12 aspectos económicos de la cinematografía cubana," *Lunes* 94 (6 February 1961): 58–60.

37. K. S. Karol, *Guerrillas in Power: The Course of the Cuban Revolution* (New York: Hill and Wang, 1970), 234.

38. Ibid., 233.

39. "Literatura y Revolución en Cuba: entrevista a Carlos Franqui," unpublished interview, 1984.

40. Carlos Franqui, *Retrato de familia con Fidel* (Barcelona: Editorial Seix Barral, 1981), 261–73.

41. It is ironic that many years later Guevara would walk a tightrope between the old and the new, and side with the latter: "Esto no quiere decir que la experiencia crítica, y el método crítico, se hayan invalidado. Ellos tienen, valor histórico el primero, y categoría de permanencia el segundo; pero sí quiere decir en cambio, que no es posible suplantar el método por la experiencia, y que lo que afirmaron los clásicos del marxismo sobre determinadas obras, no puede, sino a título de tergiversación, aplicarse a las de otra época y circunstancia" ("Algunas cuestiones de principio," Santiago Álvarez et al., *Cine y Revolución en Cuba* [Barcelona: Editorial Fontamara, 1975], 31) [This does not mean that critical experience and method have cancelled each other out. The first has historic value, and the second permanence; but it does mean, on the other hand, that it is not possible to substitute method for experience, and that what the classic Marxists affirmed about certain works cannot, except as a distortion, be applied to those of another time and circumstance (Trans. by editor)]. Later on Guevara would lose his position as vice president of culture and president of the ICAIC to the more conservative elements in the government.

"Icosaedros": The English Letters

CARLOS CUADRA

"Icosaedros" [Icosahedra] is the title of a series of articles by Guillermo Cabrera Infante published in Madrid's daily newspaper *El País* in 1977 and 1978.[1] These articles are a collection of Cabrera Infante's impressions during his first years in London, where he resides. What is striking about the articles is their heterogeneity. They are packed with seemingly unrelated topics such as the history of dandyism, dance contests shown on English television, the growth of the punk movement, renowned homosexuals, and an anthology of letters sent to the London *Times*.[2] They appear to lack any serious purpose or goal and have the charm and the aimlessness of a chat over drinks. Reading them gives one the impression of having invited the author to an aperitif in a Madrid bar, a courtesy that Cabrera Infante repays with his amusing and totally trivial conversation. Any topic—a historical oddity or a literary anecdote—gives rise to an easygoing verbal stream spiked with irony, wordplay, and intellectual gossip and of course run through with critiques of film, art, and literature, which are as authoritative as they are unexplained.

One cannot help but admire this sort of verbal striptease. The reader willingly participates in the slow unveiling of Cabrera Infante's talent and is ready to act as a devoted fan who knows when to applaud and when the star must not be interrupted, asked to explain certain attractions or aversions, or required to clarify insinuations. In exchange for reverent silence, there are rewards. For starters, one gets names—the names of writers, dandies, dancers, scientists, painters, spies, fictional characters, famous places, films, museums, philologists, and actors, among many other seductive allusions. All these names are embedded in an extensive and passionate network of cross-references and contradictory value judgments. To distract from the judgments being meted out, each article is flooded with jokes, paradoxes, personal anecdotes, and extraordinary cultural references. What more can the idle reader ask for than to observe such an exciting world?

The collection of articles gets its name from a literary reference Cabrera Infante put forward as a declaration of intent:

> ¿Qué hay en un título? En el mío, al menos en ese de ahí arriba, hay una irreverencia y quiere referirse a la broma metafísica de Jarry en su *Ubu rey.* Dice allí Acrás: "Y es cierto también que los poliedros regulares son de lo más fieles y cariñosos con su amo. Excepto que esa mañana el icosaedro se puso un poco descarado y me vi obligado, para que aprenda, a darle una bofetada en una de sus veinte caras." A esos icosaedros irreverentes y a veces abofeteables se refiere el título.[3]
>
> [What's in a title? In mine, at least in the one above, there is an irreverence that refers to Jarry's metaphysical joke in his *Ubu roi* (1896).[4] Achras says there: "And it's also quite true that the regular polyhedra are the most faithful and most devoted to their master, except that this morning the Icosahedron was a little fractious, so that I was compelled, look you, to give it a smack on one of its twenty faces." The title refers to those irreverent and sometimes smackable icosahedra.]

Cabrera Infante's rebelliousness is not as obvious in the articles as might be expected. Within the semi-puritanical context of the late 1970s Spanish "glasnost," Cabrera Infante maintained a considerable level of decorum, the fruit of his undeniable love of classicism. Instead of the series of iconoclastic acts they seem to proclaim, the "Icosaedros" are a bold attempt to salvage diverse cultural traditions. There are no political references, nor opinions on polemical topics of the day, and no direct attacks on contemporary public figures. Years have passed since the "Icosaedros" were written, and since then perspectives have changed. Swinburne's passion for flogging might have been perceived as scandalous twenty years ago; nowadays, however, it has become a reason to vindicate his poetry.[5]

The stated intent of the "Icosaedros" is no deception. While this point is open to controversy, it is instructive to consider the importance that Cabrera Infante attributes to the avant-garde revolutions, at least since his *Tres tristes tigres* (1967) [*Three Trapped Tigers* (1971)]. The key character of this novel, Bustrófedon, is an incarnation of literary genius who, with his passion for wordplay, adopts the trappings of dadaism and surrealism and identifies himself with Eugène Ionesco and Antonin Artaud.[6] For Cabrera Infante, this stance is ideological, an alternative to and against any other philosophical or political discourse imposed from without. The intellectual is one who dares to break with traditional discourse, playing with it as if it were a path to freedom. It is therefore highly improbable that the reference to Alfred Jarry is an unfulfilled promise. We need to find a more convincing solution to our problem.

A solution is not easy to find. And if we scrutinize the opening article of the "Icosaedros" series from which the above quote was taken, the matter becomes even thornier. In this article, after referring to *Ubu roi,* Cabrera Infante goes on to describe in detail the room in which he is writing, apparently with the aim of reinforcing his direct relationship with the reader. Nevertheless, the image that the writer offers of himself seems more like the beginning of a Kafka story than a *captatio benevolentaiae.*[7] The self-portrait is not exactly a cheerful one. Cabrera Infante presents himself as isolated and surrounded by danger. The page in his typewriter is "invenciblemente blanca" [unconquerably white], a reference to the panic of literary creation. The lamp illuminating the room is "una espada de Damocles eléctrica" [an electric sword of Damocles]. The window in front of him is described as "inerte" [inert] because "nada ocurre en ella por expresión, todo pasa implícitamente" [nothing occurs explicitly in it, everything happens implicitly]. The window is closed and the wall around it "recuerda al Londres de Doré: siempre sombrío" [evokes Doré's London: always gloomy].[8] But this is not the worst of it. The article ends thus:

> Los arcos de ladrillos se suceden como en una pesadilla o como en una visión de Piranesi en sus *Cárceles*: al fondo hay una escalera de caracol de hierro cuyas espirales conducen aparentemente a la nada; y al fondo del fondo, una puerta de hierro siempre cerrada. Estos arcos sucesivos son la visión diaria del escritor: mirar a través de ellos produce el vértigo horizontal para el que no hay cura posible.
>
> [The brick arches succeed each other as in a nightmare or in a vision from Piranesi's *Carceri* [*Prisons*]: at the back there is an iron spiral staircase that apparently leads to nothingness; and at the very back an iron door that is always closed. These successive arches are the writer's daily vision: looking through them produces that horizontal vertigo for which there is no possible cure.][9]

Reading these lines, one recalls the famous existential-surrealist poem by Gabriel Celaya, which begins "Es la hora de las raíces y los perros amarillos" [It is the time of roots and yellow dogs] and ends with the chilling verse: "la hora en que la luna murmura como un silencio: nada" {the time in which the moon murmurs in silence: nothing}.[10] In this poem Celaya expresses the certainty that our life lacks transcendence, one of the central themes of twentieth-century existential literature. But Cabrera Infante's description reflects more than Celaya's anguished sorrow and sense of futility. The references to Damocles, Doré, and Piranesi convey to us a concrete emotional state that can be identified with claustrophobia. Celaya looks at the moon, but Cabrera Infante can see nothing that interests him through his window. He portrays himself as isolated in a prison he cannot leave. But England—where Cabrera Infante is writing, and his permanent residence since the mid-1960s—is by antonomasia the land of freedom. To relate a sensation of claustrophobia to this country initially makes no sense. We should therefore consider the allusion to horizontal vertigo that ends the article. Cabrera Infante's prison has no limits: it refers to the disorientation of a man who has been forced to abandon his native country.

The Kafkian tone of this first article is related less to the fear of meaninglessness than to the sorrow felt by an exile. Doré's London is simply London, the place from which Cabrera Infante is writing and in which he feels imprisoned by the impossibility of return to his birthplace, Cuba. If we take this point of view, compatible with the mysterious declaration that in the window—which is to say through the writer's perspective—"nothing occurs explicitly, everything happens implicitly," light is thrown on the matter and the mysterious meaning of the title "Icosaedros" is resolved. The inexplicable aspects of the article (sorrow, the allusion to Ubu, the sword of Damocles) suddenly become coherent.

The icosahedra's irreverence refers to a supposed monarch before whom no one must kneel. Ever since *Tres tristes tigres,* that king whom Cabrera Infante attacks through surrealist discourse has had a distinct identity. Ubu is no one but Fidel Castro, and the sword of Damocles is the danger to which Cabrera Infante feels submitted in exile, a danger to which he has referred in other articles where he describes the fear that many of his writer friends and he himself have felt, due to the possible reprisals the communist government could take against them. It was not simply a matter of the threat of a forced repatriation but of the opposition of many European literary and journalistic circles sympathetic to Castro's revolution. In those articles in which Cabrera Infante writes specifically about Cuba, he describes the enmity of a number of prominent intellectuals such as Carlos Barral (the "inventor," according to some, of the Hispanic American "boom" of the 1960s) and Julio Cortázar, among many others.[11]

This theory clarifies matters somewhat but evidently has a weak point: in the "Icosaedros" Cuba is not mentioned. Some indirect allusions will be addressed later—the death of Calvert Casey or the commentaries on the way in which Latin rhythms are danced to on English television—but these articles avoid the seriousness required to discuss Castro's politics.[12] However, Cabrera Infante has indicated to us that in front of his window "nothing occurs explicitly, everything happens implicitly." If the window is what the author looks at when writing, he could very well be speaking to us about his imagination, about the way in which he intends to show us what he sees. The "inert" panorama mentioned at the beginning could hide several "implicit" surprises. Indirect exposition seems to be his modus operandi. How can we interpret such a declaration? What are his hidden intentions? In the first place, let us remember that the icosahedra have 20 faces, and that Jarry alludes to this fact. But there are many more than 20 faces in Cabrera Infante's articles; indeed, a gallery of characters parades through each article. It would be interesting to ask if these characters have something in common with the author. We are living in a century of literary alter egos. Antonio Machado, Fernando Pessoa, Jorge Luis Borges, and many other writers have resorted to fictional or historical counterparts to reveal hidden or contradictory facets of their personality.[13] Why not Cabrera Infante?

In the second place, we have seen that the indirect style of the articles is related to the way in which the author intends to show us what he cannot see through what he can see. But what does the author see? According to his personal confession it is England, an island like Cuba but with very different characteristics: a country with a grand tradition of self-expression and a culture that has been exported throughout the entire civilized world. The articles almost invariably show aspects of English culture that might be surprising or curious for a Latino. When English culture is seen through a Cuban's eyes, comparison is inescapable. Surely Cabrera Infante's comments on English eccentricities contain allusions to Cuban problems. Certain themes appear repeatedly in his other writings, and in many cases they include descriptions of his personal experience as an exile, political activist, and enemy of the Castro regime. A relationship exists between these themes and Cabrera Infante's commentaries on England in the "Icosaedros."

THE "ICOSAEDROS" AND THE *LETTERS ON ENGLAND*

It is necessary to take a short historical detour to further this critique of the "Icosaedros." In 1726 Voltaire had to exile himself to England due to a scandalous affair of honor.[14] He had challenged a powerful aristocrat to a duel, and due to his superior social status, the aristocrat sent servants to beat up Voltaire rather than confront him in person. Once Voltaire recovered from the beating, he began to publish satirical verses directed at his enemy. To avoid punishment for the crime of "lese nobility" Voltaire remained in the United Kingdom for three years. His experiences and observations during this time were collected in the *Lettres philosophiques,* also known as the *Letters on England* (1734), commentaries on institutions, literature, science, religious tolerance, and English social classes.[15] Masked by praise of England—even more convincing because in many cases they were laced with criticism and irony—the letters delivered an implicit but ferocious attack on the French political system.

In the *Letters on England* all of Voltaire's literary aptitude and his capacity for persuasion are put at the service of a concrete political ideal: liberty. But this goal is hindered by the excessively abstract content of the letters. Voltaire omits any reference to the daily life of the English and excludes any physical description of England, perhaps counting on the enlightened character of his implied reader, perhaps simply because of a certain literary inexperience that was corrected in his subsequent and more well-known works like *Candide* (1758).

If the convention of the implied reader justifies certain characteristics of the *Letters on England,* it may be useful in the study of the "Icosaedros." The "Icosaedros" appeared in Madrid's daily newspaper *El País* when Spanish public life was undergoing democratization and—after Franco's death—the majority of the political forces in the country were pro-Cuban. In his book *Mea Cuba* Cabrera Infante gives several examples of the difficulties he went through in order to publish articles criticizing the Cuban revolution in numerous intellectual and journalistic media.

> Mi delito, haber revelado en el extranjero que le acosaban [a Heberto Padilla], rompiendo por primera vez la *barrera del silencio,* . . .
>
> [My crime: having revealed abroad that they were chasing him (Heberto Padilla), breaking thus the silence barrier.][16]

Denunciatory writings such as this one began to appear in 1980 and 1981. Because of this "wall of silence," a regular column on Cuba written by Cabrera Infante in the newspaper *El País* probably would have had little likelihood of being published. On the other hand, a collection of both amusing and eulogistic notes written in the style of Voltaire and about England—the cradle of European democratic civilization—would have been well received by the progressive media in Spain. Consequently, the "Icosaedros" refer to Cuba without naming it directly.

Cabrera Infante does not analyze English politics or society, which Spanish readers are familiar with. He maintains a light and anecdotal tone, and even when he refers to the circumstances that made him move to England, he attributes them to chance. He has affirmed on more than one occasion that "Inglaterra me eligió a mí" [England chose me], although these words contradict some of his other declarations. When Carlos Barral waxed ironic over Cabrera Infante's English, calling it "inglés de inmigrante" [immigrant English], the Cuban replied: "no lo será así que pasen cinco años, será entonces inglés 'de naturalizado' " (*Mea Cuba* [1992], 35) ["it won't be once five years have passed: then it will be 'naturalized' English" (*Mea Cuba* [1994], 38)].

As already noted in the "Icosaedros," "nothing occurs explicitly, everything happens implicitly." The anecdotes related by Cabrera Infante conceal themes of burning relevance for Cuba during the late 1970s. To understand them, we need to pay attention to the opinions about England in the "Icosaedros."

Praise of England in the "Icosaedros"

"Seguramente una nación capaz de realizar hazaña tan notable es capaz de todo" [Surely a nation capable of such a remarkable feat is capable of anything]. With these words, Cabrera Infante ends one of the articles in the series, "Cartas son cartas," in which he analyzes an anthology of letters sent to the London *Times*. The phrase is not his, but taken from the last of the correspondents included in the selection. The nation to which the letter-writer refers is of course England, and the "feat" that is the focus of the article is the ability to dialogue and the love of knowledge traditionally attributed to the English people. According to Cabrera Infante, some of the polemical issues that the *Times*'s readers have taken up deal with themes apparently as insignificant as the naval capability of triremes, Byron's limp, or the day of the year on which the cuckoo's first song announces spring.[17] But this insignificance is proof of the British citizens' apparent honesty and impartiality. For example, one of the English newspaper's readers, after claiming a record for hearing the earliest song of the cuckoo (which he thought he heard on February the fourth) wrote to the newspaper again to admit that what he had heard was simply an imitation of the bird by a laborer who was working near his home.

Another article, "Homosexuales históricos," is dedicated to a book written by L. A. Rowse entitled *Homosexuals in History* (1977), in which an attempt is made to enumerate great men with this sexual preference. Cabrera Infante is very critical of Rowse's selection of characters. Nevertheless he praises the fact that Rowse himself confesses to his own bisexuality after having dedicated a good part of his efforts as a literary critic to demonstrating Shakespeare's heterosexuality. He also cites examples of aged homosexuals like the earl of Buckingham, whose pastimes were reading the Bible and sodomy.

The gentleman and the dandy are two other types—or rather two other English institutions—that merit similar commentaries in the "Icosaedros." They are treated with admiration, as aesthetic and moral examples worthy of imitation. Then come the "teds" and the "punks," to whom Cabrera Infante dedicates another article. The contrast between the appearance and the ethical code of these groups reveals the importance of clothing as an outward form of expression. Cabrera Infante quotes Wilde to remind us that there is nothing as profound as superficiality.[18] This diversity is one more example of English society's tolerance.

Spies also have a place in the articles and are studied from a dual perspective: the history of the secret services and espionage as a literary genre.[19] Cabrera Infante picks the well-known name of Kim Philby, the traitor who was at the service of Moscow intelligence, and also includes two curious characters: Mansfield Cumming, the founder of the SIS, and Lionel Crabbe, a frogman captured by the Russians as he was preparing to explore the submerged hull of a Russian destroyer.[20] Cumming is a hero, a new Lawrence of Arabia, "hombre admirable, capaz de guardar el mayor de los secretos, y ni siquiera sus íntimos amigos supieron nunca que dirigía el servicio de inteligencia" [an admirable man, capable of keeping the greatest secret, and not even his closest friends ever knew that he was directing the intelligence service].[21] Crabbe provides comic relief: a submariner who is "encantador, pero borracho e inestable" [charming, but drunk and unstable]—from the essay "Espías con salsa inglesa" [Spies with English sauce]. Philby and Cummings become a new version of the theme of the traitor and the hero, two facets of the secret services' epic. The hero is the chivalrous Cumming, the traitor the communist Philby. Crabbe, the inoffensive bungler, bends our sympathies even more toward that nation of gentlemen and tolerance.

Insofar as there is a literary subgenre of espionage novels, it is worthwhile noting that its very existence is paradoxical. Spying is an activity that exalts secrecy; literature on the contrary is public, favors communication, and has as its objective that of making information a common heritage. The fact that the English are the inventors of literary secret agents once again makes them a model of freedom to be admired.

The public character of the printed word is related to the last of the homages that Cabrera Infante pays to English society, that of literary and cultural references, a model essential to the work of this Cuban writer. The dialogic and comparative form of erudition used in the "Icosaedros" springs from the writings of authors like Laurence Sterne or Lewis Carroll, probably with the added influence of Borges.[22] For example, the article "En busca del amor ganado" [In search of love gained] consists of a comparison between the different versions of the Tristan and Isolde myth.[23] This legend is of French origin, like the quote that generates the "Icosaedros" or Voltaire's *Letters on England.* But the leitmotif of narrative diversity gives life to the article, the possibility of providing many perspectives on the same story and ultimately the fictional construction of what we call reality. All of these ideas can be disseminated only within a political system in which a certain tolerance exists.

How do the "Icosaedros" and the *Letters on England* coincide and differ? Both are a homage to the inquisitive instinct and to respect for the English people's diversity, but Cabrera Infante centers his analysis on those topics that Voltaire did not address: popular culture, daily customs, and anecdotal aspects of English life. Cabrera Infante does not quote Voltaire and nothing indicates to us that he had him in mind while writing his articles. Nevertheless, the situation of both authors was very similar. In this way, Voltaire's letters help us see that the apparently trivial and frivolous "Icosaedros" have a serious side.

The Implicit Attack on Cuban Socialism

The analysis of English culture in the "Icosaedros" is no doubt entertaining, but it only makes sense when we relate it to Castro's regimen and the situation in Cuba. Voltaire is more explicit than Cabrera Infante with allusions to his native land, and the references to France in his *Letters on England* are frequent and specific. In contrast, the "Icosaedros" almost completely avoid allusions to Cuba. In the article "Vengan bailando" [Come dancing] there is a mockery of the way in which English dancers interpret tropical rhythms:

> Pero todavía falta la mejor parte de la competencia: la categoría latinoamericana, ¡dónde se incluye el pasadoble! (Y algo llamado *jive* que debe venir de Curazao, isla sudamericana que produjo dos intoxicantes, el licor curazao y el dialecto papiamento).
>
> [But the best part of the contest is yet to come: the Latin American category, which includes the *pasadoble*! (And something called *jive* that must come from Curaçao, a South American island that produced two poisons, Curaçao liquor and the *Papiamento* dialect).]

This quotation demonstrates once more the isolation in which Cabrera Infante finds himself. Although certainly significant from the cultural point of view, the political situation in Cuba is not referred to. Another case is the following:

> Pero dio Mallarmé un paso decisivo también en Kensington: a los veintiún años se casó con María Gherard en Brompton Oratory, que es una iglesia católica donde Miriam Gómez un día de mayo de 1969 encendió una vela por Calvert Casey, que se acababa de suicidar en Roma.
>
> [But Mallarmé also took a decisive step in Kensington: at the age of 21 he married María Gherard in Brompton Oratory, a Catholic church where one day in May 1969 Miriam Gómez lit a candle for Calvert Casey, who had just committed suicide in Rome.][24]

This out-of-context allusion to Casey—a homosexual writer born in the United States but a Cuban national who committed suicide in Rome apparently because of problems with his visa—was only known to those who were up-to-date on Cuban literary and political life. But we also have to take into account that this mysterious allusion is a way of tempting the curious reader to learn about the other side of the Castro government's activities.

The themes of the "Icosaedros" are also significant with respect to Cuba. For example, homosexuality is the main focus of two of the articles, one dedicated to Rowse's book *Homosexuals in History*—which we have referred to already—and another entitled "Un poeta pervertido" [A perverted poet], which narrates the crudest details about Swinburne, who was a masochist, a homosexual, and Queen Victoria's poet laureate. The article is dated 17 September 1978, two years before the Mariel scandal.[25] Nevertheless, Castro's homophobia was already evident in the 1960s, as Cabrera Infante himself points out in another article on Calvert Casey that appeared in October 1980.

> Antón (Arrufat) volvió alegre a La Habana para encontrarse con una acusación de horrores homosexuales literarios: era su culpa, atribuida, la invitación de Allen Ginsberg a Cuba. Durante su visita . . . Ginsberg confesó su amor por el Che Guevara, pero no era un amor proletario. "Me gustaría mucho acostarme con él," declaró. . . . No hubo juicio, ni siquiera hubo causa: Antón fue despedido ipso facto de Casa (de las Américas) y la dirección de la revista fue concedida como premio al pundonor militante a Roberto Retamar.
>
> [Antón returned smiling to Havana to meet an accusation of homosexual horrors: the invitation to Cuba of Allen Ginsberg, poet and pederast, was his fault—allegedly. During his visit Ginsberg . . . confessed his love for Che Guevara—but it was not a proletarian love. "I would like very much to go to bed with him," he declared. . . . There was no sentence, there was not even a trial: Antón was dismissed *ipso facto* from *Casa* and the directorship of the review was granted as a prize for militant modesty to Roberto Retamar.][26]

It is unnecessary to point out the contrast between the treatment that (Victorian!) England gave to Swinburne, the cursed poet of pederastic love verses, and that which Cuba gave to Arrufat. The Ginsberg episode occurred in 1964. Sexual discrimination in Cuba was an open secret when the "Icosaedros" were published in 1977.

Another theme related directly to Cuba is that of the letters to the London *Times.* The freedom and the disinterest that these letters exude contrast with Castro's politics of "inviting" certain writers protected by the regime to contest the declarations about Cuba made by Cuban exiles. Cabrera Infante himself was to receive at least two "personal" letters (later disseminated through the Castro media) from Heberto Padilla reproaching him for the commentaries that he had made in his (Padilla's) defense. The "Padilla Case" gained great notoriety in Europe, and was the major reason that the Castro dictatorship began to lose prestige.[27] As is known, Padilla was forced to write the letters to Cabrera Infante and to publicly recant his previous criticism of the Revolution and his defense of Cabrera Infante in a long political confession read before high officials of the Cuban government. In the case of the letters, the link between Cuba and England is evident.

At times, the relation between England and Cuba is not one of contrast, but of parallelism. For example, the historical characters in the article "Dead Dandy" have something more in common than their elegance. Both Beau Brummel and Oscar Wilde were sent into exile for challenging the intolerance still present in England (Wilde, because of his homosexuality) or royal power (Brummel, because of his witty criticism of the Prince of Wales).[28] The other protagonist of "Dead Dandy," Caius Petronius, suffered a more radical form of punishment at the hands of the emperor Nero: he was forced to commit suicide.[29]

This last allusion leads us to note the frequency with which tyrants appear in the "Icosaedros." Ubu; Nero; Edward, Prince of Wales (only an aspirant to the crown but no less disagreeable because of this); Julius Caesar . . . In these articles we do not find as many painters or musicians or even film directors, although film criticism was Cabrera Infante's earliest vocation.[30] Only one group is larger than that of tyrants, and that is the enemies of tyranny: intellectuals, dandies, punks, and dancers—all exemplify freedom of expression in England. And they are all masks adopted by the author of these articles, as prolific in his transformations as Fantomas, Lon Chaney, and so many other beloved heroes of the screen.[31]

Translated by Lawrence Rich

Notes

1. Although all of the articles quoted here appeared in *El País* from 1977 to 1978, those published in the newspaper's weekly edition are not entitled "Icosaedros." However, since the style and themes of these articles are identical, I have treated them as a single collection.

2. These topics are the theme of five of the "Icosaedros" series published in *El País Semanal*: "Dead Dandy" (30 July 1978): 9; "Vengan bailando" [Come dancing] (4 September 1977): 11; "La resurrección de los 'Teds' " [Resurrection of the 'Teds'] (9 October 1977): 20; "Homosexuales históricos" [Historic homosexuals] (24 July 1977): 19; "Cartas son cartas" [Letter are letters] (29 May 1977): 17.

3. "Icosaedros," *El País* (17 April 1977): 19. All translations are by Lawrence Rich unless otherwise indicated.

4. Alfred Jarry (1873–1907) was a French author and precursor of romanticism, known above all for *The Ubu Plays,* a series of satires on power set in an imaginary country. *The Ubu Plays,* trans. Cyril Connoly et al., ed. and introd. Simon Watson Taylor (New York: Grove Press, 1968).

5. Algernon Swinburne (1837–1909) was an English poet laureate of the Victorian Age.

6. Eugène Ionesco (1909–1994) was a French playwright and the principal representative of the Theater of the Absurd. Antonin Artaud (1896–1948) was an actor, playwright, and theorist of French theater, affiliated with surrealism, and the creator of the Theater of the Absurd.

7. Franz Kafka (1883–1924) was a Jewish writer of German descent, born in Prague and known for the obsessive and tortured quality of his work. *Captatio benevolentiae* is a rhetorical device by which the orator manifests his/her own weaknesses, good intentions, etc., to gain the listener's sympathy.

8. Gustave Doré (1832–1883) was a French artist, known for his illustrations of world classics such as *Don Quixote,* the Bible, *Paradise Lost,* etc.

9. Giovanni Battista Piranesi (1720–1778) was an Italian engraver, artist, and architect, known for a series of lithographs entitled "Carceri" [Prisons], in which he transforms the classical ruins of ancient Italy into prisons full of torture instruments.

10. Gabriel Celaya (1911–1991) was a Spanish Basque poet associated with the "Generation of 1936" and influenced by existentialism and surrealism. Pablo Corbalán, *Poesía surrealista en España* (Madrid: Ediciones del centro, 1974), 211.

11. Carlos Barral (1914–1989) was a Catalonian poet, novelist, and publisher, the owner of Seix Barral, one of the most important Spanish-language publishing firms. Julio Cortázar (1914–1984) was an Argentinean writer known for his short stories and the novel *Rayuela* (1966). He was also a literary critic and political activist who supported the Cuban revolution.

12. Calvert Casey (1924–1969) was a Cuban writer born in the United States and known for his short stories.

13. Antonio Machado (1875–1939) was a Spanish poet of the "Generation of 1898." Machado was a Republican and died in exile shortly after the end of the Spanish Civil War. Fernando Pessoa (1888–1935) was an early twentieth-century Portuguese author. Jorge Luis Borges (1899–1985) was an Argentinean poet, essayist, and author of short stories.

14. Voltaire was the pseudonym of François-Marie Arouet (1694–1778), one of the major authors of the enlightenment and archenemy of the Church and French absolutism.

15. *Letters on England,* trans. Leonard Tancock (London: Penguin, 1980).

16. *Mea Cuba* (Barcelona: Plaza and Janés, 1992), 33; *Mea Cuba,* trans. Kenneth Hall and Guillermo Cabrera Infante (New York: Farrar, Straus, Giroux, 1994), 36; hereafter cited in the text.

17. Lord Byron (1788–1824) was an English romantic poet.

18. Oscar Wilde (1854–1900) was an Irish writer known for his wit and the victim of a terrible scandal in Victorian England due to his homosexuality.

19. "El juego de los espías" [The Spy Game], *El País Semanal* (19 February 1978): 5. See also "Espías con salsa inglesa" [Spies with English Sauce], *El País Semanal* (12 February 1978): 5.

20. Kim Philby (1912–1988) was an English spy who was secretly aiding the Russians.

21. T. E. Lawrence (1888–1935) was a politician, military leader, and Arabic scholar who aided in the Arabic peoples' revolt against Turkish domination during the First World War.

22. Laurence Sterne (1713–1768) was a novelist famous for *The Life and Opinions of Tristram Shandy, Gentleman* (1760–1767), which humorously develops the principles of Locke's philosophy. Lewis Carroll (1832–1898) was an English logician, photographer, and writer known for *Alice in Wonderland* (1865) and *Through the Looking Glass* (1871).

23. *El País Semanal* (8 January 1978): 14–15.

24. "Ellos vivieron en Kensington," *El País Semanal* (21 August 1977): 9, 26. Stephane Mallarmé (1842–1898) was a French symbolist poet.

25. On 20 April 1980 Castro announced that any Cuban who wanted to leave the country would be permitted to evacuate from the Port of Mariel. More than 120,000 Cubans joined the Freedom Flotilla for resettlement in the United States. The U.S. Immigration and Naturalization Service (INS) initially welcomed the "Marielitos," but officials soon began to notice Cuban men who were "more hardened and rougher in appearance," which led to a widespread belief, fueled by the media, that Castro was using the accord to empty Cuba's prisons and hospitals of hard-core criminals, the mentally ill, and other undesirables.

26. The article is entitled "¿Quién mató a Calvert Casey?" in *Mea Cuba* (1992), 143 ("Who Killed Calvert Casey?" *Mea Cuba* [1994], 125). Allen Ginsberg (1926–1997) was a North American poet and a major voice of the "Beat Generation."

27. The "Padilla Case" was a scandal that made public the way in which the Castro regime had jailed the Cuban writer Heberto Padilla and manipulated his public declarations.

28. Beau Brummell (1778–1840) was a famous dandy of the Victorian Age.

29. Petronius (d. A.D. 66) was a Roman poet and politician, a contemporary of Nero (A.D. 37–68).

30. Julius Caesar (100–44 B.C.) was a Roman general and politician, author of *The Gallic War,* and Cleopatra's lover.

31. Lon Chaney (1883–1930) was a Hollywood actor known for his horror films.

THE WRITER AS CINEASTE

◆

The Cinematic Imagination

RAYMOND D. SOUZA

Although Guillermo Cabrera Infante has been the recipient of major literary awards in Spain, France, and Italy, as well as a Guggenheim fellowship in the United States, he has declared on several occasions that he has received more pleasure from film than from literature. An early and decisive influence in this regard was his mother, Zoila, an avid movie fan. He fondly remembers going to the movies at a very early age in Gibara, Cuba, and many happy moments were spent at the Teatro Unión Club, the only movie house in his hometown until the opening of the Roxy and the Ideal in the last years of the 1930s.

These early and modest activities were the source of inspiration for a number of significant achievements during Cabrera Infante's career. In the 1950s he became a major film critic in Havana, and in 1967 his great experimental novel, *Tres tristes tigres* (1967) [*Three Trapped Tigers* (1971)], burst onto the international scene with a cast of characters whose views of reality and themselves were conditioned by the glamour of Hollywood or the screen personas of movie stars. After he went into exile in 1965, the writing of film scripts for movies such as *Vanishing Point* (1971) provided much-needed income. Although Cabrera Infante no longer has a regular film column, he continues to publish essays on films and the movie industry and has finished another screenplay, "The Lost City." He also has served as the honorary director of the Miami and Telluride film festivals and as a judge at Cannes.

In the numerous published chronologies of his life, Cabrera Infante has underscored the influence of films on his career. In the second entry of each chronicle, he claims to have been taken to see his first film a few weeks after his birth. "29 días. Va al cine por primera vez con su madre, a ver *Los cuatro jinetes del Apocalipsis* (reprise)" [29 days. Goes to the movies for the first time with his mother, to see *The Four Horsemen of the Apocalypse* (reprise)].[1] Since he was born in 1929, the repetition of the number 29 may reveal a whimsical preference for numerical symmetry, but the film he "saw" is even more suggestive, since it contains elements indicative of aspects of his own experience. That is, the anecdote can be regarded as a playful, but not casual, reference to disastrous events in Cabrera Infante's personal history—an individual mythology based on the collective mythology of the world of films.

The famous director of silent films D. W. Griffith once referred to *The Four Horsemen of the Apocalypse* (Metro, 1921) as "one of the greatest screen productions of the silent era."[2] It was also the favorite silent film of the English director David Lean, whose credits include *The Bridge on the River Kwai* (1957) and *Dr. Zhivago* (1965).[3] A restoration of *The Four Horsemen of the Apocalypse* was recently completed in England by Photoplay Productions under the direction of David Gill and Kevin Brownlow with a musical score by Carl Davis. This restoration allows us to view the film as its contemporaries, including Zoila, must have seen it. In retrospect, it is an exceptional multicultural production made during one of the most exciting and dynamic periods of Hollywood's history.

The person most directly responsible for bringing the Spanish novel by Vicente Blasco Ibáñez to the screen was June Mathis, the influential head of Metro's script department. Blasco Ibáñez's novel appeared in translation in the United States in 1918 and soon became a best-seller. When Mathis read it, she was convinced it would make a successful movie and she persuaded Metro to buy the film rights to the book. Blasco Ibáñez originally signed over the rights for "an advance of $20,000 against ten per cent of the royalties."[4] Shortly after the film's release in 1921, Metro offered the author $170,000 outright, an offer he accepted. By the end of 1925, a film that had cost one million dollars to make had grossed about four million dollars.[5] If Blasco Ibáñez had stuck to the original contract, he would have made $210,000, but in any event, the enterprise was a lucrative endeavor for him and opened the door to many other productions in Hollywood.

In addition to writing the script, Mathis also was responsible for the production of the film. She selected the director, the Irish-born Rex Ingram, and an unknown Italian actor, Rudolph Valentino, to play the main role of Julio Desnoyers. In every respect, Mathis was the moving spirit behind the entire production just as Zoila was the original inspiration for Cabrera Infante's love of the movies.

The multicultural and multilingual origins of *The Four Horsemen of the Apocalypse* prefigure the multicultural and multilingual aspects of Cabrera Infante's career. In the film, the story begins in the Americas and then moves to Europe, a course that Cabrera Infante would repeat when he left his native Cuba for the last time in 1965 to eventually take up permanent residence in London. The narrative fabric of *The Four Horsemen of the Apocalypse* is based on a number of dualities including the New and Old Worlds, nationalism and internationalism, and love and duty, to name just a few. In addition, the work criticizes the megalomania of ideological extremism and the folly of war. It also shows how mass movements can destroy or radically change the lives of individuals. Many of these concerns have appeared to varying degrees in the works of Cabrera Infante, particularly the contrast between the Americas and Europe, the resistance to ideological extremism, and the internationalization of culture.

Cabrera Infante has had several encounters with the four horsemen during his life. An early episode took place in 1936 when both of his parents were arrested for their activities in the Cuban Communist Party. Like most utopians, they were so dedicated to social and political change that they thought they could modify reality by changing the words that referred to it. For example, Guillermo and his younger brother Sabá were taught to address their parents by their first names rather than by traditional terms. From the perspective of the children, this practice only produced confusion. After their arrest, Zoila and Guillermo senior spent six months in prison in Santiago de Cuba. This period was stressful for their elder son, Guillermo, who had disturbing dreams, causing concern among his relatives. Reality became a nightmare and terrifying dreams tore at the fabric of everyday life. His fertile imagination, stimulated by many of the movies he had seen, began to run wild. Frankenstein and Dracula, in the guise of Boris Karloff and Bela Lugosi, were on the loose in Gibara, Cuba, and could only be dispatched back to their origins beyond the sea after the return of Zoila and Guillermo senior.[6]

Cabrera Infante had his own encounter with apocalyptic horsemen of the governmental persuasion in October 1952. He was arrested in Havana and thrown in jail with common criminals for having published a short story with English obscenities in the popular weekly magazine *Bohemia.* He emerged from his ordeal badly shaken and for several years published under pseudonyms. During the 1950s, Cabrera Infante enjoyed considerably more success as a film critic than as a creative writer, and by the end of the decade he was Havana's most prominent critic. Many of the reviews he published during those years are available in *Un oficio del siglo veinte* (1963) [*A Twentieth Century Job* (1991)], a collection of movie reviews and fictionalized meditations on the role of the critic in an ideologically committed society.[7] *Un oficio del siglo veinte* was first published in Havana and has since appeared in several editions in English and Spanish. The anti-ideological stance of the collection is due in part to events that took place in 1961 when Cabrera Infante was the editor of *Lunes de Revolución,* one of the most important journals of the early revolutionary period in Cuba.

Lunes de Revolución was an experimental and polemical publication that broke down the barriers between elite and popular culture. It played with graphics and exhibited an irreverent attitude toward authority, aesthetic or political. The journal's activities and successes eventually attracted the attention of government authorities at several levels. As a result *Lunes de Revolución* was banned and ceased publication in 1961. The four horsemen had galloped through Cabrera Infante's editorial realm, scattering him and many of the journal's supporters to the four winds. A few years later, Cabrera Infante became an exile and took up residence in Madrid. When the Franco government refused to extend his residence visa, one of the few avenues open to him was an opportunity to write film scripts in England. Like Mary Poppins two years earlier, Cabrera Infante and his family soared off to London in 1966, arriving on the winds of change.

The first years in England were economically and legally precarious. Reluctant to request political asylum, like an actor in a silent movie, he was a mute exile. By the end of 1966, the Cabrera Infante family had moved into a damp basement apartment at 18 Trebovir Road in London. Located under a hotel and next to the Earl's Court subway station, it was not a quiet or desirable location. However, in October 1967, with funds generated by the movie script "Wonderwall," they moved to a more pleasant apartment and location at 53 Gloucester Road in South Kensington, leaving behind the sounds and sensations of subway trains rumbling into the night. That ground-level apartment in a building constructed in the 1830s has been the home of Cabrera Infante and Miriam Gómez for over three decades.

Cabrera Infante produced 12 movie scripts between 1966 and 1970. Two were filmed, the British production *Wonderwall* (1969), an adaptation of a story by Gerard Brach directed by Joe Massot, and the very successful American *Vanishing Point* (1971) directed by Richard C. Sarafian and starring Barry Newman.[8] Three of Cabrera

Infante's other scripts have noteworthy literary connections. "Birthdays" (1968) was the result of a collaborative effort with Carlos Fuentes, and is based, in part, on the Mexican writer's "Tlactocatzine, del jardín de Flanders" [In a Flemish garden]. "The Jam" of 1968 (an earlier 1966 version was entitled "On the Speedway") was inspired by "Autopista del sur" [The Highway to the South] by the Argentinean/French writer Julio Cortázar. "The Jam" is a hilarious satire of contemporary society's dependence on the automobile. However, his most successful adaptation, and one that enjoys legendary status in Hollywood was based on *Under the Volcano* (1947) by the English novelist Malcolm Lowry. That particular version was written for the American director Joseph Losey but was never filmed.

Losey requested that the script follow the original novel as closely as possible. Cabrera Infante read Lowry's novel six times and worked intensely on the project for three months in 1972. Given the complex nature of Lowry's style, it was a considerable challenge, and Cabrera Infante's script was too long. In addition, Losey was in conflict with the producers of the proposed film, the Hakim brothers, and Cabrera Infante made the fatal mistake of delivering the script to Losey instead of the producers. Unfortunately for Cabrera Infante, he had violated the terms of his contract, and the Hakim brothers demanded and received the return of the $25,000 advance that he had been paid. In addition, a final payment of an equal amount was never rendered. After months of intense work, all Cabrera Infante had to show for his efforts was exhaustion. The project was an unmitigated disaster for Cabrera Infante, and when he finished the script, he was on the verge of his well-known breakdown. It was undoubtedly his most traumatic encounter with the four horsemen of the apocalypse, and the episode has cast a long shadow. Although he has had offers to publish the script, Cabrera Infante has preferred to leave that particular connection to a bitter period of his life untouched. The experience was so unpleasant that he did not return to scriptwriting until the 1990s.

Although financially lucrative, the creation of a screenplay and film is a collective endeavor, and the process can be a frustrating experience for a writer. The main responsibility of script readers is to suggest changes. It is hard to imagine such individuals not recommending modifications, since their employment is linked to revisions. During the production of most films, there is considerable tension between creative and commercial forces. Producers, directors, and sometimes even actors become involved in the process. At another level, those who control finances tend to favor formulaic approaches based on previous financial successes at the box office. It is difficult to argue with profits and the bottom line. When one takes into account all of the factors involved in the production of a movie, it is amazing that good films are ever made. Even for the nonreligious, every exceptional film is a miracle.

Despite the many frustrations that a scriptwriter can suffer during the creation of a film, Cabrera Infante's association with the production of *Vanishing Point* was an agreeable experience. He spent two months in the United States in 1970 searching for filming locations in several areas of the West and working on the script in an office located on the grounds of Twentieth Century Fox. During his stay, he met a number of notables including Robert Wise, the film editor of *Citizen Kane* (1941), and Myrna Loy and Mae West. If Zoila had been alive, she undoubtedly would have enjoyed the results of those early excursions into the movie houses of Gibara.

From a literary perspective "Vanishing Point," along with Cabrera Infante's most recent effort, "The Lost City," represent his most accomplished and original screenplays.[9] The script "Vanishing Point" was completed in January 1970 and on 24 April 1991 Cabrera Infante finished the third draft of "The Lost City" for Paramount Pictures. Although separated by 21 years and radical differences in content, the two scripts share similar structural and aesthetic features as well as central characters who confront issues of life and death.

"Vanishing Point" is set in the American West during the 1960s and concerns a young man's flight from his inner demons. Kowalski, the protagonist, expresses his internal tensions through driving a car, for "speed seems to disintoxicate the driver's soul" (41). In his attempt to go from Denver to San Francisco in less than 16 hours, Kowalski becomes involved in a battle of wits and wills with the police in several states. His spectacular driving and a series of escapes cause the authorities to become obsessed with capturing him, and their pursuit of their elusive prey becomes a deadly ballet of movement and speed. Kowalski is transformed into a cultural hero when a blind DJ is attracted to the game of cat and mouse Kowalski is playing with the police. The DJ even becomes his guide and mentor by way of his radio broadcasts, and at one point refers to Kowalski as "our Lone Driver, the Last American Hero, the electric centaur, the demi-god, the SUPER-DRIVER OF THE GOLDEN WEST" (42).[10]

The heroes in "The Lost City" struggle against successive dictatorships in Cuba between 1957 and 1961. The story unfolds in

Havana and New York and chronicles the fortunes of a Cuban family fragmented by the Cuban revolution. The main character Fico, who takes flight from the oppression of a political order, ends up in exile in the United States. In each script, the main character struggles with vague sensations of being trapped. Political disenchantment is present in "Vanishing Point," which captures the antiwar sentiments of the Vietnam period in the U.S. But discontent with the reigning order is given more prominence in "The Lost City." Music plays a major role in both scripts. "Vanishing Point" incorporates a number of forms of popular music, particularly rock, into its texture, and there are many references to specific songs and entertainers. "The Lost City," on the other hand, is a celebration of Cuban music and dance.

The importance of music in the conceptualization of "Vanishing Point" is indicated in the author's introductory comments. The intent is to integrate music into the action of the film so that it emerges from the world of the characters rather than from a superimposed sound track. As the introduction points out:

> Thus the function of lyrics and tunes will be not only to comment on the action but to control it, and furthermore, to *generate* film action . . . Consequently, visible sound sources are ever-present throughout the film, assuming "leading roles" in their own right. For instance, in all the sequences on the highway the car-radio will become a real though disembodied presence, all invisible "passengers" linking the driver to the remote DJ who is his guide through the maze of patrol cars, police forces, barricades. But this thread of a voice is as impotent as the automobile or as the electronic device itself to extricate the hero from the labyrinthine tragedy in which the film fatally, automatically ends. (ii)

Kowalski's search for oblivion ends when he hurls his white Galaxie into a roadblock, but just as he is about to die, he tries to avoid his fate by braking and attempting to maneuver his car into an about-face. The centerpiece of the barrier is an enormous bulldozer that appears in the first scene in the script as it is being transported by a twin-engine army helicopter to the location of the roadblock. The image of the bulldozer swishing through space matches the many scenes of Kowalski's speeding car. Man and machine rush toward a rendezvous with death.

Death as a heroic and wasteful act of defiance is also prominent in "The Lost City," although it is less abstract in this script than in "Vanishing Point." Since "The Lost City" is directly related to different stages of the revolutionary struggle in Cuba, many of its episodes are grounded in historical reality. Of all the film scripts that Cabrera Infante has written, "The Lost City" is the most intimately related to his own literary works and life. It is a richly textured blend of fiction, personal memories, and history. Some of the characters are fictional, others are based on people whose names have been changed, and several are well-known literary or historical figures such as José Lezama Lima, Fulgencio Batista, Che Guevara, and Commandant Alberto Mora. Mora, a close personal friend of Cabrera Infante, committed suicide in September 1972 after falling from grace in the revolutionary government. His father, Menelao Mora, was the organizer of the failed attempt to assassinate Batista at the Presidential Palace on 13 March 1957. He perished in the rash attack along with most of his companions. The depiction of this tragic episode and its aftermath is one of the most powerful sequences in the script.

Literary antecedents of "The Lost City" include episodes, characters, and scenes from the novel *Tres tristes tigres*, the collection of historical vignettes *Vista del amanecer en el trópico* (1974) [*View of Dawn in the Tropics* (1978)], and the short story "En el gran ecbó" ["The Great Ekbo"] from *Así en la paz como en la guerra* (1960) [*Writes of Passage* (1993)]. There is also material from the unpublished autobiographical novel "Itaca vuelta visitar" [Ithaca revisited]. The opening scene of "The Lost City" takes place at the Tropicana night club in Havana as a loquacious MC chatters away in Spanish and English, an episode taken from the opening of *Tres tristes tigres*. For readers of Cabrera Infante, this script is both a nostalgic homecoming and a catapult into new realms.

The story line of "The Lost City" centers on the fortunes of the Fellove family, particularly Fico, who is the central character. The owner and manager of Tropicana, Fico wages a losing battle to preserve his family and business as the revolution unfolds. One of his brothers, Luis, dies during the struggle against Batista, and another, Ricardo, embraces the revolution but eventually goes mad and commits suicide. Ricardo is the true believer of the family. At one point he announces, with all the disdain that an idealistic utopian can muster, that the revolution has killed the past. His suicide suggests that it is better to forget the past than to attempt to destroy it. Fico eventually ends up in New York City, living in exile and poverty. His living quarters are described as "the smallest hotel room in the world" (178). Fico tells a writer friend: "Exile does something to you. All you have left is memories. You don't care about the future and the present in which you live is so thin that it can be squeezed under the door" (183). In these poignant pages, one senses the residue of Cabrera Infante's early days in exile.

The third draft of "The Lost City" contains 197 pages and 300 scenes. A fourth draft has been reduced to approximately 120 pages, with most of the major episodes intact. One of the more intricate aspects of this script, and the earlier "Vanishing Point" script, is the detailed coordination of music to accompany different scenes. Specific compositions, many from popular music, are mentioned throughout the screenplay and are carefully integrated into the plot. "The Lost City" has an advocate in Hollywood in the actor Andy García who has expressed interest in directing and starring in the film. The script is a compelling read and worthy of publication. One can only hope it will be filmed or published as a screenplay or serve as the basis of a fictional work. "The Lost City" is an important story, masterfully told, that should be produced or published in some form.

Cabrera Infante has come a long way since his early days in the town of Gibara on the northeast Atlantic coast of Cuba where his mother often offered him and his brother Alberto the choice between saving money to go to a movie or eating.[11] The two boys' invariable choice of illusion over nourishment not only reinforced their mother's enthusiasm for film, it also reflected their own response to the cinema's ability to spark the imagination. Cabrera Infante enjoyed his early successes in Havana as a film critic, and when he found himself in exile casting about for a country to live in and a way to sustain his family, his cinematic talents offered the most viable avenue open to him. He has often declared that he did not choose England, England chose him. There is more than a suggestion of truth in his assertion. Once in London, earnings from film scripts enabled him to move to attractive living quarters and to send his two daughters to private school. Viable sources of income were also essential for the renewal of visas. During the early years of exile, the visa status of the entire family was in doubt, forcing him to keep a low profile. The contractual dealings that surrounded his screen version of Malcolm Lowry's *Under the Volcano* were a contributing factor to what was to be one of the most disagreeable episodes of his life, a harrowing encounter with the four horsemen. That script represents the Mr. Hyde phase of his relationship with cinema—fortunately for him, Dr. Jekyll has been the predominant persona in his connections with the film industry.

Cabrera Infante's love of the movies has also nourished his other creative work, contributing to its visual elements and conditioning some of his characters' conceptions of reality. This influence is particularly evident in the panorama of characters that populate *Tres tristes tigres.* For example, Magalena Crus declares her independence in a crude carpe diem directed at her grandmother and goes off to Havana acting like Bette Davis. In another episode Códac imagines what it would be like to wake up in the morning as Rock Hudson and find Doris Day next to him instead of La Estrella. In *La Habana para un Infante difunto* (1979) [*Infante's Inferno* (1984)], the narrator-protagonist aspires to accomplish in Havana what Rudolph Valentino carried out in the tango halls of Buenos Aires and Paris in *The Four Horsemen of the Apocalypse.* Although successful on many occasions, the narrator cannot match the number of seductions Valentino attained on the screen, except, perhaps, in the imaginative, metaphorical journey he undertakes at the end of the novel. Even *Holy Smoke* (1985), which chronicles humankind's relations with tobacco, deals as much with film as with smoking.

Written originally in English, *Holy Smoke* is another manifestation of Cabrera Infante's multicultural and multilingual orientation and of cinema's nourishment of his imagination. The cinematic image is about as close as any of us can come to safely escaping the materiality of existence. In the movies, we can experience vicariously a wide range of sensations and feelings without any risk to our physical being. Film is a major source of contemporary mythology and a dynamic contributor to world culture. In his literary and cinematic writings, Cabrera Infante blends classical and modern mythologies as well as elite and popular culture, indications that he is decidedly a creation of the twentieth century.

Active membership in the Cuban Communist Party did not prevent Zoila and Guillermo senior from introducing their sons to a range of influences, including some from the capitalistic world. Zoila's enthusiasm for the movies, baseball, and other forms of popular entertainment was contagious. She also encouraged her sons' ventures into creative activities, much to the dismay of her husband, who was more pragmatically inclined. After the family moved from Gibara to Havana in 1941, Guillermo senior enrolled his elder son in a series of night classes at an English institute, giving him direct access to the cultural and linguistic codes of the English-speaking world. Cabrera Infante's command of English brings to mind other renowned writers who have moved between different cultures and languages such as Jorge Luis Borges, Joseph Conrad, Arthur Koestler, and Vladimir Nabokov. What separates him from these distinguished writers is the extent of his commitment to film as a critic, cultural commentator, essayist, and creator of screenplays. The child who accompanied his mother into the dark world of movie theaters has emerged into the limelight.

Notes

1. "Orígenes (Cronología a la manera de Laurence Sterne)" in *O* (Barcelona: Editorial Seix Barral, 1975), 181. "(C)ave Attemptor! A Chronology (After Laurence Sterne's)," *World Literature Today* 4 (Autumn 1987): 513.

2. "Recollections of Rudolph Valentino," in *There is a New Star in Heaven . . . Valentino,* ed. Eva Orbanz (Berlin: Verlag Volker Spiess, 1979), 23.

3. Kevin Brownlow, *David Lean: A Biography* (New York: St. Martin's Press, 1996), 42.

4. Liam O'Leary, *Rex Ingram: Master of the Silent Cinema* (Udine, Italy: Le Giornate del Cinema Muto, 1993), 71.

5. Ibid., 77, 81–82.

6. Fuller accounts of this episode can be found in Danubio Torres Fierro, "Guillermo Cabrera Infante," in *Memorial Plural, Entrevistas a escritores latinoamericanos* (Buenos Aires: Editorial Sudamericana, 1986), 71–72, and in Raymond D. Souza, *Guillermo Cabrera Infante: Two Islands, Many Worlds* (Austin: University of Texas Press, 1996), 10–12.

7. *Un oficio del siglo veinte* (Havana: Ediciones R, 1963); translated by Kenneth Hall and Guillermo Cabrera Infante as *A Twentieth Century Job* (London: Faber and Faber, 1991).

8. For commentary on the scripts see Souza, *Guillermo Cabrera Infante,* 103–22. A complete listing of the screenplays can be found on pages 182–83.

9. My comments are based on the January 1970 version of "Vanishing Point" and the third draft dated 24 April 1991 of "The Lost City." Since these manuscripts are unpublished, they are listed in quotation marks. *Vanishing Point* (in italics) refers, of course, to the film. Page references hereafter cited in the text.

10. Kenneth E. Hall argues that the film combines a reworking of the Western genre with classical myths. *Guillermo Cabrera Infante and the Cinema* (Newark, Del.: Juan de la Cuesta, 1989), 114–15.

11. Juan Bonilla, "Cabrera Infante, contando y contando," *ABC Literario* 240 (7 June 1996), 19. He also relates the anecdote in Rita Guibert, *Seven Voices* (New York: Vintage Books, 1973), 401.

Movies and Mock Encomia

KENNETH HALL

For many years Guillermo Cabrera Infante has practiced the art of the mock encomium, or the playful, lightly satiric tribute to a chosen person. Ardis L. Nelson, in her study of Cabrera Infante and the Menippean tradition, dealt with this kind of approach chiefly in relation to his fiction.[1] But Cabrera Infante has cultivated a more occasional form of mock encomium. He has written a considerable number of obituaries of film personalities, mostly for newspapers and magazines in England and Spain. While some of these obituaries are serious tributes, many of them contain significant admixtures of mock encomium. Thus, titles such as " 'Sic transit' Gloria Grahame" ["So passes" Gloria Grahame] and "Por siempre Rita" [Forever Rita]—for Rita Hayworth—signal less than solemn or funereal treatments of the subject of the obituary.[2]

The mock encomium has as literary siblings the mock epic and the mock-heroic poem. All three forms, as their names imply, reverse or "mock" the intent of the original form. Thus, the mock epic is defined as "A work in verse which employs the lofty manner . . . of epic to treat of a trivial subject and theme in such a way as to make both subject and theme ridiculous" (Cuddon, "Mock-Epic").

If the encomium may be defined strictly as "formal eulogy in prose or verse glorifying people, objects, ideas or events" (Cuddon, "Encomium"), the mock encomium is an ironic or parodic encomium, often with social intent. One of the most well-known examples of such encomia is Renaissance humanist Desiderius Erasmus's *Encomium moriae* [*Praise of Folly*], in which the inappropriate subject of praise (folly) serves as the basis for the ironic functioning of the genre.[3]

As one might expect, Cabrera Infante uses the encomium in a rather different manner from Erasmus. He is not, at least in his occasional pieces on film, particularly interested in social or philosophical critique of the kind found in serious or didactic satirists like Horace, Juvenal, or Swift.[4] He *is* fascinated, as always, with the potential for punning, parody, and "neobaroque" effects such as suppression, circumlocution, and other stylistic tropes. Cabrera Infante has noted his affinity to some writers of the Spanish Golden Age, among them Miguel de Cervantes and Francisco de Quevedo.[5]

Like Quevedo, and like *Tristram Shandy* author Laurence Sterne, another of Cabrera Infante's models, Cabrera Infante has mastered the art of the left-handed tribute.[6] In his mock encomia his style bears similarities to that of the classical satirist Lucian, who almost seems baroque in his anatomical stripping away of appearances,[7] as Ronald Paulson shows in his contrasting of Lucian with Roman satirist Juvenal:

> Juvenal deals with two realities: a good one in the past and a degenerate one in the present. The good one exposes the evil of the presently accepted one. Lucian works with an appearance or an illusion and a reality, a mask and the face underneath. While in Juvenal the ideal is good and the present reality evil, in Lucian the illusion is evil and the exposed reality not good but—and this is the most important change—real. . . . His satire never explores the relation between an ideal and the falling away, or looks into the nature of evil itself. It is far too rhetorical for that; it is always persuading and arguing, revealing and surprising. More than any of the other great ancient satirists, Lucian is the rhetorician first, the moralist second, and his surprises and constant striving for effect sometimes suggest that the effect is achieved for its own sake.[8]

Nevertheless Cabrera Infante is capable of writing very serious obituaries that approach the prose elegy. Particularly moving are his tributes to his Cuban friends Néstor Almendros and Calvert Casey, both found in his recent *Mea Cuba*.[9] But even in the Casey piece, a long recounting of some of the events that preceded his tragic suicide, Cabrera Infante tries to see the humorous side of Casey and his life. The difference here is that he does not treat Casey himself ironically, as food for parody: his friendship with Casey and his obvious shock over his death do not permit such treatment.

In the film obituaries, however, Cabrera Infante works only rarely in a straight, serious mode. If these essays are not mock-heroic or mock epic, they are mock encomia, or perhaps seriocomic elegies, since they generally lack the social thrust often found in the Renaissance mock encomium or the invective found in classical satires on famous figures.[10] Still, it seems that Cabrera Infante often deflates his heroic or idealized figures by making of them surfaces, virtually one-dimensional cutouts, to be reflected in puns and baroque tropes.

One good example of such deflation, or an ironic eulogy, is "Por siempre Rita." This little gem of an obituary is often only half serious, although it does reveal true feeling and adoration on Cabrera Infante's part for the icon that was Rita Hayworth.[11] The article is based on the putatively simple concept that Hayworth was "una diosa" [a goddess]. The concept, a conceit really,[12] is expressed in true baroque form in an extended climax:

> Rita Hayworth fue más que una belleza del cine, más que una vaga vampiresa, más que el ídolo en efigie en que la convirtió el siglo. "Dios ha muerto," decretó Nietzsche pero en seguida resucitaron los dioses. Rita Hayworth fue una diosa hecha a la medida de los tiempos, . . ."
>
> [Rita Hayworth was more than a beauty of the cinema, more than a vague vamp, more than the idol in effigy into which the century made her. "God is dead," Nietzsche decreed but right away the gods were revived. Rita Hayworth was a goddess cut to fit the times.] (*Cine*, 251)

Cabrera Infante, though, immediately cuts the figure down to size: "pero curiosamente nadie con menos talento fue tan lejos" [but curiously no one with less talent went so far] (*Cine*, 251).

The conceit of the woman made goddess is established, "Su belleza se construyó poco a poco" [Her beauty was constructed little by little], and then becomes the pretext for sometimes playful exegetic commentary, not only on the notion of the constructed beauty but on the text of the expression of the conceit: "una diosa hecha a la medida de los tiempos." As María Acosta Cruz has made clear, Cabrera Infante frequently uses a baroque technique that the late Cuban writer Severo Sarduy has called "suppression" or "substitution," in which one term "hides" another but does not completely obscure it.[13] So, we are reminded throughout the piece of the dictum "Man is the measure of all things."[14] Upon this structure is built the parodic encomium of Rita Hayworth, which is furthermore based on the contrasts "appearance/reality," "Margarita Cansino/Rita Hayworth," "dark hair/red hair," "real voice/dubbed singing voice." Cabrera Infante praises Rita but never lets us forget her Hollywood-produced artificiality and the importance of her surface charms for her image and identity.

This encomium is yet more complex. It employs linguistic sleight-of-hand to place the sexual attributes of its subject onto center stage:

> su larga caballera negra [in *Gilda*] . . . era ella misma un fetiche, que es lo que todo amor quiere que sea la hembra de la especie: mamantis, amantis, mantis religiosa que promete devoraciones en público y en privado.
>
> [her long black hair . . . was itself a fetish, which is what all love wants from the female of the species: mamantis (pun on "mamá," "mammary," "mantis," "amantis"), amantis (related to "amante," "lover"), praying mantis that promises public and private devourings.] (*Cine*, 252).

And, as Gene Dubois has pointed out, a classical subtext is hidden in the following sentence: "Orson, nunca llamado Welles [who married Hayworth], entendió que Rita era algo más que cabellera longa y seso breve" [Orson, never named Welles, understood that Rita was something more than long hair and short brains] (the reference is to "ars est longa, vita brevis" [art is long, life short]).[15]

Cabrera Infante does not by "mocking" his encomia subjects thereby necessarily deprecate them: he instead flatters them with his attention, along the lines of what Linda Hutcheon calls the "reverential variety of parody."[16] Cabrera Infante can be quite Quevedesque or Swiftian in tone, as in *Mea Cuba,* but he can also present the rather odd face of one who parodies but does not judge (in other words, of one who cultivates Menippean satire). He adopts this stance in his film obituaries. His humor is perhaps more Plautan than Juvenalian.[17] So, although technically he may seem to "destroy" the subjects of his obituaries, he does not "assassinate" them as does Seneca the Emperor Claudius in his *Apocolocyntosis* or as Quevedo does with numerous figures in his *Los sueños* [The dreams].[18]

One of Cabrera Infante's favorite devices, besides his inveterate and insatiable punning, is that of ironic reversal. This device can be seen in pieces like " 'Sic transit' Gloria Grahame." As anyone who has watched this actress knows, her beauty was not of the traditional kind.[19] In fact, as Cabrera Infante shows, her very homeliness or strangeness is her great charm, as he discovered when a young man: "Fue poco después [1944] que me enamoré de Gloria Grahame para siempre: mientras más fea más fascinante" [It was not long afterward that I fell in love with Gloria Grahame forever: the homelier she was, the more fascinating she became] (*Cine,* 235). He provides a strange anatomy of her attributes that might have shocked Calixto by its irreverence:[20]

> Su pelo rubio era tan escaso como para no hacerle competencia a Verónica Lake, su frente jamás se iluminó como ese medio domo de belleza de Elizabeth Taylor, sus ojos eran chicos, de párpados pesados, y parecía siempre estar a punto de caer dormida o de no haberse despertado todavía a media tarde; su nariz no era ciertamente la de Katharine Hepburn y su boca estaba presidida por su labio superior, que se extendía peligroso más allá del labio inferior y de toda la boca, como un toldo desmedido y casi fuera de control.
>
> [Her blonde hair was thin enough so as not to compete with Veronica Lake's, her forehead never lit up like that half-dome of beauty of Elizabeth Taylor's, her eyes were tiny, with heavy lids, and she always seemed about to fall asleep or not to have awakened yet in the middle of the afternoon; her nose was certainly not Katharine Hepburn's, and her mouth was presided over by her upper lip, which extended perilously beyond her lower lip and over her whole mouth, like an outsized tarp that was almost out of control.] (*Cine*, 235)

Not content with this already negative encomium, Cabrera Infante assures us that her baroque mouth (or actually lip)

> estaba paralizado por una novocaína natural, y al hablar, Gloria Grahame dejaba escapar su vocecita fañosa de tan nasal que era y a la que su labio hacía displicente y, a veces, letal. Era el amor, sin duda.
>
> [was paralyzed by a natural novocaine, and when speaking, Gloria Grahame let slip out her little voice, breathy from being so nasal and which her lip made displeasing and, sometimes, lethal. It was love, no doubt about it.] (*Cine*, 235)

As a devotee myself of Gloria Grahame, I can fully understand his terms. Interestingly, they are not far in spirit from the sentiments expressed by the Greek epigrammatist Marcus Argentarius:

> Love is not just a function of the eyes.
> Beautiful objects will, of course, inspire
> Possessive urges—you need not despise
> Your taste. But when insatiable desire
> Inflames you for a girl who's out of fashion,
> Lacking in glamour—plain, in fact—that fire
> Is genuine; that's the authentic passion.
> Beauty, though, any critic can admire.[21]

In some cases, Cabrera Infante treats his subjects metaphorically, following a baroque tradition of circumlocution practiced by Quevedo and Luis de Góngora.[22] One of the best-realized examples of this kind of obituary is the one on Ava Gardner, "Ava se pronuncia Eva" [Ava is pronounced Eva] (*Cine,* 244–50). The obvious, but complex, pun on "Ava" and "Eva" leads Cabrera Infante in some rather unexpected directions, not the least interesting of which is the possibility of interlingual punning and homophonics: "Ava" and "Eva" are homophones between English and Spanish; while "Eva" has obvious associations with Eve—but also with Eva Perón.

In keeping with Cabrera Infante's penchant for making characters after his own taste out of the foci of his obituaries, Ava Gardner becomes a character based on her persona as actress, "una asesina de hombres" ["a mankiller"] (*Cine,* 244)—note the hidden reference to her role in Robert Siodmak's essential film noir work *The Killers* (1946)—as well as, more interestingly, a Cervantine or Quixotesque ideal.[23] Here, Cabrera Infante cleverly uses Gardner's real biographical data as a point of departure for his baroque play. In true Menippean fashion, Cabrera Infante establishes her as a type, the country girl, who in real life becomes transformed into a pop poetic ideal:

> Ava Gardner fue ese ideal de la poesía bucólica: una campesina de una belleza que sale de la tierra. Era, para tormento de todo Quijote, una Aldonza Lorenzo que es a la vez una Dulcinea toda busto.
>
> [Ava Gardner was that ideal of bucolic poetry: a peasant girl with a beauty that comes from the earth. She was, to the torment of every Quixote, an Aldonza Lorenzo who is at the same time an all-busty Dulcinea.] (*Cine*, 245)[24]

If Rita Hayworth was all surface covering the rather uninteresting Margarita Cansino, Ava Gardner is an extension; in fact, a genuinely Jonsonian "type" governed, as it were, by the "humor" of country girl innocence and attractiveness. Even her name, like Volpone's, indicates her provenance and her prominence: Ava Gardner, Eve in the garden.[25]

As should be clear by now, the term "mock encomium" is being used in a particular and restricted way. "Mock" does not necessarily mean to imply a low-mimetic or sarcastically ironic treatment of a character. Rather, it is the seriousness of the enterprise that is gently mocked or deflated, much as with those comic epitaphs that mock death rather than the dead.

The piece on Gardner maintains the note of metaphorical reversal with which it had begun, as Ava Gardner, née Lucy Johnson, returns to her true nature like the rose in Sor Juana Inés de la Cruz's sonnet "Rosa divina" [Divine rose].[26] Cabrera Infante recounts having seen Gardner on a London street near the end of her life. He writes,

> Había adoptado ella ahora la imagen real pero como se sabe la reina Isabel es la más burguesa de los monarcas. Ava había regresado. Ahora era (y parecía) Lucy Johnson.
>
> [She had adopted by now her real image, but as we know Queen Elizabeth is the most bourgeois of monarchs. Ava had returned. Now she was (and looked like) Lucy Johnson.] (*Cine*, 250)

The essay on Gardner is one of the pieces in which Cabrera Infante deals in anatomy in its literal sense, as a stripping away of appearances. A favorite technique of the baroque and a crucial question for the Renaissance, anatomy is central to Cabrera Infante's work, appearing often in forms quite as literal as in the Gardner essay.[27] Like baroque authors such as Quevedo in *Los sueños,* Sor Juana in sonnets such as "Rosa divina" and "A su retrato" [To her portrait], and Swift in the notorious "The Lady's Dressing Room," Cabrera Infante delights in revealing the truth beneath the mask—an enterprise well-suited to writing about the illusionist art of the movies.[28]

Two other essays by Cabrera Infante typify his explicit recourse to "dissection." One of these, "From Legs to Riches," is not precisely an obituary, though it contains an interestingly reductive backhanded *hommage* to George Raft.[29] The other, "El gran Cukor" [The great Cukor] is an obituary for director George Cukor.[30]

Cabrera Infante punctures the movie image of Raft in "From Legs to Riches," an introduction to the Budd Boetticher movie *The Rise and Fall of Legs Diamond*.[31] Raft's connection to the Boetticher film, he points out, is that Ray Danton, playing Prohibition-era gangster Legs Diamond, had also played Raft in *The George Raft Story*.[32] Cabrera Infante therefore has an interesting opportunity not only to "dissect" Raft but also to manipulate the relationships between biography and "real life."

Cabrera Infante recounts that he met Raft in January 1958, during his tenure as film critic (using the pseudonym "Caín") for the Havana magazine *Carteles.* Cabrera Infante's pieces and longer works often treat the theme of role-playing versus "real" life, a theme quite in line with the baroque and with the anatomical mode. In this case, Cabrera Infante plays a double game, beginning with Raft's biographical background as a potential gangster, dealing then with his assumption of that role in movies, in which he, with a "real" gangster background, played fictional gangsters, and ending by imitating his own portrayals:

> He had been the greatest romantic gangster of the movies. He became famous just by tossing a coin whose spinning was his way of courting fate. . . . The man I met in Havana was no longer a star either. He had gone back to tossing a coin by spinning a wheel. ("Legs," 1)

Raft had come to live his own role, and maintained, or pretended, "that the story of his life was a movie called *The George Raft Story*" ("Legs," 1).

Thus, Cabrera Infante sets up a system of "Chinese-box" reflections that are actually parodies: Raft parodied the real gangster (himself, potentially), then became a parody of that parody, then saw his own parody parodied and invested his identity (perhaps mockingly) in this final parody.[33] It seems that here, as in other encomia (and this little piece could be termed an encomium, in fact an obituary), Cabrera Infante comes up against the elusiveness of the identity of his subject: it is difficult to capture the "real" George Raft because his own way of life encapsulated him in so much self-reflexiveness, and Cabrera Infante compounds this conundrum with his own lightly mocking treatment.

But there is more. The story about Raft leads into a thumbnail sketch of actor Ray Danton, who played Raft in *The George Raft Story.* Thus, the connection is cemented between Raft's play on roles and appearances and the role of Legs Diamond. Diamond was himself what George Raft pretended to be:

> Legs Diamond was a crack shot and a safecracker. He was also a good dancer and because he was ruggedly handsome, a ladies man. That's why the New York tabloids were always keen to have him on the front page. Diamond loved all this but later he came to hate all publicity: it is bad for the legs. ("Legs," 2)

Like Raft, Diamond "came to hate all publicity," but for different reasons. Raft became the flip side of his youthful film image, while Diamond probably feared publicity because of its danger to him. Interestingly, Cabrera Infante turns directly from Diamond, the handsome, feckless robber, to Dutch Schultz, "the gangster with the ugliest mug" ("Legs," 2): think of feckless Raft in *Scarface* turning into ugly, aging Raft, the casino manager.

Like the essay on Raft, "Cukor visto dos veces" deals with its subject at an advanced age, well past the prime of his life and moviemaking.[34] From the opening sentence, Cabrera Infante establishes his conceit, of Cukor as "sweet," a "soft" director as contrasted with his opposite number from Cabrera Infante's perspective, Luis Buñuel:[35]

> Cukor quiere decir azúcar en checo (¿o es en eslovaco?) y George Cukor era una de las personas más dulces posibles en un negocio en que lo único dulce es el olor del éxito—y a veces ese olor, según Tony Curtis, como el de las rosas muertas, se llama hedor.
>
> [Cukor means sugar in Czech (or is it Slovak?) and George Cukor was one of the sweetest persons possible in a business in which the only thing sweet is the smell of success—and sometimes that smell, according to Tony Curtis, like that of dead roses, is called stench.] ("Cukor," 17)

The opening of this essay certainly qualifies it as an encomium, a form that, as Richard Lanham says, represents "praise of a person or thing by extolling inherent qualities."[36] It is instructive to study this brilliantly concentrated opening sentence more closely. If in "Bad Babs" Cabrera Infante merged Barbara Stanwyck's identity with a nickname, Babs, and created a picaresque character in the process, here he employs a more euphuistic tactic: Cukor's name is etymologized in order to capture his character. His name becomes his essence: he is identified semantically with his comportment in Hollywood.[37] This intriguing strategy allows the author to move into a contrast between Cukor's "sweetness" and the "stink" of Hollywood power politics. The hinge for his move is an odd parallelism between the "sweet" Cukor and the fact that in Hollywood "lo único dulce es el olor del éxito": a typically "suppressed" reference to the 1956 film *Sweet Smell of Success,* with Burt Lancaster and Tony Curtis.[38]

The Cukor piece is in fact a thorough exercise in baroque treatment of its subject. The baroque treatment here contributes strongly to the mock effect of the essay. Like Góngora, Cabrera Infante relies extensively on antithesis, as for example, "la siguiente visión fue una no-visión" [the subsequent sight was a non-sight] ("Cukor," 20).[39] The running contradictions situate the Cukor image between opposed ideas and images. Like a Menippean character, or like Tristram Shandy or Voltaire's Candide, he seems to live in the tension between two poles; his reality becomes that of a central point between two sides of a debate.[40] His literary reality is expressed by recourse to suppressed texts, as in this passage replete with such references:

> Cukor, ni ágil ni perezoso, sino cuidadoso, evitando esa losa que bosteza antes que ser sueño eterno . . . regresó a su tumbona y se tumbó y se durmió—aparente o realmente para siempre. Para el cine de veras para la eternidad. "Murió sin recobrar sus facultades," dijo el parte médico. Los buenos directores de cine, como George Cukor, sólo llegan a ser gagá y son enterrados entre los famosos en Forest Lawns [*sic*]. Los grandes directores de cine, como Luis Buñuel, viven todavía, *toujours dada.*
>
> [Cukor, neither agile nor lazy, but instead cautious, avoiding that stone that yawns before being eternal sleep . . . returned to his vault and tumbled down and fell asleep—apparently or really forever. For the movies really for eternity. "He died without regaining consciousness," said the medical report. Good movie directors, like George Cukor, only end up being gaga and are buried among the famous in Forest Lawn (a famous Hollywood cemetery). Great movie directors, like Luis Buñuel, live on still, always dada. (The reference to the deliberately nonsensical style of art during the World War I years that took the name "dada" and was a cousin of surrealism, which had significant influence on Buñuel, is also, in this case, a pun on the infantile "dada" for "father.")] ("Cukor," 20)

The suppressed allusions begin with a pop reference, as "esa losa que bosteza" interlingually parodies the old Coca-Cola slogan "the pause that refreshes"—except that this "pause" becomes "sueño eterno"—American detective novelist Raymond Chandler's "big sleep." Even more revealing, in terms of Cabrera Infante's literary influences and of the picaresque tinge to many of his mock encomia, is the clause "regresó a su tumbona y se tumbó y se durmió," an apparent travesty of the phrasing used by Lazarillo de Tormes to recount the events leading up to his father's death. Notice the similarity of phrasing in "por lo cual fue preso, y confesó y no negó, y padesció persecución por justicia":

> Pues siendo yo niño de ocho años, achacaron a mi padre ciertas sangrías mal hechas en los costales de los que allí a moler venían, *por lo cual fue preso, y confesó y no negó, y padesció persecución por justicia. . . . En este tiempo se hizo cierta armada contra moros, entre los cuales fue mi padre, . . . y con su señor, como leal criado, fenesció su vida.*

> [Now when I was about eight years old they caught my father bleeding the sacks belonging to the people who came to have their crops milled there. *So they arrested him, and he confessed, denied nothing and was punished by law. . . . About this time there was an expedition against the Moors and my father went with it. . . . and he ended his life with his master like a loyal servant.*] (emphasis added)[41]

Cabrera Infante does not always puncture or deflate images; sometimes he extends and plays upon them, turning his subjects into Plautan character-types (see note 17). Possibly the best example of this type of mock encomium is "Bad Babs," the dazzling essay on one of Hollywood's most powerful presences, Barbara Stanwyck (b. Ruby Stevens, 1907–1990). Many latter-day viewers may know her only as the matriarch of television's *The Big Valley*, but Stanwyck was a versatile actress who could play comedy or serious roles. Her greatest legacy, though, is her portrayal of the *belle dame sans merci* [beautiful lady without mercy] of the film noir of the 1940s and 1950s, as in *Double Indemnity* (1945), *The Strange Love of Martha Ivers* (1946), and *Thelma Jordan* (1950).[42] Cabrera Infante presents chiefly this image in his masterly eulogy to Stanwyck, a mock encomium that combines euphuistic, baroque wordplay with real admiration for Stanwyck's importance as an actress.

Cabrera Infante adopts a nearly picaresque strategy in this piece by causing Stanwyck's nickname "Babs" to become, more than a tag for her persona, indeed a persona of its own. As if "Babs" were Lazarillo, el Buscón, or the Artful Dodger, she becomes the exemplification of certain important traits in the Stanwyck image.[43] This exemplification is carried forward by a favorite Cabrera Infante device, the metonymic use of names:

> Babs es Barbara. Bad Babs es Barbara la Mala. . . . Barbara es Barbara Stanwyck. . . . Ella es la más mala, la más buena, la más mala de las malas, mala mala, y cuando es buena es mala, pero cuando es mala es peor.

> [Babs is Barbara. Bad Babs is Barbara the Bad (a pun in Spanish on Barbara LaMarr, a silent film actress). . . . Barbara is Barbara Stanwyck. . . . She is the worst, the best, the worst of the worst, bad bad, and when she's good she's bad, but when she's bad she's worse.] ("Bad," 11)[44]

Barbara/Babs takes a very unsentimental journey through the precarious world of film noir and suspense; Cabrera Infante treats her as a kind of reverse Candy who, instead of innocence, in *Baby Face* (1933) "proyecta la inmoralidad en movimiento, casi como una mentira a 24 cuadros por segundo" [projects immorality in motion, almost like a lie at 24 frames per second] ("Bad," 11)[45]. Even in a lighter film such as the screwball comedy *Ball of Fire* (1942, with Gary Cooper) she is a picaresque character whose "sinfulness" affords Cabrera Infante an opportunity for his preferred *conceptista* games:

> Esa piel, que ella oculta y revela como un striptease moral, aparece en *Bola de fuego* enmarcada por lúcidas lentejuelas que tienen reflejos dorados sobre sus muslos y sus piernas que pecan con pecas (Babs es pelirroja natural) paseándose provocadora entre siete eruditos como una Blanca Nieves corista y corita . . . .
>
> [That skin, which she hides and reveals like a moral striptease, appears in *Ball of Fire* marked by lucid sequins that have golden reflections on her thighs (a reference to the film *Reflections in a Golden Eye* [1967], a treatment of sexuality starring Marlon Brando[46]) and her shins that sin with freckles (Babs is a natural redhead) strolling sexily among seven scholars like Snow White from the choir and the chorus. . . .] ("Bad," 12)

As does the narrator in Cabrera Infante's 1979 book *La Habana para un Infante difunto* [*Infante's Inferno* (1984)], the essayist here identifies himself as an alter ego or double of the film characters who enter into relationships with the femme fatale. In this case, Cabrera Infante accomplishes the identification in a rather curious manner, as if differentiating himself from other film critics and viewers:

> La Stanwyck, como la llama siempre el historiador del cine John Kobal o simple pero mordaz Miss Stanwyck en la voz burlona del pintor José Miguel Rodríguez . . . Stanwyck, como la quieren las feministas, Babs para mí, su íntimo mirón, es la reina del cine negro.
>
> [La Stanwyck, as film historian John Kobal always calls her or simple but mordant Miss Stanwyck in the mocking voice of painter José Miguel Rodríguez . . . Stanwyck, as the feminists prefer her, Babs for me, her intimate peeper, is the queen of film noir.] ("Bad," 13)

The obituary for Marlene Dietrich, "Un milagro fabricado" [A fabricated miracle], contains excellent examples of Cabrera Infante's Menippean, *conceptista* wordplay.[47] The title of the piece is in fact self-referential, alluding to the artificiality of Dietrich's image ("un milagro fabricado") and signaling the technique of fabricated analogies that Cabrera Infante will employ in the essay. In this piece, Cabrera Infante's well-known wordplay shines, creating a metaphorical surface for Dietrich. The essay plays on the double conceit of Dietrich as prostitute and goddess, based on her real name, Maria Magdalena. Thus, Dietrich is a Venus in Josef Von Sternberg's *Blonde Venus* (1932), but she is, for Cabrera Infante, a Venus figure drawn from a twisting of Botticelli's vision, in a kind of comic *ekphrasis*:[48]

> *Blonde Venus* . . . es el nacimiento de Venus no de entre las aguas, sino de un símil simiesco: en vez de secuestrar King Kong a la rubia, la rubia surge ahora de un gorila.
>
> [*Blonde Venus* . . . is the birth of Venus not from the waters, but from a simian simile: instead of King Kong kidnapping the blonde, the blonde rises now from a gorilla.] ("Un milagro," 6–7)

Later in the obituary, Cabrera Infante makes explicit the virgin/whore duality of Dietrich:

> Su verdadero nombre propio, Maria Magdalena, del que Marlene es una contracción infantil, es apto para una actriz que en el cine a menudo era una santa o una puta . . .
>
> [Her real given name, Maria Magdalena, of which Marlene is a childhood contraction, is apt for an actress who often was a saint or a whore in the movies . . .] ("Un milagro," 7)

Then, as if unwilling to stay too literal, Cabrera Infante launches into an exhibition of wordplay and analogy:

> En una de sus memorias, Marlene muestra (o casi exhibe) su mala memoria y dice que le dijo a Von Sternberg: "Eres Svengali y yo soy Trilby." Pero Von Sternberg fue más que su Svengali. Fue su Cristóbal Colón (la descubrió aunque ya estaba allí), su verdadero Vespucci (le dio el nombre para el cine), su mago Magallanes (viajó alrededor de ella con su cámara), pero fue el propio Von Sternberg que dijo, en el idioma en que conversaban: "Ich bin Marlene" . . .
>
> [In one of her memoirs, Marlene shows (or almost exhibits) her poor memory and says that she told Von Sternberg: "You're Svengali and I'm Trilby." But Von Sternberg was more than her Svengali. He was her Christopher Columbus (he discovered her though she was already there), her veritable Vespucci (he gave her her stage name), her magician Magellan (he traveled around her with his camera), but it was Von Sternberg himself who said, in the language they conversed in: "Ich bin Marlene" (I am Marlene) . . .] ("Un milagro," 7)[49]

Notice here how Cabrera Infante cleverly highlights the theme of artificiality in the persona of Marlene Dietrich. By repeated use of antonomasia, he extends the metaphor in Von Sternberg's remark. Not only was Von Sternberg, who directed her in her most famous films, the Svengali to Dietrich's Trilby, he was her Columbus, her Vespucci, and her Magellan.[50] Notice the sly use of paradox to highlight Dietrich's artificiality, her false image. All the discoverers mentioned here are subjects either of controversy about their true actions or did not complete their projects. Columbus "discovered" a New World that was already there; Vespucci's name was given to the "discovery" by a quirk of publishing; Magellan did not complete his voyage, dying on the way. Thus, Von Sternberg "discovered" a Dietrich who was "already there"; he gave her a false (stage) name; and he "traveled" around her with a camera, making, incidentally, a reverse negative image, as in the case of all photography.

Even in an adulatory piece such as the obituary on Randolph Scott, "La venganza a caballo" [Vengeance on horseback] (*Cine,* 177–82), Cabrera Infante can scarcely resist a little mocking or joking.[51] He discusses Scott's investment savvy at some length, observing that Scott must indeed have had artistic reasons for appearing in Peckinpah's *Ride the High Country* (1962), "[c]omo tenía entonces suficiente dinero para retirar a un ejército a un balneario" [since he then had enough money to retire an army to a resort] (*Cine,* 181).

As in many of his other obituary pieces, Cabrera Infante rescues the marking of a sad occasion from possible sentimentality by converting his commemoration into a lighthearted, Menippean view of a memorable life. The mock encomium cultivated by Cabrera Infante is a unique contribution to the essay form. His originality has taken the journalistic obituary into the territory of the neobaroque and connects it with the classical satiric tradition.

Notes

1. Nelson, commenting on Cabrera Infante's works, characterizes Menippean satire:

> A great many characteristics of Cabrera Infante's works reflect the ancient literary tradition of Menippean satire, a serio-comic genre which arose from carnival attitudes. . . . Differing from our usual conception of satire, in which man's vices or follies are held up to ridicule with a decidedly moral or didactic purpose, Menippean satire is light-hearted and has no such moralistic end. (Ardis L. Nelson, *Cabrera Infante in the Menip-*

pean Tradition, prol. Guillermo Cabrera Infante [Newark, Del.: Juan de la Cuesta, 1983], xxiii).

J. A. Cuddon, in *A Dictionary of Literary Terms,* says that the form was "so called after Menippus, its originator, who was a philosopher and a Cynic of the 3rd c. B.C.. He satirized the follies of men (including philosophers) in a mixture of prose and verse" (J. A. Cuddon, "Menippean Satire," *A Dictionary of Literary Terms* [Garden City, N.Y.: Doubleday, 1977]; hereafter cited in the text as Cuddon).

2. Guillermo Cabrera Infante, *Cine o sardina* [Movies or meals] (Madrid: Alfaguara, 1997), 234, 251; hereafter cited in the text as *Cine.* All translations from this and other works, unless indicated otherwise, are by Kenneth Hall.

3. Erasmus was a great Renaissance humanist from Holland (1469?–1536), whose *Praise of Folly,* written in 1509, is a fantasy that starts off as a learned frivolity but turns into a full-scale ironic encomium after the manner of the Greek satirist Lucian, the first and in its way the finest example of a new form of Renaissance satire. It ends with a straightforward and touching statement of the Christian ideals that Erasmus shared notably with his English friends, John Colet and Thomas More (A. H. T. Levi, "Introduction," *Praise of Folly and Letter to Martin Dorp 1515, by Erasmus of Rotterdam,* trans. Betty Radice, introd. and notes A. H. T. Levi [Harmondsworth, Eng.: Penguin, 1971], 7).

4. Quintus Horatius Flaccus (Horace; 65–8 B.C.) was one of the greatest Roman poets. He cultivated many genres, including satire, in which he poked urbane fun at social vices and sketched vivid characters from Roman life. Decimus Junius Juvenalis (Juvenal; A.D. ?60–?130) was an important Roman satirist whose work, filled with "sarcasm, irony, innuendo and invective," "gave a new dimension to Roman satire" (D. R. Dudley, "Juvenal [Decimus Junius Juvenalis]," *Classical and Byzantine, Oriental and African Literature,* ed. D. R. Dudley and D. M. Lang [Harmondsworth, Eng.: Penguin, 1969], vol. 4 of *The Penguin Companion to Literature,* 4 vols.; hereafter cited as *Classical Literature*).

Jonathan Swift (1667–1745) was England's greatest satirist, author of the famous *Travels into Several Remote Nations of the World by Lemuel Gulliver* (1726) as well as numerous other works (Angus Ross, "Swift, Jonathan," *The Penguin Companion to English Literature,* ed. David Daiches [New York: McGraw, 1971]; hereafter cited as *English Literature*).

5. Miguel de Cervantes y Saavedra (1547–1616), was Spain's greatest writer, the author of numerous important works including the novel *El ingenioso caballero Don Quijote de la Mancha* (part 1, 1605; part 2, 1610), one of the truly monumental examples of world literature. Francisco Gómez de Quevedo y Villegas (1580–1645) was Spain's most celebrated satirist. As "the master of *conceptismo,*" he exercised his fierce wit through the use of the *concepto,* or the ingenious conceit based on linguistic play: puns, paradoxes, neologisms (word coinages), slang, and outrageous comparisons. He was the author of many works of poetry and of prose works such as *Historia de la vida del Buscón* (1626) (K. Garrad, "Quevedo y Villegas, Francisco Gómez de," *European Literature,* ed. Anthony Thorlby [Harmondsworth, Eng.: Penguin, 1969], vol. 2 of *The Penguin Companion to Literature,* 4 vols.; hereafter cited as *European Literature*).

6. Sterne (1713–1768) was one of England's most important satirists and experimental novelists. A cleric, he was the author of works such as *The Life and Opinions of Tristram Shandy* (1759–1767), a highly experimental and complex novel foreshadowing many twentieth-century techniques, and *A Sentimental Journey* (1768) (Angus Ross, "Sterne, Laurence," *English Literature*).

7. Lucian (A.D. c.115?–c.180) was a Greek satirist who drew on earlier traditions of comedy and on Plato's dialogues (many of which featured Socrates) to attack the failings of his age. His qualities are described in *The Penguin Companion to Literature* as "wit, inventiveness, formidable powers of parody and a rooted dislike of cant and superstition" (D. R. Dudley, "Lucian," *Classical Literature*). Among his best-known works are *Dialogues of the Dead* and *The True History.*

Cabrera Infante writes engagingly of the traditional practice, in composing obituaries, of "keeping up appearances" regarding the deceased, and of the changing face of obituaries, at least in the London *Times* ["*De mortuis,*" *El País* (28 April 1987): 11–12].

8. Ronald Paulson, *The Fictions of Satire* (Baltimore: Johns Hopkins University Press, 1967), 40.

9. Almendros was one of the foremost cinematographers of his generation; he died recently after a long illness. Casey was an important short-story writer who committed suicide in 1965, mainly from despair over his exile from Cuba. See "Adiós al amigo con la cámara" (396–400) and "¿Quién Mató a Calvert Casey?" (131–57) in *Mea Cuba* (Barcelona: Plaza and Janés, 1992); "Goodbye to the Friend with the Camera" (407–11) and "Who killed Calvert Casey?" (114–37) in *Mea Cuba,* trans. Kenneth Hall and Guillermo Cabrera Infante (New York: Farrar, Straus, Giroux, 1994).

10. Cabrera Infante does not treat his subject matter as "trivial" or inconsequential, and he does not employ a pretentious or "elevated" style (see quotation from Cuddon, note 1). I would not, therefore, characterize his mock encomia as mock epic or mock-heroic in the usual sense, as, for example, in this definition of the two terms from *The New Princeton Encyclopedia of Poetry and Poetics:*

> Terms used in a broad sense to describe a satiric method in poetry and prose and, more specifically, a distinct sub-genre or kind of poetry which seeks a derisive effect by combining formal and elevated lang. [*sic*] with a trivial subject (Robert P. Falk and T. V. F. Brogan, "Mock Epic, Mock Heroic," *The New Princeton Encyclopedia of Poetry and Poetics,* ed. Alex Preminger and T. V. F. Brogan [New York: MVF-Fine Communications, 1993]; hereafter cited in the text as *New Princeton*).

What I have termed the "mock encomium" in Cabrera Infante's obituary pieces shares with other "mock" styles chiefly (a) a somewhat distanced view of the subject in order to allow for comic effect and (b) parody or satire directed at the style itself—that is, the encomium or obituary itself is parodied and not so much the subject of the obituary. It is important to remember that Cabrera Infante does not consider the subjects of his obituaries to be "trivial" or worthy only of "derisive" treatment; nor does his use of the obituary or encomium form carry any of the moralizing or didacticism found, for instance, in the Augustan mock epic. See Gregory G. Colomb, *Designs on Truth: The Poetics of the Augustan Mock-Epic* (University Park, Pa.: Pennsylvania State University Press, 1992), xv.

11. Hayworth (Margarita Carmen Cansino, 1918–1987), was born in Brooklyn, New York. "Through much of the 40s," writes Ephraim Katz, "Rita was the undisputed erotic queen of Hollywood films and naturally the hottest property of Columbia [Studios]" (Ephraim Katz, *The Film Encyclopedia,* 2nd ed. [New York: HarperPerennial-HarperCollins, 1994], 607.

12. "Conceit" is a very important term in literary studies. Cuddon comments that

> By *c.* 1600 the term was still being used as a synonym for "thought," and as roughly equivalent to "concept," "idea" and "conception". It might also then denote a fanciful supposition, an ingenious act of deception or a witty or clever remark or idea. As a literary term the word has come to denote a fairly elaborate figurative device of a fanciful kind which often incorporates metaphor, simile, hyperbole or oxymoron . . . and which is intended to surprise and delight by its wit and ingenuity. The pleasure we get from many conceits is intellectual rather than sensuous. They are particularly associated with the Metaphysical Poets [such as John Donne] . . . but are to be found in abundance in the work of Italian [and Hispanic] Renaissance poets, in the love poetry of the Tudor [e. g. Shakespeare], Jacobean and Caroline poets, and in the work of Corneille, Molière and Racine. (Cuddon, "Conceit")

13. María Acosta Cruz, *The Discourse of Excess: The Latin American Neobaroque and James Joyce* (Ann Arbor, Mich.: UMI, 1985), 200, quoted in Kenneth E. Hall, *Guillermo Cabrera Infante and the Cinema,* pref. Guillermo Cabrera Infante, Estudios de Literatura Latinoamericana (Newark, Del.: Juan de la Cuesta, 1989), 40 n. 8.

14. The source for this dictum is the Greek philosopher Protagoras (c. 485–c. 410 B.C.), *Fragment I* (John Bartlett, *Familiar Quotations: A Collection of Passages, Phrases and Proverbs Traced to Their Sources in Ancient and Modern Literature,* ed. Emily Morison Beck et al., 15th ed. [Boston: Little, 1980], 78).

15. This saying is attributed to Hippocrates and is quoted, or paraphrased, by Seneca: "Inde illa maximi medicorum exclamatio est, *Vitam brevem esse, longam artem*" [Hence that exclamation of the greatest of physicians (i.e. Hippocrates) is, *That life is short, art long*]; (L. Annaeus Seneca, *Ad Paulinum,* "De brevitate vitae," *Treatises,* trans. and ed. John F. Hurst and Henry C. Whiting, rev. ed. [New York: Harper, 1877], 253, original emphasis). The form cited in the text is the one in which the concept usually appears. Lucius Annaeus Seneca, the Younger (4 B.C.–A.D. 65) was a philosopher and essayist who helped to transmit Stoic doctrines (emphasizing the brevity of life and the importance of dignity and integrity) from the Greek world to the Europe that succeeded the Roman Empire. Hippocrates of Cos (c. 460?–380 B.C.) was "the most famous of ancient physicians, and the founder of Greek medicine" (D. R. Dudley, "Hippocrates of Cos," *Classical Literature*). I am indebted for this reference to Professor Christina Dufner of the University of North Dakota.

16. Linda Hutcheon, *A Theory of Parody: The Teachings of Twentieth-Century Art Forms* (New York: Methuen, 1985), 60.

17. Titus Maccius Plautus (c. 245–184 B.C.) and Juvenal (see above, note 4) were two important Roman playwrights, who specialized in comedy. Of the two, Juvenal was much more bitter and corrosive; Plautus, more playful and genial. In the introduction to her translation of the plays of the Roman playwright Terence (Publius Terentius Afer, c. 186–59 B.C.), Betty Radice distinguishes between Terence and his near predecessor Plautus. She comments of Plautus that:

> Plautus took the stock characters of comedy, "a running slave, virtuous wives and dishonest courtesans, greedy spongers and braggart soldiers" (*The Eunuch,* 36–38), but he could not risk outraging Roman morality by

> humanizing them. Sometimes the result is caricature, but at his best Plautus created something more vigourous and exuberant than his original. . . . As well as being a master of *vis comica* [comic vigor] he has a gift for verbal extravagance and metrical technique. . . . (Betty Radice, "Introduction," in Terence, *The Comedies,* trans. and ed. Betty Radice [Harmondsworth, Eng.: Penguin, 1976], 15).

18. *Apocolocyntosis* is a scurrilous mock biography of the Emperor Tiberius Claudius Nero Germanicus (10 B.C.– A.D. 54), attributed to the philosopher Seneca the Younger (see above, note 15). D. E. W. Wormell characterizes the work as "a Menippean satire [see above, note 1] blending prose and verse and maliciously amusing on the theme of Claudius's deification" (D. E. W. Wormell, "Seneca, Lucius Annaeus, the Younger," *Classical Literature*).

The "Dreams" was an early work by Quevedo that followed the form and attitude of *Dialogues of the Dead* by classical satirist Lucian (see above, note 7); prominent figures from Hispanic and European history are satirized in the setting of the underworld.

19. Gloria Grahame (1924–1981) appeared in several interesting films of the 1940s and 1950s, including *Crossfire* (1947), *In a Lonely Place* (1950), and *The Big Heat* (1953) (Katz, *Film Encyclopedia*, 546).

20. Calixto, the hero of *La Celestina* (1499), attributed to Fernando de Rojas, recites a famous anatomy or list of his beloved Melibea's attributes. Veronica Lake (b. Constance Frances Marie Ockelman, 1919–1973) was a "sultry, provocative glamour star of Hollywood films of the 40s whose long blond hair falling over one eye started a 'peek-a-boo' style craze among the women of America." Her films included *This Gun for Hire* (1942) and *The Blue Dahlia* (1946) (Katz, *Film Encyclopedia*, 776).

21. Marcus Argentarius, "413," trans. Fleur Adcock, *The Greek Anthology and Other Ancient Greek Epigrams: A Selection in Modern Verse Translations, Edited with an Introduction by Peter Jay,* ed. Peter Jay (New York: Oxford University Press, 1973), 199. Some confusion exists as to the identity of this poet. According to the *Oxford Classical Dictionary,* he may be the same person as an orator of the Augustan period. In any case, the *Dictionary* gives an approximate date for him (fl. 1 B.C.) and says:

> [He] is the liveliest of the Graeco-Roman epigrammatists whose works crowd the Greek Anthology. A heavy drinker . . . he was poor and unsuccessful; but his vein of coarse humour never deserted him, though his sense of propriety often did. He is probably the Latin-speaking Greek rhetor cited by the elder Seneca. . . . (Gilbert Arthur Highet, "Argentarius [I]," *The Oxford Classical Dictionary,* ed. M. Cary et al. [1949; reprint, Oxford: Clarendon, 1961]).

An epigram is defined by Cuddon (230) as "a short, witty statement in verse or prose which may be complimentary, satiric or aphoristic."

22. Luis de Góngora y Argote (1561–1627) was an important writer of the Spanish baroque. He originated and perfected the literary style of *gongorismo* or *culteranismo,* which relied on convoluted syntax, classical allusions, wordplay, and complex imagery. His works include *Fábula de Polifemo y Galatea* [Fable of Polyphemus

and Galathea] (1612–1613) and *Soledades* [Solitudes] (1612–1617) (C. C. Smith, "Góngora y Argote, Luis de," *European Literature*).

23. Born in Smithfield, North Carolina in 1922, Ava Gardner, "a sensuous, sloe-eyed beauty, with a magnetic, tigresslike quality of sexuality, . . . replaced Rita Hayworth in the late 40s as Hollywood's love goddess and occupied that position until the ascent of Marilyn Monroe in the mid-50s" (Katz, *Film Encyclopedia*, 506). Gardner starred with Burt Lancaster and Edmond O'Brien in the 1946 film *The Killers*.

Film noir was a style in Hollywood film that flourished from approximately 1941 to 1955 and that featured characters with dark or unconscious motives, treacherous females, shadowy cinematography, and generally dark outcomes. It was reflective of the style of the many émigrés from the European film community, particularly from Hitler's Germany and occupied Europe, who had come to work in Hollywood, including figures such as Fritz Lang (1890–1976), Robert Siodmak (1900–1973), Edgar G. Ulmer (1904–1972) and Billy Wilder (b. 1906). Examples of the film noir style include Wilder's *Double Indemnity* (1944), Ulmer's *Detour* (1946), and Lang's *The Big Heat* (1953).

24. Aldonza Lorenzo was the real name of Don Quixote's beloved Dulcinea del Toboso: note the pun "Toboso"—"toda busto."

25. Ben Jonson (1572–1637), one of the greatest English dramatists, is often identified with an emphasis on the theory of "humours," in which human actions are explained by a predominance of a "humour" such as bile or blood. In works by Jonson such as *Everyman in His Humour* (1598), "each character is a type dominated by a ruling passion or obsession." Among his most famous works are *Volpone* (1606) and *The Alchemist* (1610) (Michael Jamieson, "Ben Jonson," *English Literature*). Volpone's name is an augmentative form of the Italian *volpe* "fox"; thus, *volpone,* "big fox," means "one greatly endowed with the qualities of a fox." So, Volpone's character is foxlike, sly, covetous. I am indebted to Gene Dubois for assistance with this point.

26. Sor Juana Inés de la Cruz (1648–1695) was a Mexican nun who became one of Spanish America's greatest writers. A poet, dramatist, and essayist, she produced many works, among them *Primero sueño* [First dream] (1692), a long philosophical poem (Enrique Amberson Imbert, *Spanish-American Literature: A History,* trans. John V. Falconieri [Detroit: Wayne State University Press, 1963]; *A Sor Juana Anthology,* trans. Alan S. Trueblood, foreword Octavio Paz [Cambridge: Harvard University Press, 1988]). Her sonnet "Rosa divina" exposes the truth of decay and death behind the rose's appearance of fragile beauty.

27. See Ardis L. Nelson, "*Holy Smoke:* Anatomy of a Vice," *Focus on Guillermo Cabrera Infante,* special issue of *World Literature Today* 61 (1987): 590–93, for remarks on Cabrera Infante and anatomy.

28. The sonnet "A su retrato," like "Rosa divina," strips away the appearance of beauty to reveal the inevitability of decay and death. "The Lady's Dressing Room," an outrageously offensive anatomy of a lady in her boudoir, was completed by Swift in 1730 and published in 1732 (Claude Rawson, Biographical Introduction, *The Character of Swift's Satire: A Revised Focus,* ed. Claude Rawson [Newark, Del.: University of Delaware Press, 1983], 20). Louise K. Barnett calls the poem "a wealth of ugly particulars held in check by a controlling comic fiction" (Louise K. Barnett, *Swift's Poetic Worlds* [Newark, Del.: University of Delaware Press, 1981], 178).

29. Guillermo Cabrera Infante, "From Legs to Riches," unpublished lecture, n.d.; hereafter cited in the text as "Legs."

30. Guillermo Cabrera Infante, "El gran Cukor," *El Nuevo Día* [Puerto Rico] (3 July 1983): 16–20; hereafter cited in the text as "Cukor."

31. Budd Boetticher (b. 1916) became an important director of Westerns in the 1950s. "In 1960," writes Katz, "Boetticher ventured into the gangster's world with his *The Rise and Fall of Legs Diamond,* a film called by critic Andrew Sarris 'a minor classic' " (Katz, *Film Encyclopedia*, 141). Raft, born George Ranft in New York City in 1895, died in 1980. His image was that of a "sleek tough guy of Hollywood gangster films, memorable as the coin-flipping Guido Rinaldo in [Howard Hawks's] *Scarface* (1932)" (Katz, *Film Encyclopedia*, 1116).

32. Ray (Raymond) Danton (1931–1992), a "leading man of Hollywood and international films, [was] at his most effective in smooth gangster roles." *The George Raft Story* appeared in 1961 (Katz, *Film Encyclopedia*, 326).

33. A "Chinese box" is a series of boxes, each fitting within the other. The boxes are removed one by one until the center is reached.

34. George Cukor (1899–1983) was an important Hollywood director with a long career. He directed many actresses, including Norma Shearer, Katharine Hepburn, and Greta Garbo. His films include *Camille* (1937, with Garbo), *The Women* (1939, with Shearer), *The Philadelphia Story* (1941, with Hepburn, Cary Grant, and James Stewart), and *Pat and Mike* (1952, a famous Hepburn and Spencer Tracy vehicle) (Katz, *Film Encyclopedia*, 310–11).

35. Buñuel (Spain, 1900–1983) was one of the cinema's greatest directors. He was often identified with surrealism, beginning with his notorious *Un Chien Andalou*/An Andalusian Dog (1928, with Salvador Dalí). His many films include *Viridiana* (1961) and *Belle de jour* (1967), starring Catherine Deneuve (Katz, *Film Encyclopedia*, 191–92).

36. Richard A. Lanham, *A Handlist of Rhetorical Terms: A Guide for Students of English Literature* (Berkeley: University of California Press, 1968), 40.

37. Guillermo Cabrera Infante, "Bad Babs" in *Diablesas y diosas (14 perversas para 14 autores),* ed. Joaquín Romaguera i Ramió and Eduardo Suárez (Barcelona: Editorial Laertes, 1990), 9–15; hereafter cited in the text as "Bad."

The picaresque type is an important one in literature (and film). The type was first popularized in the novel; as Cuddon says,

> It [the picaresque novel] tells the life of a knave or picaroon who is the servant of several masters. Through his experience the picaroon satirizes the society in which he lives. The picaresque novel originated in sixteenth century Spain, the earliest example being the anonymous *Lazarillo de Tormes* (1553). (Cuddon, "Picaresque Novel")

Lanham defines euphuism (euphuistic style) as:

> The elaborately patterned prose style of John Lyly's prose romance *Euphues* (1579). It emphasizes the figures of words that create balance, and makes frequent use of antithesis, paradox, repetitive patterns with single words, sound-plays of various sorts, amplification of all sorts, unremitting use of the sententia [pithy statement] and especially the "unnatural natural history" or simile from traditional natural history. Euphuism has now come to mean any highly figured, Asiatic style. (Lanham, *Handlist,* 47)

Euphuism is analogous to, and actually combines the tendencies of, two Spanish styles of the baroque, the so-called *culteranismo* practiced especially by Luis de Góngora (see above, note 22), and the *conceptismo* of Francisco de Quevedo and Baltasar Gracián (1601–1658).

38. The film, an anti-Hollywood and anti-public relations thesis picture, was reviewed by "Caín" (Cabrera Infante's pseudonym and alter ego) for *Carteles* (G. Cabrera Infante, *A Twentieth Century Job,* trans. Kenneth Hall and Guillermo Cabrera Infante [London: Faber and Faber, 1991], 207–11, translation of *Un oficio del siglo veinte* [Havana: Ediciones R, 1963]). Interestingly for the present essay, he employs a similar conceit in the English title of the review, "What's Rotten Smells Sweet."

39. For the point about antithesis, I am indebted to my colleague Gene Dubois.

40. Candide was the ingenuous hero of *Candide* (1759), a satirical philosophical novel by Voltaire (pseudonym of François-Marie Arouet [1694–1778]), one of the most important writers of the French Enlightenment (H. T. Mason, "Voltaire," *European Literature*).

41. I am indebted to Gene Dubois for this insight. Francisco Rico, ed., *Lazarillo de Tormes* (Madrid: Cátedra, 1987), 14–15; *Two Spanish Picaresque Novels:* Lazarillo de Tormes, *Anon,* The Swindler (El Buscón), *Francisco de Quevedo,* trans. Michael Alpert [London: Penguin, 1969]), 25.

42. Katz, *Film Encyclopedia*, 1288–89. The figure of the *belle dame sans merci* was integral to romanticism. For a full discussion of this character type in romantic literature of the nineteenth century, see Mario Praz, *The Romantic Agony,* trans. Angus Davidson, 2nd ed. (Cleveland: Meridian-World, 1956), chap. 4.

43. The reference is to three picaresque characters: Lazarillo de Tormes, protagonist of the anonymous *Lazarillo de Tormes* (1554); el Buscón, or Pablos, protagonist of *Historia de la vida del Buscón* (1626) by Quevedo; and the Artful Dodger, an important character in Dickens's *Oliver Twist* (1838).

44. As is so frequent with Cabrera Infante, we may find other texts hidden behind his inventive prose. My colleague Gene Dubois suggested to me that the foregoing sentence was based on an old rhyme; after some research, I determined that the source is very likely a poem by Henry Wadsworth Longfellow (1807–1882):

> There was a little girl
> Who had a little curl
> Right in the middle of her forehead;
> And when she was good
> She was very, very good,
> But when she was bad she was horrid.
> (Quoted in John Bartlett, *Familiar Quotations: A Collection of Passages, Phrases and Proverbs Traced to Their Sources in Ancient and Modern Literature,* ed. Emily Morison Beck, 14th ed. [Boston: Little, 1968], 625a)

45. Candy, the heroine of the comic novel *Candy* (1955), written by American novelist Terry Southern (1924–1995) and collaborator Mason Hoffenberg, was "a naïve and innocent girl . . . subjected to an outrageous series of sexual advances in various contexts" (Arnold Goldman, "Southern, Terry," *The Penguin Companion to American Literature,* ed. Malcolm Bradbury, Eric Mottram, and Jean Franco [New York: McGraw, 1971]).

46. Katz, *Film Encyclopedia*, 165.

47. Marlene Dietrich, from Berlin, was born Maria Magdalene Dietrich in 1901 and died in 1992. Due in large part to her professional relationship with director Josef Von Sternberg, she became one of film's most famous actresses: "In Hollywood, Von Sternberg [after directing her in Germany in *Der blaue Engel/The Blue Angel* (1930)] continued his transformation of Marlene from a plump fraulein into a glamorous, sensuous star and woman of mystery" in films such as *Morocco* (1930), *Shanghai Express* (1932), *Blonde Venus* (1932), and *The Devil Is a Woman* (1935). Von Sternberg (1894–1969) was born in Vienna and became one of Hollywood's most interesting directors (Katz, *Film Encyclopedia*, 366–67; 1296–97). Cabrera Infante's obituary on Marlene Dietrich is "Un milagro fabricado: Joseph von Sternberg diseñó el mito de Marlene Dietrich," *Babelia/El País* (9 May 1992): 6–7; hereafter cited in the text as "Un milagro."

48. Ekphrasis, or ecphrasis, is used here in its sense as a description of a work of art, embedded in a discourse. Lanham defines the term as "A self-contained description, often on a commonplace subject, which can be inserted at a fitting place in a discourse" (Lanham, *Handlist*, 39). *New Princeton* comments that "A tendency to limit e. [ekphrasis] to descriptions of works of art" can be found in some writers from the first centuries A.D., "but only in modern times does it bear that exclusive meaning" (William H. Race, "Ekphrasis, ecphrasis," *New Princeton*). While the example from Cabrera Infante is not a full-fledged description of a work of art, it is a capsule insertion into prose of a purely visual reference to the famous *Birth of Venus* by Italian Renaissance painter Sandro Botticelli (1444?–1510).

49. Svengali and Trilby were characters from the serial novel *Trilby*, by French-born English illustrator and author George du Maurier [Louis Palmella Busson] (1834–1896): "Trilby . . . is a variety of the harlot with the heart of gold. The story has a famous supernatural character, the sinister Svengali, exploiting the then popular interest in hypnotism" (Angus Ross, "Du Maurier, George," *English Literature*). The name Svengali has come to denote a sinister figure who controls another by force of will; thus the analogy between Von Sternberg and Svengali, as he was alleged to exercise a peculiar psychological and artistic control over Dietrich.

50. Antonomasia is defined by Lanham as the use of a "descriptive phrase for proper name or proper name for quality associated with it" (*Handlist*, 12).

51. One of the icons of Hollywood Westerns, courtly Virginian Randolph Scott was born in 1898 and died a very rich man in 1987. One of his finest roles was his last, in Sam Peckinpah's *Ride the High Country* (called *Guns in the Afternoon* in England) in 1962. Peckinpah (1925–1984) was a controversial and brilliant American director who helped to change the style of Hollywood films during the 1960s. His other films include the masterpiece *The Wild Bunch* (1969) and *Straw Dogs* (1971) (Katz, *Film Encyclopedia*, 1219–20, 1067).

Life with the Silver Screen: *Cine o sardina*

KENNETH HALL

Guillermo Cabrera Infante continues his tradition as grand raconteur in his recent collection of essays *Cine o sardina* (1997) [Movies or meals].[1] *Un oficio del siglo veinte* (1963) [*A Twentieth Century Job* (1991)] was among other things a mock biography of the late, lamented Caín, an alter ego whose criticism of film could be freely lampooned, praised, or buried by the compiler of his columns—Cabrera Infante.[2] *Cine o sardina*, whose title comes from a question his mother used to ask of Guillermo and his brother, is a history of film that delves into its subject at points selected by Cabrera Infante for their relevance to cinema or for their appropriateness to his personal geological study of film strata.[3]

Cine o sardina provides a history of film and an autobiography of Cabrera Infante's life of watching, studying, criticizing, and writing movies. As he says at the beginning of the book, "fui yo quien nació con una pantalla de plata en los ojos" [I was the one who was born with a silver screen in my eyes] (13). The book is not, however, like *Un oficio del siglo veinte*, which is a collection of film reviews, although it does contain essays on particular films. Rather it is a companion piece to *Mea Cuba*, Cabrera Infante's political autobiography and apologia; *Cine o sardina* is a less controversial book, since it is essentially nonpolitical.[4] But it does deal with the most important aspect of Cabrera Infante's own life apart from his political imbroglios with the Castroites—his lifelong involvement with the movies.

Like *Mea Cuba, Cine o sardina* is a collection of numerous pieces originally published in *Cambio 16,* the *Weekend Telegraph* of London, *American Film*, and other periodicals. A few were published first in English. Many are long treatises on aspects of the movies: musicals, dubbing, B movies, star images. Some are examples of a genre cultivated by Cabrera Infante, the film obituary, which is discussed in the preceding chapter in this volume. Others are mock encomia of living stars and movie figures.

The work consists of seven sections; the first is untitled and the remaining are titled: "Biografías íntimas" [Intimate biographies]; "Yo tengo un amigo muerto que suele venirme a ver" [I have a dead friend who comes to see me at times], a verse line from the Cuban writer José Martí;[5] "Pompas fúnebres" [Funeral ceremony]; "Vivas, bien vivas" [Alive, quite alive]; "La cinemateca de todos" [Everyone's cinema club]; and "Y la aventura va" [And the adventure goes on]. The first and most extensive section connects the history of film to the history of Cabrera Infante as commentator, viewer, and eager collector of interesting facts about movies. In one essay, he plays the role of sage adviser and sounding board for some of his friends' opinions and questions about dubbing in films.

Essays in the first section cover themes central to the movies. This section provides an impressionistic and selective but nonetheless densely detailed history of cinematic endeavor. Cabrera Infante discusses the invention of the movie camera; the differences between realist and fantastic film (as modeled on Lumière vs. Méliès);[6] the origins and development of genres; the relationship between life and film (with two major examples: Kafka's and Hemingway's works transferred to the screen); the scores for movies (and, again, an example: the essay on film composer Miklos Rozsa);[7] the development and importance of sound (and two more instances of its importance: musicals and dubbing); B movies and their flowering during the end of the studio system; stills and public relations; the star system; an enlightening and humorous history of Latin actors in Hollywood; and essays on Mexican star María Félix.[8]

The next sections are culled from Cabrera Infante's numerous film obituaries. The obituaries themselves form three sections: "Biografías íntimas"; "Yo tengo un amigo muerto que suele venirme a ver"; and "Pompas fúnebres." In the following section, "Vivas, bien vivas," Cabrera Infante pays homage to two contemporary actresses, Melanie Griffith and Sharon Stone, by no coincidence both blondes.

A collection of varied pieces comes next. "La cinemateca de todos," an oxymoronic title that subtly undermines the frequent elitism of film studies, includes some of Cabrera Infante's best writing on film and some of his most intriguing subjects, including Harry D'Arrast, Sam Fuller, Fritz Lang, "zombie" movies, the Robert Aldrich masterpiece *Kiss Me Deadly* (1955), and the David Bowie film *The Man Who Fell to Earth* (1976).[9]

The book closes with "Y la aventura va" [And the adventure goes on], as if to herald the continuous show at the movies: the rich present behind and promising future before the camera. Cabrera Infante discusses Steven Spielberg, David Lynch, Quentin Tarantino, and Pedro Almodóvar, some of the most important forces in contemporary movies. Throughout the collection Cabrera Infante displays his characteristic wit, erudition, and stylistic brilliance.

"Latinos y ladinos en Hollywood" [Latinos and Ladinos in Hollywood] is a good example of at least two of Cabrera Infante's stylistic specialties. He fully develops a neobaroque texture that displays *ingenio* [wit] and the use of paronomasia or puns, parallelism, and structural devices; and a conversational familiarity of tone that belies the considerable erudition behind the pen.

The essay is also a serious and substantial contribution to the literature on Hispanic film. At first appearance "Latinos" is a straightforward history or survey of the careers of several Hispanics in the movies. The subject matter is handled in a manner familiar to readers of Cabrera Infante. In fact, the essay is in some respects parallel to the much darker "Entre la Historia y la nada" (*Mea Cuba* [1992], 157–89) ["Between History and Nothingness" (*Mea Cuba* [1994], 138–72)]. Both essays are neobaroque in their establishment of stylistic equivalences between disparate events and personalities; both rely on a particular motif to establish this equivalence. For instance, Cabrera Infante makes an exercise in style of Hollywood suicides in "Latinos" and of Cuban political suicides in "Entre la Historia y la nada." In the *Mea Cuba* essay several of the suicides (such as Cuban revolutionary Haydée Santamaría) are carried out with a .45 automatic, by implication tying the suicides to Castro, since the .45 is his emblematic sidearm. Cabrera Infante makes Castro their killer by synecdoche.[10] In "Latinos," Lupe Vélez's notorious suicide—ending her life in grim tragicomedy when she drowns in her own toilet—occurred in midlife, which becomes the marker of other suicides in the essay:

> María Guadalupe Vélez de Villalobos tenía al morir sólo 36 años. La misma edad que otra comedianta que quería ser seria y para probarlo tomó una sobredosis de otro somnífero de moda. Se llamaba o decía llamarse Marilyn Monroe.
>
> [María Guadalupe Vélez de Villalobos was only 36 when she died. The same age as another comedienne who wanted to be serious and to prove it took an overdose of another fashionable sleeping pill. She was named or said she was named Marilyn Monroe.] (*Cine*, 109)[11]

Besides drawing parallels among Hollywood suicides, Cabrera Infante has a lot of fun with the publicity tag "Latin lovers," applying it aptly and jocosely to several Hispanic males. Although criticism of the social status of Hispanic actors is not really Cabrera Infante's main concern, the "Latin lover" epithet becomes not only a convenient description of the role to which many such actors (like Gilbert Roland and César Romero)[12] were often relegated but also a kind of comic benchmark by which to measure the actors' "performance" on the job. Did each one fulfill the requirements (whatever those might be) of the "Latin lover," as Gracián might have asked more seriously of his candidate for the status of "El héroe"?[13]

Roland could play the type to memorable effect in Vincente Minnelli's *The Bad and the Beautiful* (1952).[14] If Roland is a "modelo temprano del *latin lover*" [early model of the Latin lover] who fell right into the role, then Anthony Quinn is more of a hero-type who was ill-fitted for the "lover" role. With Quinn, as Cabrera Infante says, the studios "querían disfrazarlo de *latin lover*" [wanted to disguise him as a Latin lover] (*Cine*, 111), but the surface guise could not hide his true grit personality and talent: "Pero Quinn ha tenido en su voz un tono bronco y en sus maneras un desplante brusco como para ser no sólo una estrella muy individual, sino también un actor de carácter" [But Quinn has had in his voice a rough tone and in his mannerisms a brusque rudeness so as to be not only a very individual star, but also a character actor] (*Cine,* 111).

Cabrera Infante's presentation of Quinn is one of the little gems often found in his essays. In *Mea Cuba,* his inimitably narrated personal anecdotes about Cuban writers and personalities often provide comic relief in a sometimes grim story of Castro's Cuba. In *Cine o sardina,* the reader is saved from any danger of the book's becoming academically dry by little vignettes like the one about Quinn.

Cabrera Infante briefly describes his personal relationship with Quinn and explains how Quinn's brusqueness hides much sensitivity and an artistic temperament. He also amusingly recounts Quinn's breezy inclusion of him among Mexicans, as a fellow *cuate,* a pal, of sorts:

> Quinn me dijo: "Mira hermano, nosotros los mexicanos . . . "
> Tuve que interrumpirlo. "Tony," le dije, "yo no soy mexicano, yo soy cubano." "Cubanos, mexicanos," me aclaró. "Todos somos lo mismo. . . ."

> [Quinn said to me: "Look brother, we Mexicans . . ."
> I had to interrupt him. "Tony," I said, "I'm not Mexican, I'm

> Cuban." "Cubans, Mexicans," he enlightened me. "We're all the same. . . ."] (*Cine*, 112)

The survey of Hispanics in Hollywood also includes among its cast of true characters Antonio Moreno and Ramón Novarro, two "Latin lovers" who gave "final performances" highlighted here by Cabrera Infante.[15] Moreno's performance was a movie role, Novarro's an unfortunate scene from real life. Again we see the baroque conflation of stage role and life role. Moreno had his last film role in John Ford's *The Searchers* (1956),[16] where with great panache he plays a Mexican guerrilla-bandit leader mischievously named Emilio Figueroa: "Es un papel corto pero memorable en que se llama Don Emilio Figueroa (una broma de Ford a Emilio Fernández y su afamado fotógrafo Gabriel Figueroa)" [It's a brief role but memorable in that he's named Don Emilio Figueroa (a joke by Ford on Emilio Fernández, the Mexican director and actor, and his famed photographer Gabriel Figueroa)] (*Cine*, 105). This "Latin" actor steps out of his "lover" shoes to play a role bearing the conflated names of a director-cinematographer team famous in Mexico: thus, he "embodies" a tradition in Mexican filmmaking. And he fits himself briefly into literary and folk history. By playing an aged bandit leader, he connects to all the romantic bandits peopling the folklore of the Mexican revolution and the pages of novels like Ignacio Altamirano's *El zarco.*[17] Finally, he meets up with a legend of Hollywood film, John Wayne. As for Wayne, he provides a mirror image of Moreno's translation of his own stock role into another, that of lover to bandit, by playing himself, in a sense. Ethan Edwards (Wayne) answers Figueroa's greeting in Spanish because, as Cabrera Infante notes, Wayne the actor really knew Spanish (*Cine*, 105).

For readers of Cabrera Infante's fiction, his treatment of dubbing in films in the comically titled "Por quién doblan las películas" will come as no surprise (nor will the allusion to Hemingway).[18] Cabrera Infante laments and lampoons the institution of dubbing, especially prevalent in Spain, and recounts his discovery of that *rara avis,* that endangered species, a subtitled showing of *Mary Poppins* in Madrid. As many opponents of dubbing in foreign films can attest, dubbing destroys the original qualities of the film, since the actors' voices are replaced by those of "dubbing actors," and dubbing may even (as Cabrera Infante notes) replace or interfere with the soundtrack of the original film. As we might expect, Cabrera Infante's distaste for dubbing concerns the loss of oral uniqueness. In this essay, he uses an anecdote about one of his friends "cuya obsesión era Bogart" [whose obsession was Bogart] (*Cine*, 69) to illustrate the signal importance of sound—original sound—in the cinema. This Spanish architect was a Humphrey Bogart fanatic (not just a fan) but had never heard the actor's real voice; he was obsessed with one dimension, not two, of Bogart's screen simulacrum. His disappointment at hearing the actor's voice for the first time was akin to that of silent-film audiences when they first listened to romantic leading man John Gilbert's decidedly unromantic voice:

> ¿Era esa voz gangosa, nasal y con un ceceo atroz la voz de *Humphrey Bogart?* ¡No podía ser! Pensó que se trataba de un fallo mecánico. Seguramente esta copia estaría defectuosa: algo pasaba con el sonido. Salió del cine corriendo, corrido. Decidió volver al día siguiente. Cuando lo visitó de nuevo el espectro de Bogart hablando con acento de Brooklyn . . . le temblaban las piernas y creía que era el edificio que se venía abajo. Esa misma tarde tomó el avión de regreso a Madrid y no volvió a tratar de parecerse a Bogart . . .
>
> [Was that wheezing, nasal voice with an atrocious lisp the voice of *Humphrey Bogart?* It couldn't be! He thought it must be a case of mechanical failure. Surely this copy must be defective: something was happening with the sound. He left the theatre running, run down. He decided to return the next day. When he was again visited by Bogart's ghost speaking with a Brooklyn accent . . . his legs shook and he thought it was the building falling down. That same afternoon he took the plane back to Madrid and didn't try again to look like Bogart . . .] (*Cine*, 69)

American audiences would find such disappointment rather strange, since, as Cabrera Infante explains, "Le dije que esa voz que consideraba atroz era no sólo tan genuina como el actor sino que era la característica mayor de Humphrey Bogart después de sus ojos" [I told him (the architect) that that voice he considered atrocious was not only as genuine as the actor but that it was the greatest characteristic of Humphrey Bogart after his eyes] (*Cine*, 69–70).

But Cabrera Infante also criticizes dubbing for its inaccuracy. Dubbing results in another version of the film and sometimes a dishonest or equivocal one. Thus, one of the films that Caín reviewed for *Carteles, Sweet Smell of Success* (1957, with Burt Lancaster and Tony Curtis), suffered in the translation. One of the insults leveled at a character in the film, that of being a communist, was omitted from the dubbing, so that, as Cabrera Infante says, "había desaparecido el carnet del partido" [his party card had disappeared] (*Cine*, 70).

Cabrera Infante cites Borges, who says in effect that not only is dubbing a translation, it introduces ill-fitting elements that destroy the essence of the screen persona of, say, Hepburn or Garbo (*Cine*, 75).

As always, Cabrera Infante's "neobaroque" preoccupation with role-playing, masks, and concealment is a factor here, and in an especially compressed way. Cabrera Infante refers to the case of a dubbing actor who died and was sorely missed:

> Hace poco murió un conocido actor de doblaje especialista en doblar a un conocido actor de cine vivo, es decir capaz de seguir actuando. Cundió el pánico en la sala de doblaje hasta que apareció un actor capaz de imitar no al actor original ¡sino al actor de doblaje!
>
> [Not long ago a well-known dubbing actor died, a specialist in dubbing a well-known film actor, living, that is, capable of continuing to act. Panic in the dubbing room spread until an actor appeared capable of imitating not the original actor—but the dubbing actor!] (*Cine*, 79)

In rather a parody of Platonism, the studio sought out an imitator of the imitator: the simulacrum had become more real than the real McCoy, so to speak.[19]

Simulacra also figure prominently in another essay in the collection, "La caza del facsímil" [Fax hunt]. This piece illustrates Cabrera Infante's capacity to employ literary conventions that in themselves are metaphors for his themes: in this case, the facsimile or imitation. This kind of device is again "neobaroque."[20] A similar approach can be found in Sor Juana Inés de la Cruz or Luis de Góngora.[21] For example, in the well-known Sor Juana sonnet 168 (which begins "Al que ingrato me deja, busco amante" ["Him who ungratefully abandons me, I lovingly seek"]), the organization of the poem mirrors and exemplifies the theme. The use of anadiplotic clauses illustrates the poem's theme of the circularity of passion and the self-defeating activity through the narrative voice: "constante adoro a quien mi amor maltrata; / maltrato a quien mi amor busca constante" [I steadfastly adore him who abuses my love; / I abuse him who seeks my love steadfastly].[22]

Cabrera Infante's essay focuses on Ridley Scott's 1982 *Blade Runner,* with Harrison Ford, Sean Young, and Rutger Hauer, which has become a cult film, in part due to its postmodernist, cynical, deconstructive take on contemporary and future lifestyles.[23] "Blade runners" are android-killers. More precisely, they are policemen whose job is to kill—or, in the film's euphemistic newspeak, "retire"—renegade replicants (androids) who have escaped from their off-world exile and have come to Earth. The blade runners are themselves "facsimiles" or distorted versions of real cops, since the policeman's mission is not to search and destroy. Moreover, policemen do not—openly, anyway—answer directly to corporate executives, as does Rick Deckard's chief in the film.

Cabrera Infante is genuinely fascinated by science-fiction film, and his discussion of *Blade Runner* is thus not totally parodic. But he still engages amusingly in "smoke and mirrors," and the play on facsimiles in the essay replicates its subject. Deckard, the main character (played by Harrison Ford), is described as *not* like Bogart's Rick from *Casablanca* (after whom he was partially modeled). Nor does he follow in Bogey's footsteps; he hasn't come to Los Angeles "for the waters," as Bogart flippantly avers in the film *Casablanca* (*Cine*, 431). The technique used by Cabrera Infante is related to the *praeteritio* device made famous by Roman orator Cicero.[24] Cabrera Infante actually calls attention to the similarities between the two characters by denying the similarities.

Cabrera Infante also discerns the postmodern quality of *Blade Runner* when he extends the conceit of the facsimile that is not, perhaps, everything it seems to be to the realm of advertising. Critical literature on postmodernism has noted the tendency of postmodernist works to use advertising symbols and names as material for their imagery, often equating brand-name products—that is, ersatz and interchangeable mass-market products—with society's refuse, as in *Blade Runner,* where streets are filled with debris full of brand-name soft drink cans and the like.[25] Cabrera Infante provides his own inimitable facsimile of this process by parodying and twisting brand names: thus, "*Blade Runner,* la más excitante y perfecta de las películas de fantaciencia, de Fanta y ciencia, desde *2001*" [*Blade Runner,* the most exciting and perfect of the fantascience, the Fanta and science, movies, since *2001*]; "el séptimo sello de Alka Seltzer" [the seventh seal of Alka Seltzer] (*Cine,* 433). He also inserts snippets of song and movie titles into the text. In one instance he refers to the artificiality and the "ersatz" quality of Los Angeles in the film; hence, "Los Angeles, violentando la visión de Capra, será, es, una ciudad colmada y calma que canta en la lluvia como bajo una ducha de verde vitriolo" [Los Angeles, doing violence to Capra's vision, will be, is, a stuffed and silent city that sings in the rain under a shower of green vitriol] (*Cine,* 431). And the film itself becomes "una hermosa alucinación en glorioso technicolor: la pesadilla sin aire acondicionado" [a beautiful hallucination in glorious Technicolor: the non-air-conditioned nightmare] (*Cine,* 432), a reference to Henry Miller's *The Air-Conditioned Nightmare.*[26]

Blade Runner could be interpreted as a metaphor for Hollywood, that is, the locus of simulacra projected on large screens, with a milling, polyglot, largely semi-literate populace watching the talking heads. Whether or not Cabrera Infante would agree with such a view, he does spend a good deal of time in *Cine o sardina* dealing with simulacra and false images. Both essays in the section "Vivas, bien vivas" present and extend the conceit of the false blonde—or, conversely, of the real blonde becoming a false brunette—as a symbol of the fakery of Hollywood. While the piece on Melanie Griffith plays on the Tippi Hedren–Melanie Griffith/Alfred Hitchcock–Brian De Palma parallel, the essay on Sharon Stone more specifically reviews blondes in the movies. Beginning with Clara Bow, who was not a blonde, as a point of contrast, Cabrera Infante singles out Jean Harlow and Marilyn Monroe and mentions the current bevy of movie blondes. Among them, he finds Stone the most prominent, both for her "helada belleza perfecta" [frozen perfect beauty] and for her acting talent (*Cine,* 285). Once again, Cabrera Infante toys with a conceit, wondering whether Stone is a "bimbo" or a "bomba"—that is, a bimbo or a (blonde) bombshell. He characteristically extends the conceit: "Habrá que hacer una historia de la rubia que estalla en la pantalla (perdón por la rima) y esparce su imagen como una granada de fragmentación del sexo" [A history will have to be done of the blonde who blows to smithereens on the screen (forgive me for the rhyme) and scatters her image like a fragmentation grenade of sex] (*Cine,* 283). Though not a long or particularly substantial piece, "Sharon Stone ¿Bomba o bimbo?" [Sharon Stone, bombshell or bimbo?] nicely illustrates Cabrera Infante's inimitable style as well as his continuing interest in current cinema.

Cine o sardina, together with *Un oficio del siglo veinte,* is an extensive record of Cabrera Infante's long love affair with the movies. Ever since his mother made him many offers he couldn't refuse and introduced him to the wonderful world of movies, Cabrera Infante has made film a central part of his life and work. He continues to delight us with his humorous and stylistically innovative approach to film topics and to instruct us with his encyclopedic familiarity with the art of the twentieth century.

Notes

1. Guillermo Cabrera Infante, *Cine o sardina* (Madrid: Alfaguara, 1997). All translations from this and other works, unless indicated otherwise, are by Kenneth Hall.

2. Guillermo Cabrera Infante, *Un oficio del siglo veinte* (Havana: Ediciones R, 1963); *A Twentieth Century Job,* trans. Kenneth Hall and Guillermo Cabrera Infante (London: Faber and Faber, 1991). Caín was Cabrera Infante's pseudonym when writing film reviews for *Carteles,* a Cuban magazine, in the 1950s. Caín appears as a character in *Un oficio del siglo veinte.*

3. Cabrera Infante explains, on the book's back cover,

> En mi pueblo, cuando éramos niños, mi madre nos preguntaba a mi hermano y a mí si preferíamos ir al cine o a comer con una frase festiva: «¿Cine o sardina?». Nunca escogimos la sardina.
>
> [In my town, when we were kids, my mother used to ask my brother and me if we preferred to go to the movies or to eat with a festive phrase: "Movie or sardines?" We never chose the sardines.]

4. *Mea Cuba* (Barcelona: Plaza and Janés, 1992); *Mea Cuba,* trans. Kenneth Hall and Guillermo Cabrera Infante (New York: Farrar, Straus, Giroux, 1994).

5. José Martí (1853–1895) was a celebrated author who was at the forefront both of Cuban Independence and of the Spanish-American modernist movement in prose and poetry. He was killed in the first battle for Cuban independence from Spain.

6. Louis Lumière (1864–1948) and Georges Méliès (1861–1938) were film pioneers. Ephraim Katz summarizes their influence thus: "Lumière is revered in France and elsewhere as the 'father' of the cinema. Certain film scholars see the development of the art of film as proceeding along two distinctive avenues that eventually fused into one: the tradition of reality, originating in the films of Lumière, and the tradition of fantasy, originating in the films of Méliès" (Ephraim Katz, *The Film Encyclopedia,* 2nd ed. [New York: HarperPerennial-HarperCollins, 1994], 853–54, 926).

7. The Hungarian-born Miklos Rozsa (1907–1996) composed many film scores, including *The Thief of Baghdad* (1940), *Double Indemnity* (1944), and *Ben-Hur* (1959) (Katz, *Film Encyclopedia,* 1184).

8. María de Los Angeles Félix Guereña (b. 1915) was for many years a top star in the Hispanic cinema (Katz, *Film Encyclopedia,* 441).

9. Harry d'Abbadie D'Arrast (1897–1968) directed some early, sophisticated comedies in Hollywood. Samuel Fuller (1911–1997) was an important director usually associated with B movies, accomplished with a highly individual style, including *Pickup on South Street* (1953), *China Gate* (1957), and *The Naked Kiss* (1965). Fritz Lang (1890–1976), one of the most artistically influential directors in film history, had historic careers both in Germany and in the United States after fleeing the Nazis; his many films include *M* (1931), *You Only Live Once* (1937), *The Woman in the Window* (1944), and *The Big Heat* (1953). Robert Aldrich (1918–1983) was a major and still underrated American director; his films include *Kiss Me Deadly* (1955), *Attack!* (1955), *The Dirty Dozen* (1967), and *Twilight's Last Gleaming* (1977) (Katz, *Film Encyclopedia,* 784–87, 496, 328, 19).

10. Synecdoche is "substitution of part for whole, genus for species, or vice versa" (Richard A. Lanham, *A Handlist of Rhetorical Terms: A Guide for Students of English Literature* [Berkeley: University of California Press, 1968], 97); thus, the .45 automatic "stands for" Castro here.

11. María Guadalupe Vélez de Villalobos (1908–1944), born in Mexico, became known as the "Mexican Spitfire"; she was the star of numerous melodramas and comedies. Married for a time to Johnny Weissmuller, she committed suicide in 1944 (Katz, *Film Encyclopedia,* 1408).

12. Gilbert Roland (1905–1994) was born Luis Antonio Dámaso de Alonso in Mexico and became a "durable Latin lover of the silent and sound screen." César Romero (1907–1994), born in New York, was of Cuban background; besides gaining fame as the Joker in TV's *Batman,* he was also a very durable character actor in "Latin" parts (Katz, *Film Encyclopedia,* 1170, 1169).

13. Baltasar Gracián y Morales (1601–1658) was an influential author of the Spanish Baroque. *El héroe* [The Hero] (1637), one of his early works, had "Philip IV [of Spain] as the model hero" (J. Gibbs, "Gracián y Morales, Baltasar," *European Literature,* ed. Anthony Thorlby [Harmondsworth, Eng.: Penguin, 1969], vol. 2 of *The Penguin Companion to Literature,* 4 vols.; hereafter cited as *European Literature*).

14. Director Vincente Minnelli (1903–1986), married to Judy Garland and the father of Liza Minnelli, was one of the most influential presences in the Hollywood musical. He also made some interesting melodramas. His films include *Meet Me in St. Louis* (1944), *An American in Paris* (1951), *Brigadoon* (1954), and *Home from the Hill* (1960) (Katz, *Film Encyclopedia,* 949–50).

15. Madrid-born Antonio Garride Monteagudo (Antonio Moreno) (1886–1967) appeared in many silent films and later in sound films in smaller parts; Ramón Novarro (1899–1968), born Ramón Samaniegos in Mexico, was prototypical as the "Latin lover" but starred memorably in the silent *Ben-Hur* (1926) (Katz, *Film Encyclopedia,* 1021, 971).

16. John Ford (1895–1973), one of the greatest of American directors, was especially identified with the Western; John Wayne did his finest work under Ford's direction, especially in *The Searchers* (1956) (Katz, *Film Encyclopedia,* 471–72).

17. Ignacio Manuel Altamirano (1834–1893) was a Mexican novelist. His *El zarco* (written in 1888; published in 1901; and translated by Mary Allt as *El Zarco: The Bandit* [London: Folio Society, 1957]) "concerns a conflict between an evil blue-eyed bandit and a good steady dark-skinned villager who were rivals for the love of a girl" (Jean Franco, "Altamirano, Ignacio Manuel," *United States and Latin American Literature,* ed. M. Bradbury, E. Mottram and Jean Franco [Harmondsworth, Eng.: Penguin, 1971], vol. 3 of *The Penguin Companion to Literature,* 4 vols.; hereafter cited as *United States*).

18. The title is nearly untranslatable in its double meaning; literally, it might mean "For Whom They Dub Movies," but the verb *doblar* has, among others, the meanings of *to dub* and *to toll*; thus, Hemingway's famous novel *For Whom the Bell Tolls* could be translated as "Por quién dobla la campana," or, with some license, "Por quién doblan las campanas."

19. One of the important doctrines formulated by Greek philosopher Plato (c. 429–347 B.C.) was the notion of "ideal forms," that is, the concept that concrete objects are copies of "forms" ("the archetypes which underlie the phenomena of the world we see about us, and which are the only true objects of knowledge" [D. R. Dudley, "Plato," *Classical and Byzantine, Oriental and African Literature,* ed. D. R. Dudley and D. M. Lang (Harmondsworth, Eng.: Penguin, 1969), vol. 4 of *The Pen-*

guin Companion to Literature, 4 vols.]). From this premise Plato derived his position that the artist, copying an object in the world, is actually "imitating an imitation."

20. For a discussion of the neobaroque, see María Acosta Cruz, *The Discourse of Excess: The Latin American Neobaroque and James Joyce* (Ann Arbor, Mich.: UMI, 1985).

21. Sor Juana Inés de la Cruz (1648–1695) was a Mexican nun who became one of Spanish America's greatest writers. A poet, dramatist, and essayist, she produced many works, among them *Primero sueño* [First dream] (1692), a long philosophical poem (Enrique Amberson Imbert, *Spanish-American Literature: A History,* trans. John V. Falconieri [Detroit: Wayne State University Press, 1963; *A Sor Juana Anthology,* trans. Alan S. Trueblood, foreword Octavio Paz [Cambridge: Harvard University Press, 1988]). Luis de Góngora y Argote (1561–1627) was an important writer of the Spanish Baroque. He originated and perfected the literary style of *gongorismo* or *culteranismo,* which relied on convoluted syntax, classical allusions, wordplay, and complex imagery. His works include *Fábula de Polifemo y Galatea* [Fable of Polyphemus and Galathea] (1612–1613) and *Soledades* [Solitudes] (1612–1617) (C. C. Smith, "Góngora y Argote, Luis de," *European Literature*).

22. Anadiplosis is "repetition of the last word of one line or clause to begin the next" (Lanham, *Handlist,* 7). The Sor Juana quotations and translations are from *Renaissance and Baroque Poetry of Spain, with English Prose Translations,* ed. Elias L. Rivers (1966; reprint, Prospect Heights, Ill.: Waveland, 1988), 330.

23. Vivian Sobchack characterizes *Blade Runner* as a postmodernist film and discusses it along with other films of the type (Vivian Sobchack, *Screening Space: The American Science Fiction Film,* 2nd ed. [New York: Ungar, 1987], 264–74 *et passim*).

24. *Praeteritio,* also known as *occupatio,* is a rhetorical device by which "a speaker emphasizes something by pointedly seeming to pass over it" (Lanham, *Handlist*, 68). In this example Cicero (106–43 B.C.) is attacking Roman politician Catilina at Catilina's trial in the Senate: "And then again, think of the time when by means of your former wife's death you ensured that your house should be vacated and free for a further marriage. You supplemented that ghastly deed by another so appalling that it is scarcely believable. *But I pass the incident over and gladly allow it to be veiled in silence,* because I cannot bear people to say that such a horror could have been perpetrated in this country. . . . *I say nothing, either, about the financial ruin into which you will be plunged upon the thirteenth of this month*" (Cicero, "Against Lucius Sergius Catilina," *Selected Political Speeches of Cicero,* trans. Michael Grant [Baltimore: Penguin, 1969], 83; emphasis added).

25. The "clutter" experienced by a thoroughly commodified culture, the "new" turned into instant junk, the "pastiche" constructed by unrelated material accumulations that merely share the same space—these visible manifestations of the logic of late capitalism find their figuration in contemporary science fiction whether the films are "politically conscious" or not. . . . Certainly *Blade Runner* serves as a powerful exemplar—not only in its set design and mise-en-scène (which reveals the future as a recycled pastiche of the present) but also in its enunciation of the future through the mediation of a 1940s film noir narrative structure (Sobchack, *Screening Space*, 245–48).

26. Henry Miller (1891–1980) was one of the most important and unconventional authors of twentieth-century U.S. literature. His works include *Tropic of Cancer* (1934) and *Tropic of Capricorn* (1939). *The Air-Conditioned Nightmare* (1942) was the product of a cross-country tour and is a work "recording his repudiation of modern American life and his championing of individual American artists and eccentrics" (Brian Way and Eric Mottram, "Henry Miller," *United States*).

Literary Friends at the Movies: Guillermo Cabrera Infante and Manuel Puig

SUZANNE JILL LEVINE

Hindsight confirms what Emir Rodríguez Monegal observed in the late sixties: Guillermo Cabrera Infante and Manuel Puig were the first truly "pop" novelists of Latin America. They recognized and drew on the popular culture—Hollywood movies, Cuban boleros, Argentine tangos—and transformed everyday discourse into high literary art.[1] Cabrera Infante and Puig were small-town boys who in their youth left the provinces for the big city, but they escaped small-town tedium much earlier at the movies. "The first time I went to the movies," Cabrera Infante always says, "I was twenty-nine days old, taken by my mother who was crazy about the movies."[2] If they had to choose between flick or treat, that is, a movie outing or dinner, they chose the former. Puig was going to the movie house in town at the age of six with his mother, a film fanatic who took him to the six o'clock show every evening. Though he lived way out in the pampas where there was plenty of sky and air, Puig recalled: "As a child, the only place I breathed freely was in the darkened movie house."[3]

As a babe in arms, Cabrera Infante's first flick was *The Four Horsemen of the Apocalypse* (1921) starring the legendary Rudolph Valentino. Puig's first was at age four when his father took him to see the new projector that had just been installed in the "Spanish theater." Together they watched *The Bride of Frankenstein* (1935). This horror movie and especially the "bride," Elsa Lanchester with electrified skunk hair, was not at all reassuring, and when he wrote the first draft of his autobiographical novel, *La traición de Rita Hayworth* (1968) [*Betrayed by Rita Hayworth* (1971)], he associated his father not with Frankenstein but with Dracula, a sexual monster.

In *Tres tristes tigres* (1967) [*Three Trapped Tigers* (1971)], Cabrera Infante's alter ego Silvestre compares womanizer Cue with monsters who devour women and who had made their way to the silver screen in films such as *King Kong* (1933), *Dracula* (1931), *The Cat People* (1942), and *The Leopard Man* (1943). The best of these horror movies expressed the fears and possibly the dark desires not only of Cabrera Infante and Puig but of a whole generation of children in the 1940s. They were simultaneously terrifying and seductive.

> [E]sa, digamos, colección de imágenes influyó mucho a Manuel Puig, . . . tuvo una gran influencia, también en mí . . . en determinado momento, en los años cuarenta, era un niño capaz de sentir miedo ante esas películas, pero al mismo tiempo buscarlas como una suerte de droga. Eso le ocurrió a Puig, eso pasa conmigo.
>
> [That, shall we say, collection of images influenced Manuel Puig a lot, . . . and also had a great influence on me . . . at a certain time, in the 1940s, I was a child who could be afraid when I saw those movies, but at the same time I sought them as a sort of drug. That happened to Puig, that happens with me.][4]

"Those movies" meant Hollywood, the "dream factory" whose "Golden Age" was the thirties and forties or, as Cabrera Infante said, the period that began in 1929, the year of his birth, with the "talkies" and ended in 1949, the year his job as a film critic began. He later reflected in *Un oficio del siglo veinte* (1963) [*A Twentieth Century Job* (1991)] that 1949 was the year they made or showed *Letter from an Unknown Woman, A Double Life, On the Town, An American in Paris,* and *The Set-Up,* which formed part of his own private mythology and, of course, *Asphalt Jungle,* where that myth of all times appeared, Marilyn Monroe. For Cabrera Infante the rest is the remains of Hollywood, the decline of both a great art and the industry that made it possible.

The same was true for young Puig, or "Coco," for whom Fred Astaire and Ginger Rogers musicals were beautiful dreams. The last golden flick in his eyes, a veritable twilight of the goddesses, was *Sunset Boulevard,* directed by Billy Wilder in 1950, a film noir about the decline or swan song of a silent diva named Gloria.

Both young movie lovers set out to make movies. Each achieved this goal to a limited extent as screenwriters. Their major contribution to the medium has been their personal passion and relationship with the movies expressed in their writing. Puig's first novel, *La traición de Rita Hayworth,* began as a script. The manuscript that became *Tres tristes tigres* was motivated by the death of a singer but also by the censorship of the film *P.M.* This urtext became the section titled "Ella cantaba boleros" ["I Heard Her Sing"].

In the mid-80s Puig summarized brilliantly the essence of the great movies, the dreams that so inspired him and Cabrera Infante:

> My novels . . . always aim for a direct reconstruction of reality, hence their—for me, essential—analytic nature. Synthesis is best expressed in allegory or dreams. What better example of synthesis is there than our dreams every night? Cinema needs this spirit of synthesis, and . . . is ideally suited to allegories and dreams. Which leads me to another hypothesis: can this be why the cinema of the 1930s and 1940s has lasted so well? They really were dreams displayed in images. To take two examples, both drawn from Hollywood: an unpretentious B-movie like *Seven Sinners,* directed by Tay Garnett, and *The Best Years of Our Lives,* directed by William Wyler, a "serious" spectacular that won a bunch of Oscars and was seen as an honor for the cinema.
>
> Forty years later, what has happened to these two films? *Seven Sinners* laid no claim to reflect real life. It was an unbiased look at power and established values, a very light-weight allegory on this theme. *The Best Years of Our Lives* by contrast, was intended as a realistic portrait of US soldiers returning from the Second World War. And as such, it was successful. But, after all these years, all that can be said of this film is that it is a valid period piece, whereas *Seven Sinners* can be seen as a work of art. When I look at what survives of the history of cinema, I find increasing evidence of what little can be salvaged from all the attempts at realism, where the camera appears to slide across the surface, unable to discover the missing third dimensional photographic realism. This superficiality seems, strangely enough, to coincide with the absence of an auteur behind the camera. That is, a director with a personal viewpoint.[5]

Cabrera Infante was already writing film reviews in 1950. In 1956 Puig, who was a few years younger than Cabrera Infante, went to Rome—then known as the "Hollywood on the Tiber"—where many American producers, directors, writers, and actors had relocated, fleeing Senator Joseph McCarthy's anticommunist witch-hunts. Puig had an Argentine "Dante Society" scholarship to study filmmaking at Cinecittá. A grand disillusionment awaited him. All the instructors subscribed to the theories of Cesare Zavattini, the czar of Italian neorealism. The postwar offspring of social realism, neorealist filmmakers like Roberto Rossellini attempted to represent everyday reality, rejecting the escapist glamour of "decadent" cinema, particularly the personality cult of Hollywood.

Nostalgic for the movies of his childhood, Puig found an ally among his classmates, a Spanish-born Cuban, Néstor Almendros, who was studying cinematography at Cinecittá. It was through Almendros, an intense, serious young man destined to become the best cinematographer of his generation, that Cabrera Infante and Puig met in 1967. Almendros and Cabrera Infante had been close friends and cofounders of the Havana cinémathèque, along with Germán Puig (no relation) and other fellow Cuban film buffs. Almendros was also instrumental in bringing Manuel Puig to the attention of Juan Goytisolo, Severo Sarduy, and Rodríguez Monegal, early supporters of his first novel, *La traición de Rita Hayworth*.

Almendros and Puig were rebel students with a cause—Hollywood. They became great friends during their student days in "Dolce Vita" Rome, when Via Veneto was a cabaret of stars pursued by the paparazzi. As with Cabrera Infante, Almendros and Puig respected the good intentions of neorealism's reaction against the Hollywood system's apoliticism and mythification of personality. They knew from their own experiences back home the power of social and historical tides and the pathos of the common man; they had a passion for Hollywood as well. Meanwhile directors like Vittorio De Sica, whom Puig in particular admired for his humor as well as his humanism, produced unforgettable movies with powerful emotional intensity, notably *The Bicycle Thief* (1948). Neorealism "ended in destroying the attraction of its films for the public," observes Kenneth Hall in *Guillermo Cabrera Infante and the Cinema*. "The reaction of Cabrera Infante against neorealism in *Arcadia todas las noches* and against 'el cine de cámara' and the New Wave with its *politique des auteurs*, . . .is in effect an attack on the intellectualizing of criticism and the appropriation by self-proclaimed critics of the capacity to understand and enjoy films."[6]

Cabrera Infante and Puig were movie lovers—more than critics or filmmakers—yet they were to produce literary, and in Cabrera Infante's case, critical works that expressed what Cabrera Infante enjoyed when he first read the unpublished manuscript of *La traición de Rita Hayworth*—"for the title alone I thought it should win the Biblioteca Breve prize." *La traición de Rita Hayworth* and *Tres tristes tigres*—made of "spoken" and "celluloid" pages—achieved more empathic, authentic depictions of reality than any work of the "social realist" variety.[7] As Cabrera Infante remarks in *Arcadia todas las noches* [Arcadia every night] (1978), Puig's greatest contribution to understanding what makes movies magic is his insistence on the importance of the actor, or rather, the actresses—Jean Harlow, Marlene Dietrich, Marilyn Monroe. In Puig's worldview the feminine permeates all, even grammar, and actresses truly are goddesses.

In *Arcadia todas las noches,* Cabrera Infante's book of essays on mythic directors—Alfred Hitchcock, Orson Welles, John Huston, Howard Hawks, and Vincente Minnelli—he observes that not only does the quality of the actor's work vary according to the director, but the quality of the director's work depends equally on the actor. While the author is no longer the writer—a reality that discouraged and frustrated both Puig and Cabrera Infante—the true author, or auteur, is not only the director, as the New Wave tried to prove, but the team chemistry of actor, director, producer, writer, and cinematographer, at the very least. Expressing his disappointment with contemporary cinema in 1977, Puig wrote to Cabrera Infante from New York how certain new directors were attempting to do "auteur" cinema but the problem was "they have nothing to say. That's why the Studio system worked better."[8] In true Borgesian spirit, both Cabrera Infante and Puig carried over this subversion or questioning of "authorship" in their own fictions.

While Puig was not a critic, Cabrera Infante recognized in him one of the most lucid minds in the broad and pretentious literary landscape of their times. Responding to the marketing hype of the "boom," and to the perhaps excessive fame of certain authors, Puig composed a satirical list in 1967 entitled "M-G-M presents" in which he baptized three generations of famous Latin American writers with the names of Hollywood actresses and provided pithy descriptive critiques. Just as Puig's camp sensibility captured the sublime in the grotesque *Boquitas pintadas* (1969) [*Heartbreak Tango* (1973)], which Cabrera Infante considers among the ten best Latin American novels, along with *El beso de la mujer araña* (1976) [*Kiss of the Spiderwoman* (1984)], "M-G-M presents" displays the kitsch in so-called high art. He compares, for example, Alejo Carpentier with that "mask" Joan Crawford "oh so fiery and stilted," Mario Vargas Llosa with Esther Williams "so disciplined and boring," Carlos Fuentes with Ava Gardner "Glamour surrounds her but can she act?" and Gabriel García Márquez with Liz Taylor "beautiful face but such short legs."

Puig first wrote the list as a letter to his friend and kindred spirit Cabrera Infante, who retitled it "M-G-Monegal presents" in mischievous homage to the critic who, through his journal *Mundo Nuevo* (1966–1971), had almost single-handedly invented the notion of the "boom." Puig's "M-G-M presents" was a subversive act from the margins, in this case by a gay cinephile in a macho culture. But as a fellow cinephilic and eccentric writer, and as a political outcast for opposing censorship in his own country, Cabrera Infante empathized with Puig's maverick position.

What Puig and Cabrera Infante shared with other displaced friends like Néstor Almendros and Severo Sarduy ultimately was nostalgia: that love for old songs and singers, old movies and actresses, nostalgia for another country, the elusive past. To lose oneself at the movies, for the exiled, was a way of recovering, if only fleetingly, the double loss of childhood and one's native land.[9]

Notes

1. See Emir Rodríguez Monegal, *El Boom de la literatura latinoamericana* (Caracas: Monte Avila, 1971), chap. 5, "Los nuevos novelistas," 87–104.

2. Rita Guibert, *Seven Voices: Seven Latin American Writers Talk to Rita Guibert*, trans. Frances Partridge (New York: Knopf, 1973), 401.

3. *Manuel Puig: La Semana del Autor,* ed. J. M. García Ramos (Madrid: ICI Ediciones de Cultura Hispánica, 1991), 40.

4. Interview with Cabrera Infante cited in Kenneth Hall, *Guillermo Cabrera Infante and the Cinema* (Newark, Del.: Juan de la Cuesta, 1989), 149.

5. Manuel Puig, "Cinema and the Novel," in *Modern Latin American Fiction: A Survey,* ed. J. King (London: Faber and Faber, 1987), 288–89.

6. Hall, *Guillermo Cabrera Infante,* 39. "Cine de cámara" is a pun on camera (or objective) and chamber (or highbrow) cinema.

7. Guillermo Cabrera Infante, "La última traición de Manuel Puig," *El Pais* (24 July 1990): 22–23.

8. Letter from Manuel Puig to Guillermo Cabrera Infante, 20 January 1977, Guillermo Cabrera Infante's correspondence, Firestone Library Archives, Princeton University.

9. According to Henri Langlois, founder of the Parisian Cinématèque in Trocadero, cited in a documentary film on Langlois by Argentine cinephile Edgardo Cozarinsky.

THE WRITER AS CRITIC

◆

On Borges:
The Man Who Knew Too Much

CARLOS CUADRA

Jorge Luis Borges is often considered the grandfather of the New Latin American literature.[1] For Guillermo Cabrera Infante, Borges is not only "the most important writer in Spanish since the death of Quevedo," he is a mythical figure, a literature in and of himself, and one of the most important influences in Cabrera Infante's trajectory as a writer.[2] At the same time, Borges represents a source of anxiety for Cabrera Infante since he represents the unattainable: he is the man who knew too much. This chapter examines the dynamics between the two writers, the maestro and his disciple, on the aesthetic and the personal level.

The approach used here for examining the dynamics between Cabrera Infante and Borges is the theory of the anxiety of influence espoused by the critic Harold Bloom.[3] Bloom utilizes the Freudian concept of the Oedipus complex to explain the development of every new writer. Just as the son is influenced by his father, the youthful writer is inspired to a literary vocation by a "strong writer," in Bloom's terminology. The writer who has already established an attractive and innovative literary persona holds a great influence over the new writer even though there is no personal connection. Just as the son creates a mythic image of the father, the young writer creates a mythic image of the successful writer. In both cases the image is imbued not only with admiration but also with hatred and envy of the predecessor's superiority. Bloom's model allows us to understand the love/hate relationship between Borges, the "strong writer," and Cabrera Infante, the disciple.

Cabrera Infante's references to Borges are filled with irony, ambiguity, and passion, a language reminiscent of Hitchcock's contradictory meanings, veiled allusion, and suspense. For this reason, titles of Hitchcock's films have been chosen to head the sections of this chapter.[4]

In an interview with Emir Rodríguez Monegal at the time of the publication of *Tres tristes tigres* (1967) [*Three Trapped Tigers* (1971)], Cabrera Infante characterized Borges by three fundamental traits: intelligence, literary coherence, and aloofness. All are characteristics suggestive of Borges as a classical writer, an aesthetic enigma we will delve into in "The Wrong Man." On the personal level, what captivated Cabrera Infante "more than Borges's proverbial intelligence" was his attitude of being above most of the things that worry "the common man."[5] Borges is praised for reasons that seem to lie beyond the literary; he is dealt with mythically, superior to all others.

The Wrong Man

The "strong writer" is not a real person but rather an image constructed by a literary disciple who is a victim of the "anxiety of influence." Any successes and failures attributed to the father figure may be, in the final analysis, fictitious, based on a selective reading and interpretation by the disciple. The "strong writer" is "the wrong man," or Borges, gratuitously attributed with a series of imaginary characteristics that attempt to define not only his personality but also his works. To get at the root of Cabrera Infante's interpretation of Borges's literary theories and their application in his works, we must refer to one of the master's most important essays, "La postulación de la realidad" ["The Postulation of Reality"] in *Discusión* (1932), a statement against romanticism. In contrast to the romantic writer, who seeks to transcend language and ponder directly on existence, Borges presents the image of the classical writer:

> El clásico no desconfía del lenguaje, cree en la suficiente virtud de cada uno de sus signos. . . . El autor (del texto clásico) nos propone un juego de símbolos, organizados rigurosamente sin duda, pero cuya animación eventual queda a cargo nuestro. No es realmente expresivo: se limita a registrar una realidad, no a representarla. Los ricos hechos a cuya póstuma alusión nos convida, importaron cargadas experiencias, percepciones, reacciones; éstas pueden inferirse de su relato, pero no están en él. Dicho con mejor precisión: no escribe los primeros contactos de la realidad, sino su elaboración final en concepto. . . . [O]tra de las marcas del clasicismo: la creencia de que una vez fraguada una imagen, ésta constituye un bien público. Para el

> concepto clásico, la pluralidad de los hombres y de los tiempos es accesoria, la literatura es siempre una sola. . . . El hallazgo romántico de la personalidad no era ni presentido por ellos. Ahora, todos estamos tan absortos en él, que el hecho de negarlo o de descuidarlo es sólo una de tantas habilidades para "ser personal." (*Prosa* I, 153–56)
>
> [The classicist does not distrust language, he believes in the adequate virtue of each of its signs. . . . The author (of classical text) proposes to us a play of symbols, rigorously organized without a doubt, but whose eventual animation remains our responsibility. He is not, in fact, expressive; he limits himself to recording a reality, not representing it. The prodigious events to whose posthumous allusion he invites us imply charged experiences, perceptions, reactions: these can be inferred from the narration, but they are not in it. To state it more precisely: he does not write of initial contacts with reality, but rather of their final conceptual elaboration. . . . [A]nother of the marks of classicism: the belief that once an image has been forged, it constitutes public property. For the classical concept, the plurality of man and of time is incidental; literature is always one. . . . The romantic discovery of personality was not even foreseen by them. Now, we are all so absorbed in it that the fact of denying or forgetting it is only one of the many facilities of "being personal." (*Reader,* 30–32)]

Borges, of course, considers himself a classical writer. His artistic aloofness comes from the systematic elimination of all emotional excess and romantic expressions, according to his own particular definition. For Borges, the romantic author fails because he attempts something impossible; the expression and representation of life through literature. While the romantic writer is misleading, the classical writer succeeds by omission. There is no excess or error in his style; rather, his approach to writing is logical and at times seemingly mathematical, never attempting to communicate feelings or interpret what is going on.

In Bakhtinian terms Borges's literary voice is monologic or falsely dialogic.[6] He exerts a rigid control over the images of the various social languages, exemplars of various literary traditions. Those languages do not dialogue with one another. Borges's language is authoritarian, a voice that extinguishes other voices, a static procedure that dies because it does not evolve.

The mythical image of Borges created by Cabrera Infante is that of a classical writer who is a composite of a broad literary tradition: an author made of quotations, with an immense authority. Cabrera Infante refers to Borges's innovative capacity for joining traditions that had never before been in contact. He does not say that Borges creates something new. If to reach immortality—and become a myth, as Nietzsche would say—it is necessary to create something new, what does this innovative movement consist of but an expression of the self-inwardness, of that unique and nontransferable something that resides in each one of us?[7] Each time an example is chosen and each time the values are reversed, an expressive act is created. Borges refuses expression, not because it does not exist, but because it is not aesthetically satisfactory. The best texts, in his opinion, are those from the classics, those that do not try to recount personal experience but narrate from the simplicity of the words.

How can Borges be a quintessential classicist and at the same time be a great writer? Perhaps his authority is rooted in an extraordinarily profound knowledge of tradition. What makes Borges an inimitable writer is one of the sins he attributes to the modern writers: "Now, we are all so absorbed in [the romantic discovery of personality] that the fact of denying or forgetting it is only one of the many facilities of *being personal*" (*Reader*, 32). Borges's modesty, his renouncing the literary ego in the name of a whole tradition to which he gives form and ends up representing, is his characteristic way of being personal. Borges is not only a creator but a literary authority, considered to be a judge by a whole generation of Hispanic authors. While Borges makes the enormous richness of tradition available to us, his authority has its negative influence on other writers, as Bertrand Russell said of Aristotle in a similar vein:

> In reading any important philosopher, but most of all in reading Aristotle, it is necessary to study him in two ways: with reference to his predecessors, and with reference to his successors. In the former aspect, Aristotle's merits are enormous; in the latter, his demerits are equally enormous. For his demerits, however, his successors are more responsible than he is. He came at the end of the creative period in Greek thought, and after his death, it was two thousand years before the world produced any philosopher who could be regarded as approximately his equal. Towards the end of this long period, his authority had become almost as unquestioned as that of the Church, and in science, as well as in philosophy, had become a serious obstacle to progress.[8]

In the field of literature, the same can be said of Borges. According to Cabrera Infante, all writers of the Spanish-American "boom," including Mario Vargas Llosa, Gabriel García Márquez, Julio Cortázar, and many other first-rate authors, have been influenced by him.[9] Without a doubt the Argentine's mythical image has had a profound influence on Cabrera Infante. What does this importance consist of? "Para el concepto clásico, la pluralidad de los hombres y de los tiempos es accesoria, la literatura es siempre una sola" (*Prosa* I, 155) ["For the classical concept, the plurality of man and of time is incidental; literature is always one" (*Reader,* 32)], declares Borges in his essay "La postulación de la realidad." Nevertheless, according to Cabrera Infante, it seems that Borges has turned this situation around. Instead of taking part in classical literature, he assumes it. In this sense, the comparison that Cabrera Infante makes between Borges and Quevedo in his interview with Rodríguez Monegal becomes significant: "Francisco de Quevedo es menos un hombre que una dilatada y compleja literatura" [Francisco de Quevedo is less a man than a lengthy and complex literature] (*Prosa* II, 171) writes Borges at the end of his article about the baroque poet. When Cabrera Infante states that Borges is "the most important writer in Spanish since the death of Quevedo," he implicitly refers, through Borges's own quotation, to the value of the embodiment of "Literature," which the latter seems to represent. The reader of Borges's essays and stories has access to a vast amount of quotations that together display a philosophy and a personal style. In Cabrera Infante's own words to Rita Guibert, "Borges has [raised] reading from a state of passivity to an active one" (Guibert, 426).

The importance and the attractiveness of Borges could be intolerable for a novice writer. This uneasiness can be found in Cabrera Infante's early works. In *Arcadia todas las noches* (1978) [Arcadia every night], for example, there is an excerpt from the script of *Scarface* (1932) that is very similar to a passage in Borges's story "El Aleph" (*Prosa* II, 112–25) ["The Aleph" (*Reader,* 154–63)] in which the protagonist simultaneously watches the entire universe.[10] Despite the greater profusion of marvels alluded to in "El Aleph," the structure based on enumeration is very similar in both pieces. Paradoxically, in "El Aleph" Borges, the blind genius, bases his anaphora on the preterit of the verb *to see.* Cabrera Infante uses "remembrance" to build his argument. But remembrance is one of Borges's fundamental themes, precisely the one that allows him to quote other authors in his works, thus providing him with authority. Borges's influence is felt by Cabrera Infante, who shows symptoms of rebelliousness in his essay on Howard Hawks:

> *Tema del traidor y del héroe*
> Para los que creen en el argumento de autoridad, la realidad es un universo de citas: de verdad de verdad no hay más que citas y vacío.

> No creo en el argumento de autoridad más de lo que creo en el unicornio (aunque estoy dispuesto a creer primero en el unicornio que en las autoridades), pero la existencia de un universo poblado de citas me incita. Así puedo recordar textualmente a todos los autores posibles — y algunos que resultan imposibles. Puedo recordar a Graham Greene diciendo . . .
>
> [*The Theme of the Traitor and the Hero*
> For those who believe in the reasoning of authority, reality is a universe of quotations: in all honesty, there is nothing more than quotations and emptiness. I do not believe in the reasoning of authority any more than I believe in the unicorn (although I am more prone to believe in the unicorn than in the authorities), but the existence of a universe full of quotations excites me. This way I can remember textually all the possible authors—and some that become impossible. I can remember Graham Greene saying . . .][11]

"Tema del traidor y del héroe" is the title of one of Borges's short stories, in which the traitor and the hero turn out to be the same person. In Cabrera Infante's text the traitor, the one who questions authority, is Cabrera Infante, and the hero—the author par excellence—is Borges, whose stylistic influence is evident, especially in the selection of references and metaphors. Following Bloom's theory, the former literarily betrays the latter to find a personal writing style. But while Cabrera Infante identifies with his hero, Borges, as someone capable of producing literature of merit, there is a rebellion against a literary universe populated only by quotations, an instrument of the classical writer. Cabrera Infante clearly breaks with the authority which that universe full of quotations implies; nevertheless, he continues to imitate his master: "a universe of quotations excites me." The dialogue with Borges, what will come to be a confrontation, is still in its incipient stage. The humor and the play on words (which, as we will see later, constitute Cabrera Infante's most important expressive weapon against tradition) emerge timidly, as separate points in an attempt, most likely unconscious, to imitate the language of the classical writer, symptomatically defined as an authority. If we define "author" as "one who holds authority," the young writer must usurp the authority of the maestro in order to become an author. Cabrera Infante attempts to undermine Borges's authority by appropriating his discourse and by imitating his style disguised with humor.

Borges seems to embrace all literature, or at least all literature that is worthwhile. His mythic status limits the subjects and forms available to other writers if they believe that it is impossible to write something that can match the quality and beauty of the master's works. The artist who wants to regain his freedom needs to find an aesthetic alternative and thus free himself from the master's influence.

This task is the one that Cabrera Infante begins in *Tres tristes tigres*. Even after the publication of this novel, Cabrera Infante continues to subscribe to the theory of the classical writer, as we see in his comments about Borges in his interview with Emir Rodríguez Monegal:

> GCI: Creo que lo que es totalmente autobiográfico allí es la lectura de un cuento de Ambrose Bierce, "An Occurrence at Owl Creek Bridge" que seguro precedió la escritura del cuento de Borges. Cuando leí "El sur," no me preocupó saber si Borges se había dado un golpe al subir una escalera y si por poco muere de septicemia, ni siquiera si soñó o pensó el delirio de Dahlmann. Lo que me llamó la atención era la coincidencia del procedimiento empleado por Borges con el empleado mucho antes por Bierce. Lo que me preocupó era saber si Borges había leído o no el cuento de Bierce, que ya antes había tenido un lector tan atento como Hemingway, que yo mismo había leído y copiado, técnicamente, en un cuento titulado "Resaca."

> [GCI: I believe that what is totally autobiographical there is the reading of a story by Ambrose Bierce, "An Occurrence at Owl Creek Bridge," that surely preceded the writing of Borges's story. When I read "El sur" I did not worry about knowing if Borges had hurt himself going up a staircase and almost died of blood poisoning, not even if he dreamed or thought up Dahlmann's delirium. What got my attention was the coincidence of the process used by Borges compared with the one used much earlier by Bierce. What concerned me was finding out whether or not Borges had read Bierce's story, as he already had had a reader as attentive as Hemingway, whom I myself had read and copied, technically, in a short story entitled "Remains."][12]

In this interview Cabrera Infante defends Borges's dichotomy between the classical and romantic writer. Rodríguez Monegal wants to transform Borges into a romantic writer, one who expresses himself autobiographically through his stories. Cabrera Infante does not accept this view. For him, autobiography is derived from literary ideas drawn from other sources, which is one way of maintaining the value of the classical procedure of creation: what gives value to the story is not the personal and the expressive, as Rodríguez Monegal would like, but the perpetuation of certain schemes of imitation.

Cabrera Infante wants to justify the use of various schemes of imitation in his own work. Later in this same interview, he says that the semblance was "created" by Ambrose Bierce and copied (a procedure authorized by the classical concept of literature) by Ernest Hemingway, Borges, and himself. The imitator qualifies himself euphemistically as an "attentive reader" using Borges's own vocabulary. By means of his knowledge, Cabrera Infante is justifying his own creative (real and imaginary) limitations. What seems to excite Cabrera Infante is his ability to correctly identify the source of "El sur," because that is a way to participate in and control the creative processes of his predecessor, Borges. On this occasion, Cabrera Infante pretends to be Borges. Cabrera Infante identifies with Borges to justify why he, like Borges, borrowed—via Hemingway—Bierce's plot.[13]

In Borges and Cabrera Infante we can see the double aspect of the myth that Nietzsche spoke about: on the one hand, the heroic figure wrapped in his "aloofness," larger than life, and on the other, the real man, fallible and unpredictable.

The Shadow of a Doubt

Three essays by Cabrera Infante—"Borges y yo" [Borges and I], "Un retrato" [A portrait], and "Ellos vivieron en Kensington" [They lived in Kensington]—refer to his personal contact with Borges and illuminate the mystifying aspect of Borges.[14] Despite the seemingly harmonious interchange between Cabrera Infante and Borges, the reader is surprised again and again by dark and ambivalent references to the "strong writer." Some of Cabrera Infante's observations lead us to believe there is a shadow of a doubt behind the respect and admiration he shows for Borges. Just as the son's development requires defiance toward the father, Cabrera Infante's stance toward Borges is contentious, as the new writer grows in success and stature. "Borges y yo" chronicles the first meeting that Cabrera Infante had with the Argentine, which took place during a conference given by Borges in London. The title transforms Cabrera Infante into an alter ego of the mythical figure of Borges. The title of Cabrera Infante's essay "Borges y yo" is taken from a Borges short story of the same title in *El hacedor* (1960) (*Prosa* II, 347–48) ["Borges and I" (*Reader,* 278–79)].

> Fue allí, en la primera charla, donde por fin lo conocí personalmente. Ocurrió el jueves 13 de mayo de 1971. La fecha era memorable, y para no olvidarla guardé el talón de los boletos.
>
> [It was there, during that first lecture, where I finally got to know him personally. It happened on Thursday, 13 May 1971. It was a memorable day, and so that I would not forget it, I kept the ticket stubs.] (Cabrera Infante, "Borges y yo")

For Cabrera Infante that date assumes a cult status similar to 4 July 1862, the day Lewis Carroll went with three little girls on a boat ride and told them stories that would later result in *Alice in Wonderland*, or 16 June 1905, the date on which the action in Joyce's *Ulysses* takes place.[15]

> El público y la noche fueron de Borges. Al final el salón, lleno no sólo de espectadores sino de críticos y de escritores y hasta de editores, se volcó hacia el poeta ciego: parecían gritar nuestro Milton, nuestro Homero.
>
> [The night belonged to Borges. The whole room, filled not only with spectators, but also with critics, writers, and even editors, cheered the blind poet: they seemed to shout "our Milton our Homer."] ("Borges y yo")[16]

His indisputable success and the comparison with two of the greatest classical writers of the past places Borges in the sphere of the mythical. Cabrera Infante's essay recounts the details of the conference and of the dinner that followed, during which the two writers got to know each other better. Afterward, on their way back to the hotel, an event takes place in which Borges's "proverbial intelligence" and his aloofness seem to touch on the superhuman:

> Yendo hacia la plaza, con Miriam Gómez y Di Giovanni caminando delante, se me ocurrió de pronto que Borges no era un ciego verdadero, que su ceguera era para emular mejor a Milton y a Homero. Decidí poner a prueba la visión del argentino. Las calles que rodean a Berkeley Square traen un tráfico veloz aun tarde en la noche, casi todo compuesto por taxis ávidos en busca de trabajo a la salida del teatro. Llevé a Borges hasta el medio de la calle y lo dejé allí con un pretexto *ad hoc*. Vi los taxis venir, eludir a Borges apenas y seguir raudos. Borges no se inmutaba. Seguramente que, discípulo de Berkeley, los taxis no le concernían porque no existían al no verlos. Corrí a llevar a Borges a un sitio seguro y ni siquiera mencionó mi ausencia.

> Pero luego, de regreso al hotel, me señaló la línea amarilla junto al bordillo y me dijo: "Usted sabe, yo no veo nada ya. Solamente el color amarillo me es fiel. Esa raya que está ahí es lo único que veo de la calle." ¿Por qué me decía esto Borges? Se habría dado cuenta de mi argucia? O habría un taxi de color amarillo que le pasó de cerca y decidió hacer que no lo vio? Borges era, como se dice en sus cuentos, muy matrero.
>
> [Going towards the square, with Miriam Gómez and Di Giovanni walking in front, it occurred to me that Borges was not truly blind, that his blindness was to emulate Milton and Homer. I decided to test the sight of the Argentine. The streets around Berkeley Square have rather brisk traffic, even late at night, almost all because of taxis eager to find fares when the theater lets out. I took Borges to the middle of the street and left him there under some ad hoc pretense. I saw the taxis come, barely missing Borges and continuing rapidly. Borges did not move. Surely, being a disciple of Berkeley, the taxis did not concern him because if he could not see them they didn't exist. I ran to help Borges to a safe place and he did not even acknowledge my absence. But, later on, on our way back to the hotel, he showed me the yellow line by the curb and he told me: "You know, I cannot see anything anymore. Only the color yellow is faithful to me. That line over there is the only thing that I can see in the street." Why was Borges saying this to me? Had he become aware of my prank? Or had a yellow taxi passed close by him and he decided to pretend he didn't see it? Borges was, as it is written in his stories, very shrewd.] ("Borges y yo")[17]

Did this event actually happen? Did Cabrera Infante really place Borges's life in danger to prove that he was blind? Maybe it was just a very inopportune joke or the start of a legend that shows Borges as a wizard able to read his guide's mind. The two contradictory interpretations are easily justifiable in this anecdote, which contains many comical elements. The entire episode could have been taken from a modern-day *El Lazarillo de Tormes* (1554), with a latent homicidal bent.[18] Blindness here has symbolic meaning, for this is the element that allows Cabrera Infante to compare Borges with authors of mythical status such as Homer and Milton. The ironic reference to Berkeley is a mockery, the unreal way: because *esse est percipi* you do not see the taxis, the taxis do not exist, then what are you afraid of? Cabrera Infante seems to be saying to Borges: "What good are all these false theories on which you base your literary authority, in the face of real danger?" At any rate, Borges passes his test with high marks and his mythical status is reaffirmed, thanks to his mind-reading powers. These powers give rise to yet another association to myth; Tiresias, the archetypal soothsayer of Greek mythology, was blind. To doubt Borges's blindness is to break his symbolic link with the literary myths of the past and, thus, his strength as a myth and his authority. Cabrera Infante's rebellion, real or made up, ends in a fiasco.

The affirmation at the end of the episode merits a separate commentary. As it is written in his stories, Borges was *matrero,* very shrewd. Not only is Borges prudent, intuitive, or reserved; Cabrera Infante suggests that he is also sly, sagacious, almost deceitful. Is his shrewdness in wanting to avoid the taxis that could have run over him? Did he guess Cabrera Infante's quasi-homicidal intentions? We do not know whether this is a fact or only the author's paranoid speculation. Where is his shrewdness or his will to deceive? This occasion was not the only one on which Borges, referring to his blindness, has spoken of the color yellow as the only color he could still distinguish. This episode, with all its sadistic pretenses, reveals that the anxiety of influence expressed in Cabrera Infante's first novel is still in full force in 1986.

This attempt at demythification is not the only one to which Borges is submitted in these articles. While Cabrera Infante's direct statements about Borges are always full of praise and respect, certain incidents show him under a different light, more humane, yet less alluring:

> Cuando entré al camerino, Borges estaba apoyado en su grueso bastón escocés, y sentado ante una mesa tenía frente a sí una botella de brandy medio vacía y un vaso lleno. Pensé que Di Giovanni (el apoderado de Borges) se fortalecía antes de apoderarse del público. Pero mi curiosidad se volvió asombro al ver a Borges coger el vaso de coñá firmemente y apurarlo de un trago. Nunca hubiera creído que Borges, tan moderado en todo, bebía.
>
> [When I entered the dressing room, Borges was sitting in front of a table, leaning on his thick Scottish cane. Before him was a half-empty bottle of brandy and a full glass. I thought that Di Giovanni (Borges's agent) strengthened himself before facing the public. My curiosity turned into amazement when I saw Borges grasp the glass of cognac and drink it all at once. I would have never believed that Borges, so moderate in everything else, would take a drink.] ("Borges y yo")

And in another selection:

> "Pero a usted no le interesa nada el dinero." Borges me miró con esos ojos que no veían más que las rayas amarillas en el asfalto y se sonrió un poco. Cuando habló había un aire pícaro en su voz: "En cuanto al dinero, no crea, ayuda." Y disolvió la confusión en una carcajada de sus grandes dientes postizos. Todos, por supuesto nos reímos. Borges era, como los indios de la Pampa, un contradictorio.
>
> ["But you are not interested in money." Borges looked at me with those eyes that could only distinguish the yellow line of the pavement and smiled a little. When he spoke there was a mischievous air in his voice: "With respect to money, believe me, it helps." He then dissolved the confusion with a guffaw showing his large dentures. Of course we all laughed. Borges was, like the Pampa Indians, a contradictory person.] ("Borges y yo")

Within the warm and benevolent tone of the confidences shared by Cabrera Infante, the insinuations appear: Borges suffers from some dipsomania (he quickly drinks no less than a full glass of brandy in one gulp) and much avarice. In the second quote, the joke is innocent, but it seems to produce "confusion," and Borges is labeled not as amusing but as "contradictory." Cabrera Infante could have simply praised the fine irony of the commentary about the value of money. Instead, he ingeniously treats his statement as if it were one of Borges's ideological principles. This technique is typical of the mythical treatment of a subject, whose words, always considered significant, are attributed with a plausible, albeit unjustified, profundity.

The word "contradictory" has a special meaning for Cabrera Infante, evident in this excerpt from one of his articles, "Centenario en el espejo" [Centenary in the mirror]:

> ¿Ya saben ustedes qué es un contradictorio?
> CONTRADICTORIO (del B. Lat. "Contradictorius" de "contra" y "dicere" decir lo contrario). Que tiene contradicción con otra cosa." Más que una tribu [los contradictorios] eran una casta dentro de la tribu, los samurai (sí, esa palabra es un plural de majestad) de la pradera, soldados de raza. Los guerreros, cuando no había guerras que hacer, eran los aristócratas, como en todas partes. . . .
>
> La cuestión, el meollo, a donde quiere llegar este artículo hace rato (eso que los académicos llaman "mi tesis") es que más que una casta, los contradictorios son una categoría humana: hay contradictorios donde quiera. . . . Donde más hay es en la literatura. Petronio, por ejemplo, es un contradictorio temprano, y Hemingway un contradic-

torio actual, sin tener en cuenta que una vez me dijo que tenía sangre india. Hay más, allá, de donde vengo. Cientos de ellos: Cervantes, Quevedo, Marlowe, Shakespeare, Byron, . . .

[Do you know what a contradictory is?
CONTRADICTORY (From B. Lat. "Contradictorius, from "contra" and "dicere" to say the opposite). That has a contradiction with something else. More than a tribe [the contradictories] were a caste within the tribe, the samurai (yes, that word is plural for majesty) of the prairie, soldiers by lineage. The warriors, when there were no wars for them to fight, were aristocrats, like everywhere else. . . .
The question, the essence of where this article has wanted to go for some time (what is called in the parlance of academia "my thesis") is that more than a caste, the contradictories are a human category: there are contradictories everywhere. . . . Where most are found is in literature. Petronius, for example, is an early contradictory, and Hemingway is a contemporary contradictory, without taking into account that he once told me he had Indian blood. There are more, there, where I am coming from. Hundreds of them: Cervantes, Quevedo, Marlowe, Shakespeare, Byron . . .][19]

This article entitled "Centenario en el espejo" was written in 1967, about the same time as *Tres tristes tigres,* and is dedicated to Lewis Carroll. The above-mentioned authors greatly influenced this novel. The great absentee, the author not mentioned in the article, is Borges, who has to wait until 1986 to obtain this encoded praise. The contradictories are a special breed of aristocrats, and Cabrera Infante obviously admires them. The article—and also *Tres tristes tigres*—is a product of "active reading," the method practiced by Borges, according to the actual expression used in the interview with Rita Guibert. Cabrera Infante, who has acknowledged the debt that his generation owes to Borges, excludes him as a direct antecedent in his first novel because he is the giant from whose influence he wants to free himself. To do so he takes Borges's methods to the ultimate extreme and creates a new myth, Bustrófedon, the great contradictory. Twenty years later, in Cabrera Infante's essay on Lewis Carroll, this process is acknowledged, and Borges is included among the aristocracy, although in secret, that has given life to the literary ideal of Bustrófedon. As in the anecdote about blindness, it is Borges who earns his own place in Cabrera Infante's literary hierarchy.

Despite this secret recovery, the explicit tone that predominates in "Ellos vivieron en Kensington" and "Borges y yo" lies between frank admiration and a critique with humorous overtones. The most direct attacks are on Borges's knowledge and authority based on memory, that is, on his reliance on literary tradition. These attacks occur in two similar anecdotes, each in relation to two of Borges's favorite authors, Robert Louis Stevenson and G. K. Chesterton.[20] The first, related to the author of *Treasure Island* (1886), is as follows:

> La noche siguiente fuímos Miriam Gómez y yo a cenar a su hotel. . . . Como entrante, Borges me dijo casi en confidencia: "Usted sabe, Stevenson se hospedaba aquí cada vez que venía a Londres."
>
> [The following night, Miriam Gómez and I went to have dinner at his hotel. . . . For starters, Borges told me almost in confidence: "Do you know, Stevenson stayed here every time he came to London?"] ("Borges y yo")

Years later, Borges and Cabrera Infante get together again in the same hotel, and the Cuban reminds him:

> "Borges," le dije, "recuerda que a este hotel venía Stevenson cada vez que visitaba Londres?" Me miró asombrado y me dijo: "¡No me diga! No lo sabía. Gracias por dejármelo saber." No le dije, claro, que era él quién me había contado esa anécdota. Pero al entrar al restaurante cogió del brazo a uno de los dos angloargentinos que lo acompañaban (mientras el otro escoltaba a María Kodama, cada vez más inescrutable) y oí como Borges le decía a su acompañante: "Usted sabía que Stevenson cuando visitaba Londres venía a este hotel?" El angloargentino movió su cabeza en ignorancia absoluta. Fue entonces cuando Borges compuso su mejor bocadillo: "Me lo acaban de decir ahí afuera."
>
> ["Borges," I said, "do you remember that this is the hotel where Stevenson stayed every time he came to London?" He looked at me amazed and said: "You don't say! I didn't know. Thanks for telling me." Of course, I did not remind him that it was he who had told me this anecdote. But when we entered the restaurant, he grabbed the arm of one of the two Anglo-Argentines that were with him (while the other one accompanied Maria Kodama, ever more inscrutable) and I heard Borges tell him: "Did you know that Stevenson used to come to this hotel whenever he visited London?" The Anglo-Argentine moved his head in absolute ignorance. It was then that Borges composed his best line: "They just old me that outside."] ("Borges y yo")

What does it matter that an older person forgets absolutely minor facts through the years? The only explanation for Cabrera Infante's emphasizing this unimportant detail is the mythical value of memory, that is, of Borges's knowledge of literature and his intellectual superiority. As is well-known, Cabrera Infante has a tremendous memory, although on several occasions he has apologized for what he considered to be his limited literary education compared to his knowledge about movies. The literary rivalry—or maybe, the anxiety of influence—becomes significant in the arena of memory, what the two of them have forgotten or what they can remember. Another anecdote is very similar:

> Cenando con Borges una noche de 1971 en el hotel Brown's en Mayfair, el argentino me preguntó abruptamente: "Y dónde vive usted en Londres?" "En Kensington," le respondí, "porque es más fácil decir Kensington que decir Gloucester Road." "Ah," dijo Borges en seguida, "ahí vivió Chesterton."
>
> [Having dinner with Borges one night in 1971 at Brown's Hotel of Mayfair, the Argentine abruptly asked me: "Where do you live in London?" "In Kensington," I answered, "because it is easier to say Kensington than to say Gloucester Road." "Ah!" said Borges immediately, "Chesterton lived there."] ("Ellos vivieron en Kensington")

Cabrera Infante confesses that he did not know this fact but proceeded to use it as a pretense to write the article "Ellos vivieron en Kensington." With a mixture of frustration and irony he comments: "Ahora armado con la primera edición de la Oxford Literary Guide to the British Isles, puedo aguardar confiado una nueva reunión con Borges" [Now, armed with the first edition of the Oxford Literary Guide to the British Isles, I can confidently manage another meeting with Borges].

He then devotes himself to a superficial review of Chesterton's biography and details about other artists who lived in the same area of London. These details begin as simple curiosities, like the different addresses where Henry James or Mallarmé lived, and quickly slip into darker subjects, such as contemplating the suicide of Shelley's first wife in a shallow pond, or W. M. Thackeray's impudent remarks to the chlorotic Charlotte Brontë.[21]

In this essay Cabrera Infante parodies Borges's level of erudition. The inference that the origin of all Borges's knowledge is a dictionary completely changes our perception of the learned and apparently humble style of Borges's literary essays. His prodigious knowledge is identified as being available to anyone, and his literary idols are reduced to mere entries in an encyclopedia.

The anxiety of influence, the literary reflection of the oedipal ambivalence described by Freud, always offers us two contradictory faces. Let us compare the articles we have been analyzing with one entitled "Un retrato" [A portrait], primarily the description of a photograph Borges dedicated to Guillermo Cabrera Infante. In it he brags about the affection the Argentine author had for him:

> Pero luego me dijo: "Sabe una cosa?" [Borges a Cabrera Infante] "Anoche estaba en mi habitación, ya tarde, y me dije: mañana voy a decirle a Cabrera que Fulano de Tal y Zutano han muerto en Buenos Aires. De pronto reflexioné y me dije: 'Pero ¡qué estupidez! ¿Cómo voy a decirle a Cabrera que esos viejos amigos han muerto cuando seguramente ni siquiera ha oído hablar de ellos?' ¿Qué le parece?" No pude decirle nada. "¿Sabe lo que es?" me explicó. "Es que yo lo consideraba a usted un amigo tan viejo que tenía que conocer a mis viejos amigos." Por supuesto, yo no conocía a esos amigos de Borges, muertos seguramente de vejez en Buenos Aires, aunque luego supe que uno de ellos era escritor. Pero lo extraordinario es que Borges, que nunca debió oír hablar de mí, que no me había conocido hasta una semana antes en Oxford y luego me viera en una cena en el Brown's Hotel, hiciera esa distinción. La atribuyo, por supuesto, no a dotes que no poseo, sino a un don de Borges: su generosidad.
>
> [But later he said to me: "You know?" (Borges to Cabrera Infante) "Late last night in my room, I said to myself: Tomorrow I must tell Cabrera Infante that so-and-so and so-and-so have died in Buenos Aires. But then I thought it over and said to myself: 'How stupid! How can I tell Cabrera that those old friends have died when surely he has never even heard of them?' What do you think?" I could say nothing. "Do you know what it is?' he explained. "It's that I considered you such an old friend that you had to know my old friends." Of course I did not know any of Borges's old friends, who surely had died of old age in Buenos Aires, although later on I found out that one of them was a writer. But the amazing part is that Borges, who had probably never heard of me until a week earlier in Oxford, and later on he would meet me for dinner at Brown's Hotel, would make that distinction. I attribute this, of course, not to talents I don't have, but to a quality of Borges: his generosity.] ("Un retrato")

On this occasion, Borges—previously indirectly accused of being a miser—becomes generous because of flattery. What stands out in this piece is, above all, the way in which Cabrera Infante proclaims his being distinguished by his idol's friendship "at first sight." To attribute this friendship exclusively to Borges's generosity would be a touch of false modesty, since Cabrera Infante has written the article to proclaim this distinction.

In summary, we have in "Un retrato" some contradicting attitudes, coinciding with the ambivalence described by Harold Bloom in *The Anxiety of Influence.* Cabrera Infante officially praises Borges, the invincible and consecrated writer, while at the same time he tries to undermine his authority. Finally, he declares himself worthy of praise from the very author he tries to diminish.

The most interesting part of this process is that it both utilizes and destroys the very themes and literary processes consecrated by Borges himself: respect for the "great ones" of literary tradition, memory and knowledge, and blindness. The examples analyzed here are not merely anecdotes, but rather, they are a part of the process of artistic transformation, the destruction of Borges as myth. The only suitable weapons available to the disciple for confronting his predecessor are irony, treason, and even symbolic murder.

Vertigo

For the writer under the inflluence of anxiety literary tradition is an unending vertigo. Borges comes from a place of skepticism with respect to literary creativity that allows him to have written with exceptional originality, basing his work on the apparent preeminence of the written word over the ego and its emotional expression. Cabrera Infante began writing in a style modeled after Borges. Later he detached himself from the master and adopted the most recent form of romantic rebellion, surrealism, in search of his own voice. Starting from the canon, he finds himself connected with the iconoclastic tradition. This concept, discussed extensively by Octavio Paz, among others, is in itself highly paradoxical.[22] In Cabrera Infante's case, it results in a mixture of auto-affirmation and knowledge, moral assertion and ruthless satire, popular culture taken seriously and higher education submitted to ridicule. In this broken tradition one does not maintain the illusion of an ego autonomous from language or a clear dividing line between literature and life. Language is a shared and unavoidable element, but it is also a repressive mechanism, the product of exploitation and yet the most effective guard of individual liberty. Cabrera Infante finds it necessary to flee from meaning, expose its deceptions, and turn its mechanisms around.

Paradoxically, Borges is also a precursor of this process. His reactionary political opinions and his stories, poems, and articles make us look at the infinite projected onto two opposing mirrors.

For Borges, this presents a horrific image. Cabrera Infante, on the other hand, seems to look at that emptiness as a kind of hope and freedom.

Translated by Birgit Kuban Austin

Notes

1. Jorge Luis Borges (1898–1985) was a world-famous Argentine writer of erudite poems and essays and fantastic short stories. References to his works in this chapter are from *Prosa completa,* 2 vols. (Barcelona: Editorial Bruguera, 1980); hereafter cited in the text as *Prosa* I or II, and *Borges, A Reader: A Selection from the Writings of Jorge Luis Borges,* eds. Emir Rodríguez Monegal and Alastair Reid (New York: E. P. Dutton, 1981); hereafter cited in the text as *Reader.*

2. Rita Guibert, *Seven Voices: Seven Latin American Writers Talk to Rita Guibert.* (New York: Alfred A. Knopf, 1973), 426. Francisco de Quevedo (1588–1645) was a satirical Spanish poet.

3. Harold Bloom, who wrote *The Anxiety of Influence: A Theory of Poetry* (New York: Oxford University Press, 1973), is an American literary critic and author of a large array of essays on literature. In *The Western Canon: The Books and School of the Ages* (1994), Bloom attempts to establish which writers form the canon of occidental literature.

4. Alfred Hitchcock (1899–1981) was an English film director and a master of suspense.

5. Emir Rodríguez Monegal (1927–1986) was an Uruguayan literary critic who had great influence in the analysis of the authors of the Latin American boom. The article referred to is "Las fuentes de la narración" *Mundo Nuevo* 25 (July 1968): 41–58.

6. Mikhail Bakhtin (1895–1975) was a Russian literary critic whose conception of the novel is a carnivalesque ceremony in which different social languages are in a dialogue. See Mikhail Bakhtin, *The Dialogic Imagination,* ed. Michel Holquist, trans. Caryl Emerson and Michael Holquist (Austin: University of Texas Press, 1981).

7. Friedrich Nietzsche (1844–1900) was a German philosopher, critic of Christianity, and defender of the theory of the eternal return.

8. Aristotle (384–322 B.C.) was a Greek philosopher, disciple of Plato, and teacher of Alexander the Great. His authority was undisputed until the scientific revolution of the Renaissance. Bertrand Russell (1872–1970) was an English mathematician and philosopher. Known for his essays on logic, Russell together with Alfred North Whitehead wrote *Principa Mathematica* (1913) and later was known as a technician of philosophy, a revolutionary, and a pacifist. The citation is from his *History of Western Philosophy and its Connection with Political and Social Circumstances from the Earliest Times to Present Day,* 2nd ed. (London: George Allen and Unwin, 1961), 173.

9. Mario Vargas Llosa (b. 1936) is a Peruvian novelist, author of *La ciudad y los perros* (1963), *Conversación en la catedral* (1969), and *La guerra del fin del mundo* (1981). Gabriel García Márquez (b. 1928) is a Nobel laureate in literature, author of

Cien años de soledad (1967) [*One Hundred Years of Solitude* (1970)], and one of the best writers of the twentieth century. Julio Cortázar (1910–1974) was an Argentine writer who lived for many years in Paris and was greatly influenced by the European vanguard.

10. Guillermo Cabrera Infante, *Arcadia todas las noches* (Barcelona: Editorial Seix Barral, 1978), 92-93.

11. Ibid., 87. Howard Hawks (1904–1972) was an American movie director of *His Girl Friday* (1938) and other films. Graham Greene (1904–1991) was an English novelist, greatly influenced by Catholicism. Some of his most famous works are *The Third Man* (1950) and *Of Power and Glory* (1940).

12. Monegal, "Las fuentes," 47. Ambrose Bierce (1842–1914) was an American storyteller and journalist, lost without a trace in the Mexican revolution. Ernest Hemingway (1899–1961) was a North American writer who won the Nobel Prize in literature in 1954.

13. The Borges story "El sur" (*Prosa* I, 529–35) ["The South," *Reader*, 252–57] employs the technique of a flashback, in a similar fashion to that used in "An Occurrence at Owl Creek Bridge." In "El sur" Juan Dahlmann falls ill of blood poisoning and in his delirium recalls a childhood memory in which he is traveling to the family ranch south of Buenos Aires. This flashback seems to be Dahlmann's reality, when in fact he is on an operating table in the hospital.

14. "Borges y yo," *El País* (16 June 1986): 34; "Un retrato," *El País* (26 August 1979): IV–V. Section: Arte y pensamiento; "Ellos vivieron en Kensington," *El País* (21 August 1977): 9, 26.

15. Lewis Carroll (1832–1898) was an English photographer, logician, and writer, known for his fantasy stories originally written for children. James Joyce (1882–1941) was an Irish writer who revolutionized world literature with his novels *Ulysses* (1922) and *Finnegan's Wake* (1939).

16. John Milton (1608–1674) was an English poet and the author of *Paradise Lost* (1667). Like Homer, he lost his sight. Homer was the mythical Greek rhapsodist, author of the *Iliad* and the *Odyssey.*

17. George Berkeley (1685–1753) was an Irish philosopher and bishop who created an idealistic system based on John Locke's empiricism.

18. *El Lazarillo de Tormes* was the first novel of chivalry in Spanish literature, published at the end of the reign of King Carlos I.

19. "Centenario en el espejo," *Mundo Nuevo* 13 (July 1967): 62–66. Cayo Petronio Arbiter (d. A.D. 66) was the reputed author of the *Satyricon,* a literary portrait of Roman society in the first century A.D. Miguel de Cervantes (1547–1616) was a Spanish writer and author of *Don Quixote,* the first modern novel. Christopher Marlowe (1564–1593) was an English dramatist of the Elizabethan era. William Shakespeare (1564–1616) was an English dramatist, considered by many to be the greatest literary genius of all times. George Gordon, Lord Byron (1788–1824) was an English romantic poet known for his long poems "Childe Harold" and "Don Juan" and his life of debauchery.

20. Robert Louis Stevenson (1850–1894) was a Scottish writer who died prematurely due to tuberculosis. He was a strong influence on Borges's style. G. K. Chesterton (1874–1936) was an English writer, famous for his taste for irony and paradox.

21. Henry James (1843–1916) was an American novelist, short-story writer, dramatist, and critic. He spent most of his life in England and is famous for the complexity and subtlety of his literary works. Stéphane Mallarmé (1842–1898) was

a French poet, probably the most important exponent of the symbolist movement, who considered poetry as a new form of religion. Percy Bysshe Shelley (1792–1822) was an English romantic poet who drowned at an early age in a boating accident. W. M. Thackeray (1811–1863) was an English novelist, essayist, and illustrator whose masterpiece is *Vanity Fair.* Charlotte Brontë (1816–1855) was an English novelist and a pioneer in the modern treatment of feminine characters. Her most popular novel is *Jane Eyre* (1847).

22. Octavio Paz, *Children of the Mire* (Cambridge: Harvard University Press, 1974).

The Translator Within: A Conversation with Guillermo Cabrera Infante

Suzanne Jill Levine

SJL: Hemingway seems to have produced an anxiety of influence for generations, Latin American writers among them. Do you consider yourself among those touched by this influence, or anxiety, or both? What aspect of Hemingway, his style or the man, has influenced you most?

GCI: Probably his fame.

SJL: How about his style?

GCI: Fame first, style later.

SJL: *View of Dawn in the Tropics* ends with a quotation from Hemingway's *The Green Hills of Africa,* just to cite one of the many allusions to Hemingway in your books.

GCI: Remember that he lived down there in Havana, so it was impossible to escape, not only his bulk but also his fame. He was the model of *the* successful writer living in Cuba. So why not imitate him? Not as an influential writer per se, like James Joyce, if you wish, but as a famous writer living right there. In *el patio* as it were. He was inescapable. As far as quotations in that book, there are quotations from Martí, from Borges, from Faulkner—and even from Arthur Koestler, for Christ's sake!

SJL: Would you say that Faulkner's literary vision had a greater impact on your work than Hemingway's?

GCI: I would separate impact from influence. I read Faulkner when I was 16, 17, 18, and he was for me the epitome of the American novelist. But that influence disappeared very soon. What is certain is that I wasn't as keen reading Hemingway as I was when I was reading Faulkner. So there is a great difference between an influence and the fun of a fan. I was (and I am) a great fan of Alfred Hitchcock, but I don't think he has influenced my writing.

SJL: I can't help thinking about the resonances. . . .

GCI: There are bits of Hemingway here and there, such as the format of *Así en la paz como en la guerra,* which comes from Hemingway's first book. But even in this first book of mine there are certain short stories that are closer to Faulkner than to Hemingway. For instance, "Un rato de tenmeallá" at a first reading will look much more Faulknerian than Hemingwayesque, with the device of having a child for a narrator of the solecist soliloquy, as in *As I Lay Dying.* Though of course the total lack of punctuation comes from Joyce. By the way, I hadn't read him when I wrote my monologue.

SJL: I'm wondering if you read these writers in translation or in the original English. Did the translations produce a different effect upon you as a reader?

GCI: I read them in both translation and the original, though I first read Faulkner in Borges's translation, *The Wild Palms,* in 1946. After I read it in the original, years later, I considered it to be a better book in Spanish than in English. Because it's organized by Borges, a classic who is very different than the kind of loose romantic Faulkner was. It is like Baudelaire translating Poe in fact. Faulkner was, you might say, a very unkempt writer—the total opposite of Borges. Then I read *Light in August*—which by the way means giving birth in August: an impossible pun in Spanish—, and then I read *Sanctuary.* Or perhaps *Sanctuary* first. Both in translation. Then all of a sudden there were available in Havana the Signet paperbacks, a treasure trove. That's how I met *Intruder in the Dust* and the short stories in *Knight's Gambit.* By the time I was 20 I had read all the Faulkner I cared to read. As it happens with *For Whom the Bell Tolls* (a book I wouldn't want to have to read again in my life!) so it happened with most of Faulkner's books—with the exception again of *The Wild Palms,* in Spanish in the Sudamericana editions. Because to read it was to read a master, Borges, reorganizing the world of a very loose kind of poet in prose—which is what Faulkner was, after all. But then I read other books by Hemingway, such as *The Sun Also Rises.* It's very funny, I read *For Whom the Bell Tolls* first and *The Sun Also Rises* after. It should have been the other way around.

SJL: In English or in Spanish?

GCI: In English. I read "The Killers" in Spanish, because it wasn't available in English at the time. Then when I got married in 1953, a man, a Spaniard where I worked, the old librarian in *Carteles,* gave me as a present *The Fifth Column and the First Forty-Nine,* the collected short stories by Hemingway. But before that, I had read in English in *Life Magazine* "The Old Man and the Sea." It wasn't until many years later that I read the Lino Novás Calvo version. I was surprised that Hemingway considered him his best translator, because right at the end, not exactly in a secluded cove, was Lino Novás's flagrant mistake with the lions: calling the lions of the beach *sea* lions. That really struck me as curiouser, first for being a translation by Novás, authorized by Hemingway, who apparently knew Spanish. The times I met Hemingway in Havana he always spoke English, not Spanish. Once he tried to speak Spanish and it was like Inspector Clousseau speaking English! From that you could infer that he really didn't even read the Spanish version of "The Old Man and the Sea," though he recommended it.

SJL: So, in a sense, Lino Novás Calvo represents for you not a great translator, but the archetype of the translator as betrayer, a producer of mistakes. Or both, like most great translators.

GCI: He was a great translator, no doubt about that. Remember that he translated Faulkner into Spanish before anybody else and he translated not only short stories by Faulkner but also novels like *Sanctuary.* He was the official translator from English for Ortega y Gasset's *Revista de Occidente.* He did many translations in Cuba for *Bohemia.* He translated everything that appeared there as taken from American English. But I found it very awkward to have that enormous mistake so conspicuous right at the end of the book. I kept it in mind for many years and when I wrote the "Bachata" section of *Tres tristes tigres,* I mischievously elaborated on this gross error. But, at the same time, Lino was himself a great influence on me, not as a translator but as a writer of short stories who used the Cuban mode, Cuban speech as a kind of literary language. Also his characters were very new, very much from the Havana of the '20s, all from the lumpen. I was some kind of follower for a while—but not for many years. At the same time I was surprised that nobody who has read, reviewed, or criticized Alejo Carpentier's *El acoso (The Chase)* has mentioned "La noche de Ramón Yendía" by Lino Novás Calvo, which is a much earlier short story. I could say that "La noche" is a better novella—because that is what Carpentier's novel is.

SJL: Does it have the same plot?

GCI: It is *very* similar. In the case of Lino Novás, the main character is some sort of stool pigeon for the Machado police, who imagines that he is being persecuted all over Havana by the revolutionary police, right after the fall of Machado, and is finally killed in error. In the case of *El acoso* it is a stoolie who is truly persecuted all over

Havana by his former colleagues or the police or whatever. Frankly, they are so similar that I'm sure Carpentier had read the short story by Novás Calvo before writing *El acoso.* Because Lino was considered a master before anybody heard of Carpentier in Cuba—or anywhere else. As a matter of fact Carpentier came back to France in 1940 and wrote only one short story in Cuba, "Viaje a la semilla" ("Journey to the Source") in 1942 or '43. Then he wrote a book about Cuban music that was published in Mexico but written in Caracas—and it was there that he wrote all the best novels. He was never considered a real Cuban writer. He was, as a writer, as alien as the way he talked.

SJL: Novás Calvo was born in Spain but moved to Cuba when he was very young, isn't that so?

GCI: Carpentier was apparently born in Havana; Lino Novás was actually born in Galicia. It's a total reversal: Carpentier came by his own choice to sound and to look very foreign in Havana, while Lino became very Cuban in Cuba. Not only that. He was, for a time, a taxi driver, and at that time driving a taxi in Havana was truly the most Cuban of all possible professions. I wouldn't imagine Alejo Carpentier driving a taxi. A passenger yes; a chauffeur never.

SJL: Since Lino Novás first began translating for *Revista de Occidente,* I imagine he translated his first Faulkner pieces while still living in Spain. Who else did he translate in that period?

GCI: He also was translating Lawrence and Hardy. And *Huxley* I mean. He was a professional translator in Madrid, in the early 1930s.

SJL: Did he begin writing as a translator?

GCI: Not at all. Before then he had already become a writer in Cuba. He then went back to Spain as a correspondent. Later he got involved with Ortega y Gasset and the writers around Ortega y Gasset and then got ensnared in the Civil War and was almost killed. He always had a very awkward kind of behavior, all his life. He was what you could call not an anti-hero but a non-hero. Caught in heroic situations in Cuba, later in the Civil War in Spain, and later again in Cuba. And even later when he was associated with another translator who was also a writer, Rolando Masferrer, a communist man of action who became a corrupt gangster and a Batista sbirro. Finally Lino landed in *Bohemia,* becoming the managing editor of the magazine. He left Cuba after the revolution because Miguel Angel Quevedo, the owner of *Bohemia,* and his cronies all left. So he was more or less compelled to leave. I think he was also extremely wary of communists, because of what he saw in Spain during the Civil

War—terrible things he used to tell, like when he was almost tried and shot after an anonymous letter. But then again, why did he land in literary *Hoy,* which was the magazine of the communist newspaper? I'm talking about 1940, 1941, and 1942—that's when I met him. I was very young at the time, barely 14, but I remember these people very well. Novás Calvo, Masferrer, Montenegro—all of them working for *Hoy.* Perhaps you can say that Lino Novás was terribly gregarious with the wrong people.

SJL: Which is not to say *greguerías.*[1]

GCI: This is not to say that he led a charmed life. Not in Cuba first, not in Spain later, not during the Spanish Civil War, not back in Cuba at *Hoy.* By 1953–54—that's when I saw him again—I was then the movie reviewer of *Carteles* magazine and Lino's wife was the editor in chief of a very successful women's magazine called *Vanidades.* By then he had the curious notion that you shouldn't write novels or short stories, that this was completely passé. You should write reportage, newspaper items, articles. That was exactly where the fiction writer ended up. So from 1949 probably—when he published in *Bohemia* an incredibly good story called "*Angusola y los cuchillos*"—until he left Cuba in 1960, he didn't write one single short story! He only wrote the Hemingway translation and that's all. It surprised me that when he became an exile in the U.S.A. and was teaching at Syracuse University, he had taken up writing again. I mean writing short stories. That was exactly what he knew best. But, somehow, exile hasn't been too kind to Novás Calvo.

SJL: Has the idea of fiction being passé and of reportage being the real thing influenced you too as a writer?

GCI: Not at all! I was very cross at Lino for saying these things—especially saying such silly things to young writers. I was then 24 and I knew what I wanted and how to get it. But there were young writers, 18 or 19 years old at the time, who came to him and he always told them this rigmarole over and over: You shouldn't write fiction, you should write reportage, you should write for newspapers, forget about books, forget about short stories. I don't know why he did this. I thought it could have been understandable if he were totally through as a writer. But he wasn't, unlike the case of Carlos Montenegro, who stopped writing completely long ago. I never knew what was really going on. Lino was truly a very awkward man. At the same time he chided me because I was on television. I had a TV program then, and he was saying to me every time I saw him, with that thin voice of his, "You're going to end up as an actor." A silly sally coming from a man who was obviously very intelligent.

I do not know why he did all these weird things. Why did he start trying to regain some sort of recognition when he was already in exile, many years later? Why didn't he do what Carpentier did, writing and publishing his own material, paying for the publication of his novels and his short stories if necessary. I never understood it. I tend to think that Carpentier had more faith in literature and in himself than Lino ever had.

SJL: Do you think that Hemingway's "The Killers" had any repercussions on "La noche de Ramón Yendía" being, in a way, a model gangster story?

GCI: Hard to tell, really, "The Killers" had been published many years before Lino Novás even imagined the situation in his story, but something very strange happens with the language in that Cuban short story; it's not at all like Hemingway, it's something different.

SJL: What do you mean?

GCI: The language—and I don't mean only his characters' idiom—is so particularly Havanan or what Lino Novás made us believe was Havanan. I'm not terribly sure that they ever spoke like that. I'm only sure that he approached the material with an idea of idioms, of colloquialism, of popular language, which is very different from Hemingway. Hemingway was interested always in the situation and then the language came after. He had always in mind a given character in a given situation, with given leanings, as happens in *The Sun Also Rises.* And then the language came after. He gave you the impression of being tremendously original. That probably attracted Novás Calvo. Or perhaps it was that he lived close by.

SJL: In Havana?

GCI: Yes. I can tell you something about "The Killers." "The Killers" influenced my story "Balada de plomo y yerro" a lot. In that story there were only characters and situations, but because, as the gangsters were Cuban gangsters, they were very different from the gangsters in "The Killers." Very different also from "La noche de Ramón Yendía," in which there is only one point of view: the squealer's and this anguish, certain or imagined, of him being hunted. In "The Killers," as in "Balada," the point of view comes from the killers, not from the prey. In "Balada" there is also a humorous twist at the end, which makes it slightly different. But I must really confess, under terrible duress, that my short story came after reading "The Killers." I don't think that either Lino Novás Calvo or Carpentier would make a similar confession.

SJL: Well, that makes you the most honest man, to misquote our own W. C. Fields.

GCI: Oh no! It's that I have a compulsion to tell all. Just ask me about something and I will tell you instantly what I know. You don't have to invent the ways of making me talk. I'll always do the talking. In fact, I'm very close to Mr. Memory in Hitchcock's *The Thirty-nine Steps.* I tell the truth in spite of myself—even if it will cost me dearly.

SJL: Back to the possible influence of the translations . . .

GCI: Remember that when I began to read American literature at the age of 15 or 16, I didn't read English. I was a reader of translations forcibly, even with French literature, because I didn't know any French then either. Also some of these translations were very good. They were not though, as you could say of Coca-Cola, the real thing. But very acceptable translations were being made in Argentina, Mexico, Chile—and even in Cuba. So it was the only way to know these authors. It was an agreeable way because the Argentine translation of Erskine Caldwell had a certain piquant: it was a Spanish that wasn't exactly Spanish. The translator was trying to imitate the rhythm and voices of both the narration and the characters but using Argentinisms. For instance, *God's Little Acre* was called in 1946 *La Chacrita de Dios.* That was quite amusing because I had to find out what *Chacrita* meant in Spanish. *Chacrita* doesn't mean anything in Cuba.[2]

SJL: So these translations were full of, not only Americanisms, but Argentinisms.

GCI: Yes, the Chilenisms, Mexicanisms. This was part of the flavor, and I enjoyed those books immensely in translation. The only problem is that there were not enough translations at the time. And then came a blessing in disguise, Signet Books, a publishing house that brought out all those American writers in paperback around 1948.

SJL: And then?

GCI: I was able to read all those Faulkner novels I told you about. I was able to read Erskine Caldwell's *Trouble in July.* I was able to read Steinbeck and dos Passos all in English. Not because I was after some original literary land where all these writers dwelled, but because before they were simply not available.

SJL: Getting back to Lino, what was his very first translation?

GCI: He translated Faulkner's "All the Dead Pilots" for *Revista de Occidente* in Madrid and another story whose title I don't remember. Then he translated *Sanctuary.* Very well done; I read *Sanctuary* again in English, in the '50s. His version proved quite readable, entertaining, even.

SJL: It's interesting that perhaps your first contact with the linguistic flavor of other Latin American countries seems to have been through these translations.

GCI: There were other books that were not translations, like *Don Segundo Sombra* or *Martín Fierro,* or some other Argentine books. But basically I met this kind of strange language, where gasoline was called *nafta* and a boy a *pibe,* through translations from the English into Spanish. I don't know if that makes it more interesting but that's how it happened. Regional relations.

SJL: I guess I'm thinking of all the games you play with vocabulary and accents and dialects and about how linguistic realities seem to matter more to you than the world behind the words.

GCI: I'm not so sure about that. I think reading those books was simply a question of enjoyment, not of looking for models. Pure pleasure.

SJL: A unique aspect of your work is that you're always rewriting texts, in a sense. Indeed the translations into English of your own work have inspired you often to rewrite the text in English, then elaborate on it. As you did with the story "A Nest of Sparrows," which became "Nest, Door, Neighbours," or recently with the British edition of *View of Dawn in the Tropics.* Or *Así en la paz como en la guerra* transformed in English into *Writes of Passage,* the same yet not the same book, whose title winks in homage to the subversive scribe.

GCI: But it also happens in Spanish. I am always rewriting. I don't have a problem with the blank page at all. I just write whatever I imagine or concoct. And then comes *the* problem—which is rewriting. And not only in books like *Tres tristes tigres* or *La Habana para un Infante difunto.* Even with articles in Spanish or English that I write now in London, I can rewrite them forever. I actually lose money on those articles. Because they should take me only one afternoon but sometimes they take more than a week. But that's only because for me in English, in Spanish, in French, words are not solitary.

SJL: You mean words are not a game of solitaire but a pas de deux, a two-step so to speak?

GCI: One word gives in turn the possibility of not merely two but three more words that are there because the first word suggested them. This doesn't only happen in translation. It happens in all I write.

SJL: As you say, the pure pleasure of the text. Your remarks here remind me not only of Lino Novás's barbs but a phrase somewhere in *Tres tristes tigres* where you say that writers make the best actors, because they write their own dialogues. In a sense you're really saying they are the best interpreters, no?

GCI: I did say they're the best interpreters of what they've written. The only problem is that writers are truly coy people. They want to be praised, but they don't want to have too much praise piled up on them because excessive praise always engenders embarrassment. But then again, writers want praise at any price. So there is a dichotomy there. If I tell you how good I was when I was writing this, it would appear extremely vain, but it could also be facetious and not implying the truth. That is, if I respond, "Well, that's not terribly good," I might then be fishing for compliments. It's a position not totally unlike that of actors, but actors can be vain and nobody blames them. They say that Greta Garbo said, "I want to be alone." Well, that's not true. She never said that. It was said by a character in a movie called *Grand Hotel.* But, that's something only an actor would say, and not meaning it at all. With writers it's different. I want to be a lone wolf—but never a steppenwolf. To live only in the imagination brings solitude.

SJL: Do you think that your "relationship" with Hemingway was that of an actor with the role he'd like to play? In a sense, you wanted *to be* Hemingway.

GCI: I wanted to be as famous as he was. It's not a question of being influenced by his style. Or his characters. But rather by his way of life, if you will. Influenced by his living style. Though of course, with the passing of time I believe that he did something that writers do a lot. He spent so much time in futile endeavors that it's baffling. I mean, that ritual of going every day at 11 o'clock in the morning down to Cojimar, onto his boat and into the ocean and the Gulf Stream to try and fish the biggest fish possible was sheer lunacy. Having nothing to do with real living, it had everything to do with fantasy. I went once in his boat into the ocean across the Gulf Stream—and it was hideously boring. From six o'clock in the morning until four o'clock in the afternoon, all he did was to get drunk. Get drunk on vodka and end up lying on the deck, completely knocked out for the whole day—or most of the day. Then all of a sudden he was up again: the effect of the vodka faded, and he was now heading the boat back to Cojimar, back to port. I couldn't understand it! If that was a way of life, believe me, I never wanted to lead it. Or to go to Africa to kill animals in order to get a terrible case of dysentery, then having the runs most of the time when he was supposed to be killing elephants, buffaloes, or whatever. Or going all over Spain after some bullfighters because he wanted to watch every good bullfighter that lived while he lived. He was truly a madman. No doubt about that. But at the same time he lived in a very beautiful villa outside Havana, with everything he wanted, with an orchard full of tropical fruits, a large library. He came to Havana driving a Mercury convertible, went to the Floridita or the Zaragozana to eat and to drink. That was certainly appetizing, but the rest of his life was not appealing but appalling. And that's something writers do a lot: wasting time. Faulkner believed he was a Southern gentleman who should ride after the fox every Saturday.

SJL: In muggy Mississippi!

GCI: In that sense, European writers were more professional. You couldn't imagine Joyce going on a hunt in Ireland. Or trying to catch a marlin in the English Channel. Or going after bullfighters in southern France. He led a very conscientious life. He was consequent with himself and with his family and with his writing. The only problem with Joyce was his aloofness, his tremendous vanity, and the fact that he was a drunk like most Irish. Drinking was also a wretched waste of time. Why was I telling you this?

SJL: We were talking about aspects of famous foreign writers, which did, or did not, have an impact on your own life and work. You have often spoken about your affinities with English culture, like Borges, and, speaking specifically of Joyce, you recently translated *Dubliners.* "The Dead," which you translated as "Los muertos"—the dead in plural—has been considered one of the greatest stories in the English language. Besides its incredible musicality, what strikes you most about this story?

GCI: That's because "el muerto" (in singular) sounds funny in Spanish.

SJL: It's also the title of a story by Borges. Your choice of the plural seems most appropriate because the story is not only about one dead boy . . .

GCI: "The Dead" is the most autobiographical of Joyce's stories. He was very jealous of a past love of his wife, a man, or rather a boy who died young. Joyce's wife Nora laughed at his jealousy over the dead, but for Joyce it was very real, and that young man is the Michael Fury in this story. Of course, the dead are more than just Michael Fury; it is also dead illusions and the past and the author himself.

SJL: Very much, I suppose, like the Havana of a Dead Infante.

GCI: *¿Quién sabe?*

Notes

1. The word *greguería* means "outcry" and is the name of a unique literary genre invented by Ramón Gómez de la Serna (1888–1963), a vanguardist Spanish writer who anticipated surrealism in literature. The *greguería* is a hybrid between the incongruous poetic metaphor and the prose aphorism.

2. A *chacra* is a farm or ranch; *chacrita* is the diminutive form of the same word.

Critical Readings from Exile

JUSTO C. ULLOA AND LEONOR A. ULLOA

Unlike many of his contemporaries, Guillermo Cabrera Infante has not written on the interdependence of fiction and history in the works of contemporary Spanish American authors. Nevertheless, his unconventional readings of some authors, especially Cuban intellectuals both in exile and on the island, have produced a thought-provoking discourse that reveals how their fiction is shaped not only by historical events but also by their often marginalized existence. *Mea Cuba* is a compilation of essays on the life and work of some of the most important twentieth-century Cuban writers: José Lezama Lima, Virgilio Piñera, Reinaldo Arenas, Nicolás Guillén, and Alejo Carpentier.[1] Through suggestive pun-laden vignettes Cabrera Infante consciously invades the writers' private spheres to provide readers with rare insights into the relationship between their lives and their literary voices.

The impact of the Cuban revolution and the frustration Cabrera Infante experienced as a political exile is clearly evident in his character portrayal of each writer. Cabrera Infante goes to great lengths to expose the negative effects of the Cuban revolution, especially with respect to persecution of homosexuals and censorship of individual works. He and his colleagues had first hand knowledge of inhumane government policies that encouraged self-condemnation and efforts to marginalize exiled writers and render them invisible.

Without apology, Cabrera Infante intertwines his own pained vision of an expatriate with unorthodox literary observations and personal anecdotes in a manner that can touch even readers not interested in the critical analysis of a writer's work. Through his vignettes Cabrera Infante becomes a modern-day portraitist and caricaturist whose expert knowledge of Cuban politics and culture and passion for these subjects generate sketches that capture the tenuous relationships between the authors' literary creations and their lives in post-republican Cuba. His disregard for the boundaries between traditional literary analysis and biographical sketch belies the commonly held assumption that one can know writers best through scholarly dissection and interpretation.

Cabrera Infante goes beyond the straight biographical sketch. He has blurred the distinction between the psychological and the physical, between fact and fiction, between portrait and caricature. Psychological insight along with physical description became essential elements in portrait creation around the time of Sigmund Freud's studies on the importance of dreams and the unconscious in the late nineteenth century. In Cabrera Infante's early biographical sketches it is not uncommon to find references to external and salient aspects of the body, which in some cases had been previously outlined in portraits and caricatures. These two faces of the biographical sketch—the psychological and the physical—form an integral part of most life stories and serve to articulate the mini-biographies included in *Mea Cuba.*[2]

Cuban history and the impact of the Cuban revolution on writers is the raison d'être for these vignettes, and this imperative is revealed in the epigraph to "Vidas para leerlas" [Parallax Lives]: "Toda biografía aspira siempre a la condición de historia" (*Mea Cuba* [1992], 315) ["All biography constantly aspires towards the condition of history" (*Mea Cuba* [1994], 329)]. Cabrera Infante has produced a hybrid genre that seeks to provide a place in history for those revolutionary Cuban writers like himself who are no longer in favor with the political left and who have been ostracized for their beliefs. He has culled previously unknown and unexpected biographical data that allows him to contrast the lives of persecuted artists with those writers favored by the Cuban regime.

Each essay is structured in chronological order and generally begins with references to the source of Cabrera Infante's privileged information. He then dutifully informs the reader of his first encounter with his subject, the circumstances surrounding their acquaintance, and the details involving his participation in the events described. He ends his mini-biographies with the writers' death or information related to the last time he saw them. His prose tends to be conversational and confessional, full of humor, gossip, puns, and colloquial phrases that in themselves could provide a fruitful source of study on oral expressions of the period. The tone is mainly parodic, indeed, to such an extent that some of the sketches are caricatures rather than biographies. Typically there are three general themes: sex, a denunciation of the Cuban revolution, and Cabrera Infante's opinions about the author's literary production and professional standing in the intellectual community. He is unabashedly biased in the selection of the details included, frequently taking sides in the political squabbles of the characters and dwelling mercilessly and intentionally on the flaws of his subjects.

The vignettes in *Mea Cuba* dealing with contemporary Cuban artists and writers are grouped together under a section entitled "Vidas para leerlas." Although all of these stories are grouped within a single section, they do not form an organic whole but rather a series of self-contained anecdotes Cabrera Infante has drawn on from his apparent experience. He freely offers the historical and cultural background necessary for readers to comprehend the significance of a given sketch. In fact, readers of "Vidas para leerlas" not familiar with intimate or confidential details surrounding the lifestyles of the authors described would come away feeling familiar with the author, if not well informed.

"Tema del héroe y la heroína" ["Two Wrote Together"] is the title of the first essay of "Vidas para leerlas," the original title of the essay first published in 1980. As the quizzical title of the entire section suggests, it deals with the parallel but different lives and works of two Cuban authors who shared a common intellectual space.[3] By resorting to alliteration, puns, parody, and Cuban *choteo,* Cabrera Infante creates a poignant biographical essay. Even in their similitude, the main characters of "Tema del héroe y la heroína" are different, for if the poet José Lezama Lima preferred, for example, young and handsome male sexual partners, the playwright Virgilio Piñera favored rough and scruffy-looking individuals who would make him scream in ecstasy:

> Tanto Virgilio como Lezama abominaban de la felación mutua y el "cruce de espadas." Pero la misma militancia marcaba diferencias de aspecto y de comportamiento público. Virgilio era muy afeminado, apocado. Lezama tenía una virilidad valiente, que lo acercaba a lo que el personaje de comedia bufa Sopeira, gallego gallardo, llamaba un "caballero español." Lezama era un caballero cubano. Aun un mismo vicio los separaba: los dos fumaban mucho, pero mientras Virgilio, de perfil dantesco, encendía un cigarrillo tras otro y los sorbía con un abandono lánguido que parecía propio de Marlene Dietrich, Lezama, de rostro rudo, mordía un enorme puro eterno. . . . (*Mea Cuba* [1992], 320)

> [Both Virgilio and Lezama abhorred mutual fellatio and the "cross of the swords." But the same militancy marked differences of appear-

ance and of public conduct. Virgilio was very effeminate and shy. A valiant virility made Lezama what the comic opera character Sopeira, a gallant Galician, used to call a "Spanish gentleman." Lezama was a Cuban gentleman. Even an identical vice separated them. The two of them smoked a lot, but while Virgilio, he of a Dantesque profile, would light one cigarette after another and would inhale them with a languid abandon that would seem strange to Marlene Dietrich, Lezama, he of the rough face, would bite a cigar like a bullet. (*Mea Cuba* [1994], 334)]

From the very first lines of "Tema del héroe y la heroína," Cabrera Infante weaves his literary observations through passages describing specific physical and psychological idiosyncrasies of Lezama Lima and Piñera, making sure that the most prickly personal details support his critical observations. If, for example, both precocious writers began publishing about the same time in the late 1930s or early 1940s, the "fatter" one, Lezama Lima, did so with poems that were already marked by his "barroco y oscuro" (*Mea Cuba* [1992], 318) ["baroque and obscure" (*Mea Cuba* [1994], 332)] style, while the "thin" one showed himself to be "simple, casi callejero" (*Mea Cuba* [1992], 318) ["colloquial, almost street wise" (*Mea Cuba* [1994], 332)].

Cabrera Infante's succinct review of the major pieces published by these two legendary writers captures the essence of their works with well-timed metaphors that express the inseparability and interdependence of the writers' lifestyles and their writings. Lezama Lima's obesity and "valiant virility" and Piñera's "Dantesque" gauntness find their equivalence in the baroque and obscure prose of the former and the colloquial and direct writings of the latter. Skeptics may point out, and perhaps rightly so, that Cabrera Infante relies on the readers' previously acquired knowledge of the authors for them to understand the connection between the writing style, the lifestyle, and physical appearance of both writers. But what is important here is that readers of Cabrera Infante's piece, whether academic critics or simply interested aficionados, will be able to grasp swiftly what is in essence one of the major differences in Lezama Lima's and Piñera's writing.

Cabrera Infante cannot resist the temptation to dwell irreverently on his subjects' sexuality. There seems to be an intentional diminishing of his subjects' creative imagination when he attributes the origin of certain stories included in their works to simple recreations of homosexual misadventures whether real or apocryphal. Nothing illustrates this better than Cabrera Infante's explanation of a questionable source for the first homoerotic episode in chapter 2 of Lezama Lima's first novel, *Paradiso* (1966). According to Cabrera Infante, *Paradiso* "rose" to the public precisely because of an episode in the novel dealing with a Malay painter and "una blonda criatura púber" (*Mea Cuba* [1992], 322) ["a blond pubescent creature" (*Mea Cuba* [1994], 335)] who was living with him and who at night received the Asian painter's "gusano" [worm] *per angostam via.* This description, motivated by Lezama Lima's hurt pride after being rejected and ridiculed by the "blond pubescent creature" in a printed story entitled "The Fat Man," indeed endows *Paradiso* with elements characteristic of the roman à clef. Cabrera Infante's version of the story adds a link of causality for those readers not familiar with Lezama Lima's intimate life. Cabrera Infante concedes that "Tal vez ambas historias sean apócrifas pero lo que queda hoy es mala literatura de 'El hombre gordo' contra la prosa poderosa del relato del pintor malayo . . . De ese infierno íntimo surgió público *Paradiso*" (*Mea Cuba* [1992], 322) ["Maybe both stories are apocryphal, but what remains today is the bad writing of the 'Fat Man' contrasted with the powerful prose of the tale of the Malay painter . . . From that particular inferno *Paradiso* rose to the public" (*Mea Cuba* [1994], 335)]. As most writers would admit—Cabrera Infante included—this episode may have been the source of inspiration for this story. However, to attribute such importance to a story not fully confirmed, as Cabrera Infante does to Lezama Lima's alleged homoerotic misadventures, is a form of disfigurement that accentuates the burlesque propensities of the two sketches in "Tema del héroe y la heroína."

Despite the frivolity, Cabrera Infante gives a sound rendition of the literary contributions of both authors, their involvement in the development of Cuban intellectual and cultural life of the period, and their relationship with the extraordinary set of circumstances brought forth by the revolution. Initially both authors publicly expressed their reaction to the changes taking place in post-1959 Cuba. Piñera openly declared that he felt very frightened, while Lezama Lima "se limitó a hablar de literatura, de la eternidad del arte y la permanencia de la cultura" (*Mea Cuba* [1992], 332) ["limited himself to speaking of literature, of the eternity of art and the permanence of culture" (*Mea Cuba* [1994], 345)]. Although in different ways, both Piñera and Lezama Lima were deeply affected by the changes and the new rules established by the revolutionary government.

Piñera was arrested during the raids that took place the "Night of the Three P's" (aimed at prostitutes, pimps, and pederasts) and accused of "assault on revolutionary morality" because of his homosexual tendencies.[4] He was systematically persecuted, intimidated, exiled, and excommunicated on Cuban soil. He told Cabrera Infante that part of his ordeal during the period of incarceration "fue encontrarse entre presos contrarrevolucionarios que al saber no que era un poeta pederasta prisionero sino un colaborador de *Revolución,* lo trataron como un colaboracionista y le pegaron y amenazaron con pelarlo al rape" (*Mea Cuba* [1992], 336) ["was finding himself among counter-revolutionary prisoners who upon learning that he was not merely a pederast poet prisoner but a contributor to *Revolución,* treated him like a collaborator and beat him and threatened to crop his head Paris-style" (*Mea Cuba* [1994], 348)]. In spite of the persecution he suffered, Piñera could not live outside of Cuba, much less away from Havana. Shunned by the government, he withdrew silently into his house and became an invisible person immersed "en otra querida costumbre: jugar canasta con varias viejas damas retiradas" (*Mea Cuba* [1992], 345) ["in another cherished custom: playing canasta with several retired old ladies" (*Mea Cuba* [1994], 357)].

Lezama Lima, on the other hand, was not a direct target during the period of oppression of homosexuals in Cuba, but he wrote a silent protest opposing the government's homophobic campaign. Although the homosexual chapters of *Paradiso* constituted an act of defiance, the novel was not banned along with other undesirable manuscripts because of the direct intervention of Fidel Castro, who allowed the first printing of the novel in Cuba. However, like Piñera, Lezama Lima was ostracized, especially after the Padilla Affair in 1971:

> Pero a partir de 1971 y la delación de Padilla, cayó sobre el poeta y *Paradiso* un doble domo de silencio y cuando ganó un premio en Italia y fue invitado a Roma le fue negado el permiso de salida. Igualmente le impidieron viajar a México, aunque ya no habría llegado a la Montego Bay con su alborozo auroral. Su vida se hizo más difícil de lo que había sido nunca y . . . murió de una crisis pulmonar en un hospital, en una sala anónima, sin ser reconocido el más grande poeta que ha dado Cuba. . . . (*Mea Cuba* [1992], 346)

> [But after 1971 and Padilla's recantation a double dome of silence fell on the poet and on *Paradiso* and when he won a prize in Italy and he was invited to Rome he was denied an exit visa. They also prevented him from traveling to Mexico, although he wouldn't have got to Montego Bay with his double auroral exultation of love. His life became more difficult than it had ever been and . . . he died of a pulmonary oedema in a nondescript hospital, in an anonymous room, without being recognized as the greatest poet Cuba has produced. . . . (*Mea Cuba* [1994], 358)]

Government attempts to undermine the literary acclaim of both writers were, of course, not entirely successful. Against all odds, today both are well-known writers in Latin America and around the world.

Cabrera Infante's renditions of significant events in the lives of Lezama Lima and Piñera are enriched with details that only a contemporary witness to these happenings can furnish. The fact that he was, like Lezama Lima and Piñera, a member of the intellectual elite, that he witnessed Piñera's persecution and tried to help him during this fearful period, and that he himself suffered the alienation and oppressive tactics of the revolution, make these insightful vignettes all the more poignant. They add tantalizing nuances to the parallels between Cabrera Infante's experiences and the incidents that affected the lives and works of Lezama Lima and Piñera.

As in the case of Piñera, passive sex ruled the life of Reinaldo Arenas, probably the most widely persecuted Cuban homosexual novelist of the 1980s. In 1973 Arenas was charged with "ideological deviation" by Fidel Castro's regime: he was summarily convicted, and sent to prison. Arenas spent most of the 1970s in and out of prison or hiding from his persecutors until he finally managed to escape from Cuba during the Mariel exodus in May of 1980. In "Reinaldo Arenas o la destrucción por el sexo" [Reinaldo Arenas, or Destruction by Sex] Cabrera Infante examines the relationship between Arenas's political beliefs, his scabrous sexual life, and his largely fantastic literary production. To Cabrera Infante Arenas's life was "una azarosa aventura en un bosque penetrable de penes, dejando detrás la señal de su semen y de su escritura" (*Mea Cuba* [1992], 403) ["a hazardous trek in a penetrable forest of penises, leaving behind the sign of his semen and of his writing" (*Mea Cuba* [1994], 414)]. In addition, he was committed to fighting the homophobic dictatorship that ruled his country. The initial paragraph summarizes his biographical sketch as follows:

> Tres pasiones rigieron la vida y la muerte de Reinaldo Arenas: la literatura no como juego sino como fuego que consume, el sexo pasivo y la política activa. De las tres, la pasión dominante era, es evidente, el sexo. No sólo en su vida sino en su obra. Fue el cronista de un país regido no por Fidel Castro, ya impotente, sino por el sexo. (*Mea Cuba* [1992], 400)

> [Three passions ruled the life and death of Reinaldo Arenas: literature, not as a game but as a flame that consumes, passive sex and active politics. Of the three, the dominant passion was sex. Not only

> in his life, but in his work. He was the chronicler of a country ruled not by Fidel Castro, already impotent, but by sex. (*Mea Cuba* [1994], 412)]

This essay offers Cabrera Infante the opportunity to discuss briefly the role of sexuality in Cuban culture. For him, it is a culture dominated by sexuality. He alludes to the Spanish crown's reaction in 1516 to the sexual customs of the Indians and to the present-day erotic activities of the *jineteros,* a Cuban term for hustlers, mainly associated with prostitutes of both sexes. This new kind of sexual imperialism practiced by men from Western countries buying up Cuba's youngest *jineteras,* and the dictatorship's obsession with rampant pederasty, have led to the creation of *sidarios* for those who have contracted AIDS and to a series of other institutional measures predominantly against homosexuals.

El "caso Arenas," as Cabrera Infante calls it, is not as well known as "el caso Padilla" within Cuban circles but aptly illustrates the persecution and suffering of those caught by the State Security agents. Sentenced for pederasty, Arenas was able to chronicle the anguish of persecuted homosexuals. Cabrera Infante's sketch captures the fusion between Arenas's life and his work as a rare combination of "penes y penas" (*Mea Cuba* [1992], 405) ["penises and pain" (*Mea Cuba* [1994], 416)]. He sees Arenas as a pansexual being, "indecent and innocent," who breaks the canon and the interdiction with actions and writings that go beyond Lezama Lima's, Piñera's, and Severo Sarduy's homoerotic and irreverent creations:[5]

> [S]u clase de sexo se manifiesta entre niños, con muchachos, con adolescentes, con bestias de corral y de carga, con árboles, con sus troncos y sus frutos, comestibles o no, con el agua, con la lluvia, con los ríos ¡y con el mar mismo! Y hasta con la tierra. Su pansexualismo es, siempre, homosexual. Lo que lo hace una versión cubana y campesina de un Walt Whitman de la prosa y, a veces, de una prosa poética que es un lastre de ocasión en ocasión. (*Mea Cuba* [1992], 402)

> [His kind of sex is man infested: with children, with boys, with adolescents, with beasts from the barnyard and of burden, in the yard, with trees, with their trunks and their fruits, edible or not, with water, with rain, with rivers and—with the sea itself! (And even with the earth.) His pansexuality is always homosexual. Which makes him a country Cuban version of Walt Whitman of prose and, at times, of a poetic prose that is on occasions a brown man's burden. (*Mea Cuba* [1994], 413)]

Cabrera Infante recognizes Arenas's genius as a writer. He also understands that had he stayed in Cuba, he never would have produced the masterpieces he was able to write in exile. Persecution and political vendettas pushed many writers to the edge and almost destroyed their lives, as was the case of Piñera. Both Lezama Lima, exiled in his own Cuba, and Arenas, exiled in the United States, were affected by the political repression that castigated deviations of any kind. Yet there were other writers such as Nicolás Guillén and Alejo Carpentier who managed to flourish under Cuba's dictatorial system.

Most of Cabrera Infante's literary portraits were published in newspapers and literary magazines and were extensively revised before being gathered into his best-known collection of essays. For example, his original essay on Nicolás Guillén, "Un poeta de vuelo popular," published in Spanish in the March 1990 issue of the well-known Mexican journal *Vuelta*, went through a series of modifications before its inclusion in the original Spanish version of *Mea Cuba* (363–70) and then in the English translation as "A Poet of a Popular Parnassus" (376–82).[6] An English magazine adaptation entitled "Nicolás Guillén: Poet and Partisan" was published concurrently in the January–June 1990 issue of *Review.*[7] Since this version is considerably shorter and more general than the one published in *Vuelta,* it can be assumed that it is a translation based on the Spanish magazine account of the same year. In comparing all four pieces—the original Spanish in *Vuelta,* the original English one in *Review,* as well as the revised ones in the Spanish and English editions of *Mea Cuba*—it is evident that the changes incorporated into all four renditions have to do not only with the place of publication but also with Cabrera Infante's desire to draw an unforgettable caricature of Guillén, accentuating a series of negative events related in one way or another to the Cuban revolution and its "Maximum Leader."

Even though Cabrera Infante recognizes Guillén's ability as a poet in each version, he emphasizes Guillén's personal and professional compromises in the most recent English account. Here Guillén's talent is described as having evolved to become "craft" and his poetry "political propaganda." If the story of Guillén's poetic evolution is correct, then it is easy to see why he seems to have had a history of conforming to whatever was most advantageous to his literary ambitions: in the 1930s he imitated the Spanish poet Federico García Lorca, whom he had met during one of his visits to Cuba, and became a member of the Cuban Communist Party. In a section of *Mea Cuba* entitled "Perversions of History" (*Mea Cuba* [1994], 9–48),

Cabrera Infante alludes to Guillén's habit of singing the praises of whomever was in power:

> Nicolás Guillén es un viejo ruiseñor de emperadores. Comenzó como censor de Prensa de Machado en 1932 y desde entonces no ha dejado de servir a todos los tiranos: con su pluma alegre: encomendó Stalin a la protección de sus dioses afrocubanos, regocijaba a Batista con cuentos verdes narrados en su voz congolesa en los años cuarenta, escribía para Aníbal Escalante y todavía compone letras de guarachas en loa a Fidel Castro. (*Mea Cuba* [1992], 52–53)

> [Nicolás Guillén is an old nightingale of emperors. He started out as a press censor for Machado in 1932 and since then he has not ceased to serve all the tyrants with his cheerful pen: he commended Stalin to the protection of his Afro-Cuban gods, he regaled Batista with off-colour stories narrated in his Congolese voice in the forties, he wrote for Aníbal Escalante and he still composes *guaracha* lyrics in praise of Fidel Castro. (*Mea Cuba* [1994], 28)]

Cabrera Infante's exposé of Guillén's life suggests then that he was in essence what most *habaneros* would call both an *aprovechado* and an *acomplejado,* a sponger and an insecure man who became a communist when he was at his peak and then went on to find a comfortable "niche" in the Soviet-style communism that took root in post-revolutionary Cuba.

The shorter 1990 magazine version in English emphasizes two separate incidents related first to Guillén's race and second to his deteriorating relationship with Fidel Castro. The first is directly associated with the fact that the Cuban poet thought of himself as a *mulato* and not as a *negro.* The second is based on Castro's dissatisfaction with Guillén's performance as a revolutionary poet. The two anecdotes underscore that Guillén's problems in Cuba were both racial and political in nature. Cabrera Infante indicates that on one occasion, Guillén corrected an American publisher who had referred to him as "el gran poeta negro!" ["the great black poet!"]. "Negro no, mulato" ["Not black, mulatto"], retorted Guillén in Spanish to the embarrassment of the journalist, who was not familiar with the distinction made among Hispanics between blacks and mulattos (*Mea Cuba* [1992], 366; *Mea Cuba* [1994], 378–79). In the other instance Cabrera Infante cites Guillén's intense discontent with the way Castro was treating him personally, alluding to a negative epithet the Cuban leader had used in one of his visits to the University of Havana in which he commented on Guillén's unproductive professional life. Castro thought that Guillén was overpaid as the poet laureate of the revolution, since he was producing hardly a poem a year while less well-known poets were publishing several a week. Castro called Guillén a "lazybones" and condoned the "poetical lynching party" that ensued after his derogatory remarks: a group of university students marched down to the street where Guillén lived, shouting to the tune of an improvised chant reminiscent of one of the mulatto poet's better-known poems:

> ¡Nicolás, tú no trabaja ma!
> ¡Nicolás, no ere poeta ni na!
> (*Mea Cuba* [1992], 368)

> [Nicolás, you don do no work, man!
> Nicolás, you ain no poet, you ain nuthin!
> ("Guillén," *Review* [1990], 32)]

These same anecdotes are retold in a longer and more specific way in the English version of *Mea Cuba*. The students' chant, for example, has been revised to better capture the Afro-Cuban rhythm of the original Spanish composition:

> Nicolás, don't work no mo'!
> Nicolás, you ain't a poe!
> No mo', no mo', no mo'!
> (*Mea Cuba* [1994], 380)

The more recent account in *Mea Cuba* is also more illustrative of the tense relationship that Cabrera Infante noticed between Guillén and Castro. Cabrera Infante discards the "lazybones" epithet for a more suitable one that better exemplifies Castro's true feelings about Guillén. Moreover, if in both the first and second versions Cabrera Infante quotes Guillén as saying that Castro was a "son of a bitch," in the latter Castro does not call the poet a "lazybones" but instead a "good-for-nothing bum"—indeed, a more appropriate description from the Cuban leader who fancies himself a literary critic and, of course, a defender of public funds. Unlike the first anecdote, which in essence does not relate with enough force the little-known feud between the *mulato* poet and the *gallego* leader, the second English account is not skittish about portraying the mutual dislike between the two Cubans. It is much more realistic and politically aggressive, and it even makes better sense as a story of opportunistic behavior on the part of an oversensitive individual who aspired to be the "Great

Poet of America" but had fallen from grace with Cuba's self-appointed guardian of aesthetic and fiscal morality.

As is the case with the vignette dealing with the "Vidas para leerlas" of Lezama Lima and Piñera, the anecdotes in *Mea Cuba* dealing with Guillén are associated with the life of another important contemporary literary figure. In this instance, however, the writer is not Cuban but Chilean and heterosexual rather than homosexual. Guillén's life is ever so briefly contrasted with that of Pablo Neruda who, in his memoirs *Confieso que he vivido* (1974) [*Memoirs* (1977)], had given the Cuban poet the nickname of "Guillén the bad," negatively comparing him with the then better-known Spanish poet Jorge Guillén. The fact that in *Mea Cuba* Cabrera Infante expands the allusions of the English version of 1990 to include Neruda is indicative of the author's constant rewriting to adapt the original piece to the section of the book where parallel lives are singled out. His continual rewriting also reveals an intent to sharpen the picture of Guillén as a frustrated writer and lover who followed the party line but was not able to achieve the success of his Chilean counterpart. Both Guillén and Neruda were nominated for the Nobel Prize, but only the Chilean received it. Although neither was homosexual, the Cuban's dwarf-like physical stature hindered his love life with the opposite sex, while the taller Nobel laureate was reputed to have had a long list of paramours.

The debunking of Carpentier is more poignant than that of Guillén. Cabrera Infante's objective in "Carpentier, Cubano a la Cañona" (*Mea Cuba* [1992], 370–88) ["Alejo Carpentier: A Shotgun Cuban" (*Mea Cuba* [1994], 383–99] is to systematically undermine what he considers to be the overblown reputation of a literary and political figure fabricated by Carpentier himself and by the huge propaganda machinery of the Cuban Revolution. Despite Cabrera Infante's claims of friendship with this "official" Cuban novelist, a careful reading of the sketch reveals that he is convinced that Carpentier was a fake as an author, as a person, and as a government bureaucrat. The author of *Mea Cuba* deftly manipulates a series of personal and professional facts to give credence to his argument. Not taking any chances at being misunderstood, he deconstructs Carpentier's physical characteristics, his intellectual acumen, and his professional comportment. Irony and contempt surround everything he writes about Carpentier the writer and Carpentier the person. He manipulates his firsthand knowledge of events surrounding Carpentier's life to belittle the author whom critics like Raymond D. Souza, for example, have referred to as the "dean of Cuban novelists."[8]

But Cabrera Infante had not always disputed Carpentier's literary legacy or taken sides in the squabbles about Carpentier's politics. In a review of Alfred MacAdam's translation of *El acoso* [*The Chase*] (1956) by Carpentier, Cabrera Infante is surprised that Carpentier is not better known in London. He quotes literary critics who have praised Carpentier's remarkable literary career, and he himself brags about his industry and the baroque style of his fellow compatriot:

> Architect, musician, novelist, Alejo Carpentier is a Cuban writer because he is utterly baroque: not in the sense of Borges (who said that baroque is the style that contains its own parody) but as a continuation of the Cuban writers of the nineteenth century such as José Martí, who thought language as opaque as a steamed window.[9]

As a matter of fact, Cabrera Infante's review says little about the merits of MacAdam's translation, but it is not shy in praising Carpentier's impeccably crafted original version, which he considers to be "one of the few perfect novellas in Spanish."

Cabrera Infante's praises are limited, in this piece at least, to Carpentier's literary production. In the review, he corrects a statement on the dust jacket of MacAdam's translation that attributes to Carpentier the creation of "magical realism." Cabrera Infante points out that "what Carpentier did originate, in his prologue to *El reino de este mundo* (1949) [*The Kingdom of this World* (1957)] (but omitted in the English and French editions), is 'the marvelous in the real.' " He goes on to say that Carpentier had borrowed the phrase "from a minor French surrealist who invited him to Haiti in 1943." He is right when he sets the record straight again concerning the origin of the two terms in question. It is pertinent to mention here that literary critics like Jean Franco, for example, routinely affirm that the term "magic realism" was coined by Carpentier in the late 1940s.[10] And it is also common practice to laud the prologue of *El reino de este mundo* as highly influential in broadcasting his notion of "the marvelous in the real," even though the novel itself has been deemed to be immature as a literary work. Whatever the case, the association of "magical realism" and "the marvelous in the real" with the author of *El acoso* initially brought an unusual amount of attention to his novelistic production—attention that Carpentier never seemed to have dismissed. In Cabrera Infante's initial questioning of the origin of these two terms, it is possible to see the beginning of a strategy to erode Carpentier's reputation as the dean of Cuban novelists. In *Mea Cuba,* Cabrera Infante goes on to prove the facts as he sees them and, after providing additional anecdotes in support of his assertions, concludes once and for all that "No ya el realismo mágico sino siquiera lo real maravilloso pertenecen a Carpentier" (*Mea Cuba* [1992], 374) ["No longer does magic realism or even the marvelous in the real belong to Carpentier" (*Mea Cuba* [1994], 386)].

The "facts" of Carpentier's personal life cannot be readily summarized. The little that is known comes mainly from the novelist's own recollection. Fully aware of the existing biographical lacunae and desirous of reducing his personal stature to naught, Cabrera Infante draws heavily from his own experience to recast Carpentier the man according to his vision. His approach clearly tends to diminish Carpentier, whom he sees almost as a tragic figure who supported the revolution for his own personal gains and not out of conviction. The image that emerges is clearly that of a trapped individual obsessed with his self-worth.

It is not surprising that Cabrera Infante manipulates to his advantage a series of little-known anecdotes surrounding the novelist's birth. He knows that there are no documents proving that Carpentier, the son of a Frenchman and a Russian woman, was born in Cuba. The author of "Carpentier, Cubano a la Cañona" believes that Carpentier was indeed not born in Cuba and that the "official" stories surrounding his childhood are nothing but self-serving tales created by the novelist's fertile imagination. To convince his readers, Cabrera Infante unearths a copy of a birth certificate issued in Switzerland that—he believes—proves his assertions that the "shotgun Cuban" is nothing but a fake:

> El documento desvelaba las múltiples y sucesivas invenciones de Carpentier por ser Alejo, por qué Lydia Cabrera, conocedora, lo llamaba siempre Alexis, por qué Alejo desplegó ese duradero rencor contra Padilla, el hombre que sabía demasiado, en Cambridge, y por qué Carpentier siempre había tomado a La Habana, como los ingleses, por un puerto de escala y, todavía más terrible, por qué se había comportado toda su vida tan mal con Cuba: cómo se había prestado a todas las canalladas para servir a dos amos, el comunismo y Castro, a quien debió tener por un usurpador pero era su embajador muchas veces extraordinario, usando su prestigio para un desprestigio. (*Mea Cuba* [1992], 387)

> [The document uncovered the multiple and successive inventions of Carpentier to be Alejo, why Lydia Cabrera, knowingly, always called him Alexis, why Alejo displayed that lasting rancour against Padilla (the man who knew too much) in Cambridge, and why Carpentier

> had always, like the English, taken Havana as a port of call and, still more terrible, why he had behaved so badly with Cuba all his life: how he had lent himself to every dirty trick to serve two masters, Communism and Castro, whom he must have seen as a usurper but was his ambassador extraordinary many times using his fame for an infamy. (*Mea Cuba* [1994], 398)]

Carpentier's reputation as a Cuban novelist will remain strong among intellectuals of opposing political convictions on both sides of the Atlantic. Guillén's poems will maintain their value as committed texts that capture the sorrow of the less fortunate. Arenas's brilliant account of his never-ending fight against a corrupt regime will also remain a part of literary history. And Lezama Lima's poetry and his *Paradiso,* as well as Piñera's plays and stories, will be read as masterpieces of an era when homosexual writers were savagely persecuted. That Cabrera Infante has been able to shuffle some of these reputations around is indicative of his resolve to combat the tyranny of efforts to render dissidents invisible and to aggrandize supporters. Despite the often burlesque tone of his sketches, he brings to light new sources of documentation that stress the destructive impact of the revolution on the Cuban people. The terseness of these mini-biographies is enriched by the confessional tone of a masterful storyteller.

Notes

1. José Lezama Lima (1910–1976) was a poet, novelist, essayist, and short-story writer. He was the intellectual leader of a generation of writers in Cuba. His works include *Muerte de Narciso* (1937), *Enemigo rumor* (1941), *Paradiso* (1966), and *Poesía completa* (1970). Virgilio Piñera Llera (1912–1979) was a novelist, short-story writer, playwright, poet, and literary critic. His works include *Electra Garrigó* (1943), *La carne de René* (1953), *Cuentos fríos* (1956), and *Dos viejos pánicos* (1968).

Reinaldo Arenas (1943–1990) was a novelist, short-story writer, and poet. His first novel *Celestino antes del alba* (1967) was published in Cuba, but his subsequent works had to be smuggled out and published elsewhere. Those works include *El mundo alucinante* (1969) and *El palacio de las blanquísimas mofetas* (1980). Nicolás Guillén (1902–1989) was a poet who received numerous nominations for the Nobel Prize in literature. His works include *Motivos de son* (1930), *Sóngoro Cosongo* (1931), *Páginas vueltas: Memorias* (1982), and *El libro de los sonetos* (1984). Alejo Carpentier (1904–1980) was a novelist, short-story writer, and essayist. His works include *Los pasos perdidos* (1953), *Guerra del tiempo* (1958) [*War of Time* (1970)], *Tientos y diferencias: Ensayos* (1964), and *El arpa y la sombra* (1979).

2. Guillermo Cabrera Infante, *Mea Cuba* (Barcelona: Plaza and Janés, 1992); *Mea Cuba,* trans. Kenneth Hall and Guillermo Cabrera Infante (New York: Farrar, Straus, Giroux, 1994); hereafter cited in the text.

3. Cabrera Infante, "Vidas para leerlas," *Vuelta* 4, 41 (April 1980): 4–16.

4. The "Night of the Three P's" took place in 1961. Cabrera Infante discusses this incident in "En espera del Piñera total," *El País* (26 December 1983): 3. Section: Libros.

5. Severo Sarduy (1937–1993) was a Cuban novelist, essayist, and poet. His works include *De donde son los cantantes* (1967) [*From Cuba with a Song* (1972)], *Escrito sobre un cuerpo: Ensayos de crítica* (1969), *Maitreya* (1978), and *Colibrí* (1984).

6. "Un poeta de vuelo popular," *Vuelta* 14, 160 (March 1990): 45–47.

7. "Nicolás Guillén: Poet and Partisan," *Review: Latin American Literature and Arts* 42 (January–June 1990): 31–33.

8. Raymond D. Souza, *Major Cuban Novelists: Innovation and Tradition* (Columbia: University of Missouri Press, 1976), 30.

9. "More haunted than hunted," review of *The Chase,* by Alejo Carpentier, trans. Alfred MacAdam, *Sunday Review,* supplement of the *Independent on Sunday* (London) (18 March 1990): 19.

10. Jean Franco, "Remapping Culture," in *Americas: New Interpretive Essays,* ed. Alfred Stepan. (New York: Oxford University Press, 1992), 179.

THE WRITER AS COMMENTATOR: ARTS, LEISURE, AND MEMOIRS

◆

On Buñuel and Surrealism: The Art of Audacity

ARDIS L. NELSON

Guillermo Cabrera Infante's notoriety in life and in literature can be traced to events in his youth that led to his audacious attitude and style of writing and link him with the surrealists. At the age of 22 he was thrown in jail for using English profanity in the short story "Balada de plomo y yerro" ["Ballad of Bullets and Bull's-Eyes"].[1] In 1965 he experienced the trauma of undesired exile and the offense of undeserved censorship and ostracism. His somewhat predictable life as an editor and film critic was transformed into the life of an exiled writer whose physical and emotional pain is translated into biting puns and who in turn seeks to unsettle his readers in the very spirit of the surrealists. Cabrera Infante's anti-Castro stance has made him unpopular in many circles. His works even elicited bomb threats in Mexico in 1995. His philosophy on life, liberty, and language shares some striking similarities with the surrealist filmmaker Luis Buñuel Portolés, the subject of several of Cabrera Infante's essays.

Cabrera Infante first met and interviewed Buñuel in 1957, when he could not have known that his life was about to follow a path similar to that of the Spanish director, then residing in Mexico. Both experienced the rejection and censure of their works in their homeland. Both have extolled the vices and virtues of beautiful women in their works. Both have had a keen interest in the literature of horror. And although they crossed the Atlantic in opposite directions, both chose to live in exile rather than under tyranny.

Their mothers not only were supportive of their career choices but also were instrumental in the initial stages of their careers. Cabrera Infante's mother, an avid moviegoer, took Guillermo to the cinema with her when he was but a babe in arms. He was brought up on movies, so to speak, and many of the adventures told in his novel

La Habana para un Infante difunto (1979) [*Infante's Inferno* (1984)] take place in movie theaters. This aspect of his upbringing served him well when he became a film critic, since, as he puts it, he had already done a lot of "research." Buñuel's mother helped finance his first film, the famous *Un Chien andalou* [An Andalusian Dog] (1928). In 1934 she lent him enough money to start coproducing commercial films with Ricardo Urgoiti in Spain. They made 18 films together, which overall were a financial success. Buñuel's name does not appear on the credits of any of these films, the main condition of their business arrangement. He did not want to be associated with second-rate melodramas.

Cabrera Infante hid his identity on some of his early writing but due to entirely different circumstances. Part of the sentence handed down to him for publishing obscenities, besides five days in jail and a two-year suspension from journalism school, was a prohibition from using his name on anything he wrote. It was at this point that he adopted the pseudonym G. Caín, as well as some less frequently used, such as Jonás Castro and S. del Pastora Niño.

In their youth, Cabrera Infante and Buñuel gave talks on films at the cinémathèque, which they had cofounded respectively in Havana and Madrid. They wrote film reviews and scripts and were directly involved with filmmaking. Buñuel had a nearly 20-year hiatus between his surrealist films and his Mexican films but then achieved fame, if not fortune, that extended over the rest of his life. Cabrera Infante has written 13 film scripts, but only 2 have come to fruition on the screen.

Evidence shows that Buñuel influenced Cabrera Infante in his attitude toward music in film and perhaps in his writing. In his 1957 interview with Buñuel, published as "El elefante de Buñuel" [Buñuel's elephant], there is a discussion about the disastrous effect of the excessive background music in Buñuel's *Abismos de pasión* [Wuthering Heights] (1954).[2] Buñuel attributed this problem to his departure for the Cannes Film Festival before the editing was completed, which meant the musical decisions were left to the composer, Raúl Lavista.

> Por otra parte, detesto la música en el cine. . . . Me he propuesto que mis próximas films no lleven comentario musical. La única música será la música como personaje: un radio que alguien conecta, una orquesta en un baile, una canción cantada. Música realista como se dice. Eso de utilizar la música para subrayar un sentimiento me parece deleznable, muy poco legítimo.

[Besides, I detest music in movies . . . I have promised myself that my next films will not have any musical commentary. The only music will be music as a character: a radio that someone turns on, an orchestra at a dance, a song that is sung. Realistic music you might say. The idea of using music to emphasize an emotion seems to me very weak and hardly legitimate.] ("Elefante," 42)

In *Vanishing Point* (1971) performed music and music played by a radio station disc jockey function as surreal or disembodied characters, an effect that Cabrera Infante may owe in part to Buñuel. Raymond D. Souza points out this feature of the film and cites from the foreword of the unpublished script:

Our intention is to create (or rather *to try*) a new form, the true *melo*-drama—a musical drama using pop songs as Wagner used opera. Thus the function of lyrics and tunes will be not only to comment on the action but to control it, and furthermore, to *generate* film action. . . . For instance, in all the sequences on the highway the car-radio will become a real though disembodied presence, all invisible "passengers" linking the driver to the remote DJ who is his guide through the maze of patrol cars, police forces, barricades.[3]

The likelihood of a Buñuelian influence is heightened by Cabrera Infante's mention here of Wagner as an example, since Wagner was used by Buñuel as the score for *Un Chien andalou* and *Abismos de pasión,* which made a favorable impression on Cabrera Infante ("Elefante," 44).

Cabrera Infante has often been quoted as saying that his writing is music in another form: *Tres tristes tigres* (1967) [*Three Trapped Tigers* (1971)] is a rhapsody, for example, and the real protagonist of his film script for "The Lost City" is music.[4] In the 1957 interview Buñuel said that the happy ending of his darkly humorous film *Ensayo de un crimen* [*The Criminal Life of Archibaldo de la Cruz*] (1955) was added because of the musical structure of this film: "Se trata de un *scherzo*" [It's a matter of a scherzo].

In contrast to Buñuel, who was practically deaf, Cabrera Infante loves to listen to music and is very conscious of the musical effects of his writing: "Music, all kinds of music is music to my ear and to my eyes and to my writing hands. When I write I always try to make the sentence, the phrase, and the word sound right to me. I of course pay more attention to sound than to sense. If the sound, the written sound, is right I don't particularly care about the sense. In fact, if there is no sense, more power to the prose. All it can become is nonsense" ("Wit and Wile," 28–29). Cabrera Infante's preference for sound over meaning betrays a kinship with the surrealists, who could care less for logic.

In *Man's Rage for Chaos* Morse Peckham suggests that art is a counterbalance to society's tendency to order, logic, and compartmentalizing. Art, especially surrealist art, provides the mind with a training ground for future challenges and disruptive influences. Cabrera Infante successfully takes on the role of jester as he transforms language into a high art.[5] His uncategorizable writing may shock the senses into a new way of perceiving reality, a transformation desired by the surrealists.

The idea of transformation goes back to ancient times, when alchemy was practiced. The purpose of the alchemical process was to transmute base metal lead into gold, but it was really a metaphor for the idea that mankind is capable of a perfectibility, developing from his base nature into something sublime, if not divine. The surrealists were cognizant of the goal of the alchemists and shared their belief in the perfectibility of mankind.[6] They sought to liberate the subconscious through startling visual and verbal metaphors created by "automatic writing"—uncensored spontaneous expression.

Among the precursors of surrealism were the romantic poets, who yearned for freedom and euphoria. What was to become the epitome of the surrealist metaphor was coined in the nineteenth century by Lautréamont, who described the image of "the fortuitous encounter of a sewing machine and an umbrella on a dissecting table." Freudian dream symbolism also influenced the surrealists, who relied heavily on their own dreams for self-expression, especially in the visual arts.

The use of surprise, or even shock, which originated with the dada movement (1916–1923), was adopted by the surrealists to *épater le bourgeoisie* [kick the bourgeoisie], to get the comfortable, apathetic citizen to see reality from a new perspective. The goal was *donner a voir* [to give sight]. *Amour fou* [mad love] was extolled. Passion was desirable and encouraged as a means of liberation from straightjacketed emotions and hypocritical moral restraint.

The French writer and poet André Bréton (1896–1966), who was active in the dadaist movement in Paris (1919–1921), founded the surrealist movement in 1924 with the publication of his *Surrealist Manifesto.* His writings are the most important theoretical statements of the surrealist movement and include *L'amour fou* [*Mad Love*] (1937) and *Nadja* (1928), a mystery dedicated to mad love. Bréton's circle of friends were creative thinkers and artists who shared a desire to live and love with great intensity, free from the constraints of societal norms and the mundane use of language. They met daily in Parisian cafés to expound upon their beliefs and discuss their projects and their dreams of achieving freedom through rebellion, revolt, and surprise.

In *On Surrealism in its Living Works* (1953) Bréton looks back at the surrealist movement and states that the point of it all was to revitalize language, to rescue it from its "increasingly utilitarian usage" and its "depreciation."[7] Language was viewed as the key to revolution, and several techniques were practiced as a means to achieve a realism above and beyond ordinary reality: *sur-reality.* Automatic writing was the attempt to write from the subconscious level, bypassing the logical mind. Through automatic writing, one has access to "the prime matter of language, . . . where desire arises unconstrained . . . [and] where myths take wing. . . . [In order to] bring language back to true life . . . the name must *germinate,* so to speak, or otherwise it is false" (299). Objective hazard was the term coined to describe the metaphor created by chance association and encounter. Dream images, based on Freudian psychology, were given more credence than ordinary reality. The paranoid-critical method, defined by Bréton as "the ultra-confusional activity that arises from an obsessive idea," was one of Salvador Dalí's contributions to the repertoire of surrealist techniques.[8] And black bile was their name for black humor, an irreverent, sinister humor that holds nothing sacred.

The surrealists wanted to change the world by showing the way to a new perception of reality, jolting the complacent into an awareness of the vibrant beauty of life—beauty was required to be "convulsive"—and into an awareness of the inequities of life suffered by the poor and unfortunate. Contrary to the generally accepted understanding that surrealism was an artistic movement, for the surrealists as expressed by Buñuel in "El elefante de Buñuel," "lo importante era la vida, la manera de ver al hombre, la libertad, el amor: la vida. El arte era un subproducto despreciable" [The important thing was life, the way of seeing man, liberty, love: life. Art was a despicable by-product](42).

The horror genre meshes well with the surrealist agenda, and perhaps this is why the surrealists were enamored of the silent film *Nosferatu* (Germany, 1922), the expressionistic film based on Bram Stoker's *Dracula* (1897). The shock effect of a hair-raising scene in a horror story, whether literary or cinematic, may bring to conscious awareness the ambivalent nature of man. As the characters confront the vampire, the werewolf, or Frankenstein's monster, the ordinary rules of life do not apply. Good and evil are no longer helpful categories for dealing with the reality at hand. The reader or viewer, faced with the paradox of good and evil, and of human potential and limitations, is shocked into a radical change in perspective.[9]

For the surrealists the motivating force behind transformation is desire, and it is here that the link between surrealism and the horror genre becomes clear. An essential ingredient in horror is the insinuation of passion and mad love taken to their illogical extremes. The juxtaposition of the human and the monstrous opens a Pandora's box of enigmas about the nature of man. The vampire's lust for eternal life is satisfied by drinking human blood. The werewolf metamorphoses from man to beast and back. Both creatures are doomed to eternal suffering in a limbo-like state, driven by uncontrollable passion. Frankenstein's monster is assembled by a man who wants to experience the godlike thrill of creation but subsequently is tortured by guilt because of the destruction his monster wreaks on the world.

According to James B. Twitchell, the subliminal message of the horror story teaches the young the consequences of sexual taboos, especially incest.[10] Linda Badley believes that "horror descends into primal fear and desire. It is a loss of ego in cellular chaos."[11] It is that elemental desire that the surrealists wanted to tap into. Bréton believed that man has been separated from his own desire and that he "could regain contact with his unconscious through words."[12] It is at this point that the relationship between the surrealists and the monster of the horror story comes into focus. The monster, as in the surrealist metaphor, is totally out of the reach of reason, thus requiring involvement on the part of the reader or viewer in order to make new connections, to learn something new.

Bréton describes the surrealist metaphor as resulting from "the fortuitous juxtaposition" of two terms from which "*the light of the image*" has sprung: "The value of the image depends upon the beauty of the spark obtained; it is, consequently, a function of the difference of potential between the two conductors. When the difference exists only slightly, as in a comparison, the spark is lacking." The terminology used here vividly brings to mind the creation of Frankenstein's monster and his other offspring, by electrical conductors that sparkle and fizz. These images from horror films even suggest Bréton's "invisible ray" of surrealism, as life is infused into creatures made up of body parts from a corpse.[13] In a literary context the two conductors would be two words or poetic images juxtaposed to create a surrealist metaphor.

Some of Cabrera Infante's earliest writing reveals his familiarity with surrealism and its origins. In a 1959 review he says that *Vertigo*

(1958) is the best Hitchcock movie he has ever seen and calls it "the first great surrealist film."[14] Indeed, he says that *Vertigo* is the only great surrealist film. He was so taken with the film and its magical play on time, memory, and mad love that he saw it three times. In *Vertigo* James Stewart plays the role of a man whose mad love leads him to "disaster, madness, and death." Kim Novak plays the role of both Madeleine and Judy, projecting "a morbid sensuality, decadent and at the same time highly attractive" (*Job,* 283). Cabrera Infante goes on to discuss three literary works prominent in the surrealist canon that he considers to have influenced Hitchcock in *Vertigo*: *Aurelia* (1932), an oneiric, hallucinatory tale by the French romantic writer Gerard de Nerval (1808–1855); *The Monk* (1796), a Gothic novel by the English novelist Matthew Gregory Lewis (1775–1818), translated into French by Antonin Artaud (Buñuel tried to adapt *The Monk* to film, but had to abandon the project for lack of a willing producer); and *Nadja* (1928), Bréton's mystery novel dedicated to mad love.

Buñuel was one of the most important figures in the surrealist movement of the twentieth-century. He was a practicing surrealist even before he met Bréton and the core group in 1929. In fact, it was because of his film *Un Chien andalou* that they met. The surrealists were the first to see the film and helped Buñuel arrange for its public showing.

Un Chien andalou was a joint endeavor of Buñuel and Dalí, made up of a series of dream images recalled by the two artists. Their aim was to shock the viewer, following Dalí's paranoid-critical technique, "the critical and systematic objectivization of delirious associations and interpretations" and to expose "the omnipotence of desire," one of the beliefs underlying all surrealist thought.[15] Concerned that the Parisian audience was not sufficiently outraged by the film itself, Buñuel added a preface to the film script published in two journals indicating that the film was "a desperate, impassioned call for murder. . . . Despite its success, many people complained to the police about its 'cruelty' and 'obscenity,' but this was only the beginning of a lifetime of threats and insults."[16]

Some of the insults came from his friend and collaborator Dalí, even before the filming of *Un Chien andalou*. Buñuel went to Dalí with an idea for making a surrealist film based on newspaper stories. Dalí adamantly rejected Buñuel's idea. Sixty years later Cabrera Infante vindicates Buñuel's original idea in his 1988 essay "Un perro murciano" [A Murcian Dog] by citing and commenting on a headline in *Diario 16*: "Un enfermo rasura el pubis de una mujer que iba a ser operada de la cabeza en Murcia" [Sick man shaves pubic hair of woman whose head was to be operated on in Murcia]. This headline elicits a surreal image from *Un Chien andalou*, that of pubic hair on the woman's underarm. Cabrera Infante supports Buñuel's idea by saying that "En España cada diario, cada día, es un guión de cine, siempre surreal" [In Spain every newspaper, every day, is a film script, always surreal].[17]

In "Manuscrito encontrado en una botella" ["Manuscript Found in a Bottle"] Cabrera Infante includes *Un Chien andalou* as one of the three great silent films of the world: "this anarchist, *nadaist* film is one of the indubitable, durable masterworks of the cinema." It has had a tremendous influence on other filmmakers, beginning with Alfred Hitchcock, Ingmar Bergman, and Roberto Rossellini. Cabrera Infante credits Buñuel with being an influence on Hitchcock's "technique of the latent shock" called "suspense." Bergman was influenced by the surrealist's nihilism, and the whole New Wave film movement was influenced by the aforementioned, according to Cabrera Infante (*Oficio*, 245–46; *Job,* 183).

For Cabrera Infante, all of Buñuel's films sprang "by spontaneous generation" (*Job,* 183) from the embryo of *Un Chien andalou* and *L'Age d'or* [The Golden Age] (1930). *L'Age d'or* was only the second or third sound film made in France, and it created a real scandal. After playing for six days to packed houses at the Studio 28 theater, on 3 December 1930 members of the Catholic Youth group, the Patriotic League, and the Anti-Jewish League "damaged the screen with oxide and ink, tore up the cinema seats, and destroyed the exhibition of surrealist painting that was being held in the foyer."[18] On 11 December the film was banned, the theater manager fined, and all copies of the film were seized the next day. *L'Age d'or* was not shown again for 50 years, when it played in New York City in 1980 and then in Paris in 1981.

Even though Buñuel and Dalí made *L'Age d'or* together, it was their last collaborative effort. Cabrera Infante presents Buñuel's description of his falling out with Dalí in the 1957 interview. He quotes Buñuel as saying that Dalí had nothing to do with the filming of *L'Age d'or:* "Dalí no intervino para nada en su filmación. Puse su nombre junto al mío por consideración al amigo y este regalo él lo recibió de buen grado" [Dalí was not involved in any way in the filming. I put his name next to mine out of consideration for my friend and he was very pleased with this gift] ("Elefante," 43). Years later Dalí repaid Buñuel by defaming him in his autobiography, claiming that Buñuel did not share his awe and obsession with Catholicism.

Rather, "Buñuel, con ingenuidad y tozudería aragonesa, desvió todo esto hacia un anticlericalismo elemental. Tenía siempre que detenerle" [Buñuel, with ingenuousness and Aragonese obstinacy, diverted all this towards an elemental anticlericalism. I always had to hold him back] ("Elefante," 43). In the McCarthy era of the 1950s anything close to atheism could be construed as communism, so Buñuel was forced to resign from his job at the Museum of Modern Art in New York City. In a 1988 essay Cabrera Infante cites Dalí's defamation of Buñuel to support his own critique of *L'Age d'or* "por poco católica cuando sólo era caótica" [for barely being catholic when it was only chaotic] ("Un perro murciano" [A Murcian dog] 46).

Buñuel is not included in *Arcadia todas las noches* [Arcadia every night] (1978), Cabrera Infante's book of essays on five directors, yet Cabrera Infante was favorably impressed by some of Buñuel's Mexican films. *El* [*This Strange Passion*] (1953) is on the list of G. Caín's 12 most important films in "Manuscrito encontrado en una botella" (*Oficio,* 243) ["Manuscript Found in a Bottle" (*Job,* 181)]. Although there is no known review of this film by Caín, he does state that "un gran maestro toma a Freud por las barbas y le muestra el bien que puede hacer la paranoia" (*Oficio,* 243) [A great master pulls Freud's whiskers and shows him all the good that paranoia can do (*Job,* 181)].

Cabrera Infante's early work belies more than a passing fancy for surrealist ideology. In "El absurdo se muerde las colas" (*Oficio,* 41–45) ["The absurd eating the absurd" (*Job,* 24–27)] his sentiments about "la perversión de los oficios" [the perversion of jobs] echo the surrealists' attack on the bourgeois ideal of work as sacred: "Si la Revolución francesa nos trajo el fin de la artesanía, las revoluciones de este siglo de revoluciones verán el fin de los oficios" (*Oficio,* 41) [If the French Revolution brought us the end of artisanry, the revolutions of this century of revolutions will see the end of jobs (*Job,* 24).] Cabrera Infante then lists three pages of professions in chaotic enumeration.

The surrealists held the work ethic to be a false and enslaving deception promoted by those with money and power. Buñuel incorporates this rebellious attitude in his film *Tristana* (1970) based on the Benito Pérez Galdós novel of the same title in the character of Don Lope, who refuses to work: "I say to hell with the work you have to do to earn a living! . . . But the work you do because you like to do it, because you've heard the call, you've got a vocation—that's ennobling! We should all be able to work like that. Look at me, Saturno—I don't work. And I don't care if they hang me, I *won't* work!

Yet I'm alive! I may live badly, but at least I don't have to work to do it!" (*My Last Sigh,* 123–24). Buñuel puts a surrealist twist on his films whenever possible. In this case he changed Galdós's critique of laziness to praise.

The rejection of the puritan work ethic is but one product of the self-imposed moral imperative of Buñuel and Cabrera Infante. They are intransigent against fanaticism of any kind, including communism. Cabrera Infante expressed his admiration for Buñuel's political views in his obituary for the filmmaker, whom he calls "un wespañol sin fronteras, . . . era no un ácrata a la moda, sino un verdadero anarquista, y su arte iba dirigido a subvertir todas las ideologías, sean de izquierda o de derecha. . . . Buñuel quería decir, quiere decir, ser sordo a los ayes de todo poder, por poder, por joder" [a West-Spaniard without frontiers, he was not just a rebel without a cause, but a true anarchist, and his art was directed toward the subversion of all ideologies, both left and right. . . . Buñuel wanted to say, wants to say, be deaf to all the yes-men of power, for power, for perversity].[19]

Buñuel attributes his moral foundation to the realization gained through his experience with surrealism of "the profound conflict between the prevailing moral code and my own personal morality, born of instinct and experience. . . . More than the artistic innovations or the refinement of my tastes and ideas, the aspect of surrealism that has remained a part of me all these years is a clear and inviolate moral exigency" (*My Last Sigh,* 124). Cabrera Infante's extreme honesty, in his own words "a compulsion to tell all," may be interpreted as his moral exigency. "I tell the truth in spite of myself—even if it will cost me dearly" (see the interview with Suzanne Jill Levine in this volume). For Cabrera Infante, the pain of leaving Cuba was so great that he eventually made his views public in an interview published in the Argentine magazine *Primera Plana* (5 August 1968). Despite the fact that speaking out against Castro was not in vogue in the 1960s, Cabrera Infante was forthright about his October 1965 escape from an increasingly totalitarian Cuba. Consequently he suffered personal and professional ostracism. His anti-Castro confession halted further printings of *Tres tristes tigres* until 1970, when his Spanish publisher Carlos Barral retired. To this day, many consider Cabrera Infante politically incorrect as he continues to denounce Castro's betrayal of the Cuban people.

In the early days of the Cuban revolution (1959) Buñuel was at a stage in his life where he felt a longing for Cuba. He had never been to Cuba, but his father had lived there for many years and owned a hardware store. Buñuel was excited about the possibility of shooting his new film *Los náufragos de la calle Providencia* [Shipwrecked on Providence Street] in Cuba. Cabrera Infante, a member of the ICAIC [Cuban Film Institute], supported the idea wholeheartedly, but Alfredo Guevara, the director of ICAIC, turned the project down. He considered the film script an apology for the bourgeoisie. Clearly Guevara did not understand surrealism or the thrust of Buñuel's work. By the time the film was premiered in Mexico City it had been renamed *El ángel exterminador* [*Exterminating Angel*] (1962) and was one of the most devastating attacks on the sterility of the bourgeoisie ever filmed.[20]

Cabrera Infante traveled to Mexico City to interview Buñuel in 1957. He turned the experience into a story as well as an interview, which he published in *Carteles* as "El elefante de Buñuel." In the story he recounts that, while waiting in a car for Buñuel's producer Manuel Barbachano Ponce to arrange the interview with the filmmaker, he hears two or three gunshots in the distance. He later discovers that a neighborhood policeman had acted on an impulse, resulting in the death of a six-year-old girl. This anecdote recalls the dadaist concept of random acts, such as a man entering a public place with a gun and firing indiscriminately into the crowd.

The reader begins to doubt the veracity of the story included in Cabrera Infante's preface to his interview with Buñuel, not only because of what comes later in the article, but also because in his subsequent essays on Buñuel there is a different version of that evening's events. At the end of "El elefante de Buñuel," for example, there is a separate column dedicated to Buñuel's comments on a film he hopes to make in the near future, entitled *Ilegible, hijo de flauta* [Illegible, son of a flute]. In the script a policeman commits suicide, his death symbolizing the freeing of the creative imagination from the censure and repression of human consciousness. Cabrera Infante suggests a connection between the above anecdote about the policeman shooting a six-year-old girl and the film script Buñuel is writing.

In "Buñuel al desnudo" [Buñuel in the nude] (1983), however, the story takes a different turn. This time Cabrera Infante enters the house with Barbachano Ponce and in an inner sanctum they find Buñuel completely nude, doing target practice with a pistol, a pastime he says he inherited from Alfred Jarry, "su antepasado dramático y antiguo artífice de la agresión purificadora. Las balas para Buñuel, más que una solución, eran una absolución" [his dramatic ancestor and ancient artifice of purifying aggression. Bullets for Buñuel, more than a solution, were an absolution] ("Buñuel al desnudo," 23). Is this scenario an exercise in poetic license, or is it prudence on the part of Cabrera Infante, who waited until the death of the filmmaker to reveal that Buñuel did target practice in the nude? In "Un perro murciano" Cabrera Infante indicates that he met Buñuel two times: the first time was the 1957 interview and the second time was at his house, where Buñuel was doing target practice in his garage.

In "Buñuel al desnudo," written as an obituary, Cabrera Infante lauds Buñuel's sense of humor, which ranged from the surrealist black humor of *El* and *Ensayo de un crimen* to a more playful humor displayed in his daily life. In the 1957 interview, for example, he noticed that Buñuel heard the questions he wanted to respond to but could not hear the ones that he did not like. His 1983 essay recounts an incident that took place on the set of *Nazarín*. Buñuel had hired the Spanish actor Paco Rabal to play the role of Nazarín but wanted him to sound like a Mexican, so he hired an expert in Spanish pronunciation to prompt Rabal. One day the expert complained to Buñuel that Rabal was speaking with the *ces* and *zetas* of Castillian Spanish. Buñuel put his hand to his ear with the usual "¿Cómo dice?" [What's that?] but then followed it with: "¿Y qué quiere que haga? ¿Usted no ve que Rabal es español? ¿Con qué acento va a hablar? ¿De Veracruz?" [And what do you want me to do? Don't you see that Rabal is Spanish? With what accent is he going to speak? From Veracruz?]

Cabrera Infante then follows through with the theme of ears, comparing Buñuel with Francisco de Goya and Vincent Van Gogh: "Desde los días de Goya, no ha habido un sordo más oído en las artes visuales. De cierta manera la oreja de Buñuel, siempre la misma, era como la oreja de Van Gogh, pero todavía en funciones. . . . Buñuel, es evidente, no tenía oído: tenía oreja" [Since the days of Goya, there has not been a deaf man heard as much in the visual arts. In a way Buñuel's ear, always the same, was like Van Gogh's ear, but still functioning. . . . Buñuel clearly couldn't hear: he had an ear] ("Buñuel al desnudo," 23).

Cabrera Infante admired the rebel Buñuel and the surrealists, with whom he shared the perversity of finding a certain delight in the macabre. Buñuel had hoped to make a film one day based on the Gothic novel *The Monk*, but he was unable to realize that dream. Monster-like characters made their way into Buñuel's films, albeit without a physical metamorphosis. Cabrera Infante pays tribute to the horror genre in his short story "The Phantom of the Essoldo" (1983) and in the essays on horror literature and film discussed in this chapter.[21] It is via the literature of horror that Cabrera Infante is finally able to exorcise his demons.

Cabrera Infante's writing on the horrific began in 1978 with "La vuelta de Jack el Destripador" [The Return of Jack the Ripper], in which he details what is known of the history of the man who committed an infamous series of murders in 1888.[22] This essay was prompted by a series of more recent murders committed in London in the 1970s. Another retrospective essay published that year, "Vuelve Drácula" [Dracula returns], chronicles the history of Dracula in legend, literature, and film.[23] Petronius's *Satyricon,* perhaps the earliest literary influence on Cabrera Infante, contains a werewolf story that Cabrera Infante describes in detail years later in his 1987 essay "Lobos, licántropos y manía lupina" [Wolves, werewolves, and lupine mania].[24] It seems that this essay was prompted by a real-life event in London: a man who believes he is a wolf is brought into the police station by a prostitute. Cabrera Infante takes advantage of this news item to combine a discussion of ancient literature and folklore with a current event, turning what would be a journalistic report into a punning parody, the adventure of an idea: man metamorphosizes into beast.

The lengthy essay chronicles the history of lycanthropy beginning with Plato and its early literary appearances, such as in *The Thousand and One Nights,* and critiques some of the better known filmic versions, such as *Dr. Jekyll and Mr. Hyde* (1941), *The Wolfman* (1941), and *An American Werewolf in London* (1981). Referring to Oscar Wilde's pronouncement that nature always imitates art, Cabrera Infante adds that nature also imitates the movies. An article in the *Independent* entitled "The Hallucination of Lycanthropy" covers the story of "the wolf-man of Essex." This final segment of Cabrera Infante's essay mixes the surrealist headline with a fictionalized commentary by a local psychoanalyst frustrated by his repeatedly failed attempts to light a pipe during the talk. Cabrera Infante's interjections add humor to the already absurd situation: the prostitute who brought in the wolf-man said, "gruñía y aullaba, cosa curiosa, sin auxilio del sexo" [he growled and howled, strangely, without having sex] ("Lobos," 181). Cabrera Infante comments to the analyst that prostitutes were called *lobas* [wolves] by the Romans. He notes that lycanthropy is no longer a crime and that the woman was also released, "aunque se le podría acusar de comercio carnal con bestias" [although she could be accused of carnal commerce with beasts] ("Lobos," 181).

Cabrera Infante's essays on werewolves and the Dr. Jekyll and Mr. Hyde variation on this theme began in 1986 on the occasion of the 100-year anniversary of the publication of Robert Louis Stevenson's *The Strange Case of Dr. Jekyll and Mr. Hyde* (1886). In "Centenario del Dr. Jekyll y Mr. Hyde" Javier Marías writes on "Esencial de Jekyll" [The Essential Jekyll] and Cabrera Infante writes on "Formal de Hyde," a play on the word "formaldehyde," referring to the lab in which Hyde was created.[25]

In "Formal de Hyde" Cabrera Infante describes the monster that has subsequently inspired more than 20 cinematic versions. In his literary analysis he notes that "[la] capacidad de narrar pertenece solo a los caballeros" [only gentlemen are capable of narrating/writing] (31), while Hyde is the evil force without a voice that all the other characters are trying to exorcise. His critique focuses on the lack of humor in the text and includes the wry observation that not enough description is given even to provide a make-up technician instructions for recreating Mr. Hyde on stage. He finds only one example of wordplay, which provides "el único alivio verbal de un libro tenebroso" [the only verbal relief in a dark book] (31), when Utterson says: "If be [*sic*] Dr. De Hyde, I shall be Mr. Seek."

Cabrera Infante also discovers and plays on a parallel between Stevenson's characters and his relationship with the Argentine master Jorge Luis Borges. Part of a writer's development involves the breaking away from the influences of the parent/creator, portrayed in the extremely violent sadism of Mr. Hyde toward his creator Dr. Jekyll.[26] Cabrera Infante sees the relevance of this mythic theme in his own life and accordingly makes fun of Borges's comments on Hyde as being limited and defective.[27] Cabrera Infante says that Borges does not understand Hyde, as Borges refers to him as "an odd writer" (32), when Cabrera Infante has just indicated that Hyde is the only character in the novel who does not narrate, rather he is referred to in the third person.

The climax of "Formal de Hyde" gives a fictionalized twist to the incident previously told in "Borges y yo" [Borges and I].[28] As Cabrera Infante and Borges take an evening stroll by Berkeley Square, Cabrera Infante suddenly notices some physical changes in his hand, exactly like those of Mr. Hyde as described by Dr. Jekyll:

> observo que en la mano que lleva al poeta del brazo se ha producido un cambio, un temblor y siento que mis tendones sobresalen de la piel y mi brazo habitualmente lampiño se cubre con profusos pelos. . . . A mis labios viene una canción como inspirada por un

> trago amargo y liberador. ¿Ha cambiado mi cara? Nadie puede verla."
>
> [I observe that my hand that leads the poet by the arm has changed, it trembles, and I feel that my tendons are jumping out of my skin and my normally clean arm is covered with a profusion of hair. . . . A song comes to my lips inspired by a bitter and liberating drink. Has my face changed? No one can see it.] ("Formal de Hyde," 32)

The drink refers to the potion that Dr. Jekyll created over many years of experimentation in order to liberate a second self in his desire to be free from the imperfections and emotions suffered by humans.

By equating Dr. Jekyll with Borges and Hyde with himself, Cabrera Infante writes his own horror story, complete with a surrealist metamorphosis from man to beast. The transformed Cabrera Infante leaves Borges alone in the middle of the busy street and retreats to the safety of the sidewalk: "Entre las sombras me escondo para poder ver mi desatino y su destino. Somos ahora una sola invención" [I hide among the shadows to be able to see my wildness and his destiny. Now we are one single invention] (32). Whereas in the earlier essay, "Borges y yo," Cabrera Infante was testing Borges to find out whether or not he is truly blind, in this essay he has identified the pair as Jekyll and Hyde in a graphic depiction of wishful deicide. Little does he know that if Jekyll is killed, Hyde too will die. Hyde and Cabrera Infante want to be liberated from the constraints of their respective creators, the bourgeois doctor Jekyll/Borges, generator of the new Latin American Narrative. The desire for transformation and liberation is at the core of the horror genre and surrealism, and these values are espoused by both Buñuel and Cabrera Infante, each in his chosen medium.

At the time of the 1957 interview, "El elefante de Buñuel," Cabrera Infante did not have an in-depth understanding of Buñuel's charisma and intellectual rigor, having seen only those Buñuel films that had been shown in Havana. Three years after his interview with Buñuel, Cabrera Infante wrote a review of *Nazarín* (1959), a film based on the nineteenth-century Spanish novel of the same title by Benito Pérez Galdós.[29] By then Cabrera Infante had seen most of Buñuel's films. Nazarín is a country priest who lives the Christian ideal to such an extreme that he has lost touch with reality. He is so kind, generous, and altruistic that the church fathers disdain him and the locals do not take him seriously. Instead of helping others, as he truly desires, he creates havoc in the lives of all those whose paths he crosses. He begs for alms and follows the moral principles of the church, but when he lands in jail and is mistreated even by common criminals, he begins to understand that his cherished beliefs have imprisoned him and robbed him of his humanity.

In his analysis of the film, Cabrera Infante asserts that when Nazarín hesitates and then decides to accept the gift of a pineapple from a fruit vendor in the final scene, he has become a true rebel, for he has acted in a conscious manner for the first time. "Es un toque genial de Buñuel haber transformado al anticlericalismo español del siglo XIX en un real problema de duda y negación de los valores cristianos, pasando el original que Galdós mantenía en la casuística, al plano de la teología" (*Oficio,* 414) [It is a brilliant touch of Buñuel's to have transformed the Spanish anti-clericalism of the nineteenth-century into a real problem of doubt and negation of all Christian values, moving the original that Galdós confined to mere casuistry to the level of theology (*Job,* 317)].

We see the surrealist influence in *Nazarín,* in its antireligion, indeed, antiestablishment stance. Cabrera Infante calls *Nazarín* "the first philosophical film" (*Job,* 318) and a masterpiece due to the ambiguity of its message. He also suggests a Freudian interpretation of Nazarín's excessive piety and messianic character as the sublimation of a compulsive neurosis, a nod to the surrealists' love affair with Freud.

Buñuel's films span five decades, from *Un Chien andalou* (1928) to *That Obscure Object of Desire* (1977). His last film ends with an explosion in a shop window as the couple walks away, satisfying the surrealist desire to "blow up reality" (*My Last Sigh*, 108). Cabrera Infante's interest in Buñuel spans 33 years, from the early film reviews of the 1950s to "Un perro murciano" in 1988. The 1957 interview is pivotal in understanding Cabrera Infante's relationship with Buñuel and surrealism. The title of that interview was inspired by the surrealist proverb "Elephants are contagious" and presents Buñuel as a figure who was as surreal in his life as in his films. The proverb juxtaposes two incongruous elements or "conductors," creating a mental "sparkle and fizz" that plays on our ideas about elephants and contagion. By making a metaphor that juxtaposes Buñuel and an elephant, Cabrera Infante intimates that Buñuel would make a lasting impression on him.

Buñuel shared with Cabrera Infante his love for wordplay when he showed him surreal headlines from the daily paper in 1957, still toying nearly 30 years later with his original idea for *Un Chien andalou*. One of the headlines that day was "Un Venado y un Cocodrilo chocan en Reforma" [A deer and a crocodile crash on Reform] ("Buñuel al desnudo," 23). The mundane interpretation is that two taxis collided on Reform Avenue, but without knowing that the names refer to taxis and a street, the headline conjures up a surreal image.

Cabrera Infante acknowledges his debt to Buñuel and surrealism in the titles of his essays and books. His last essay on Buñuel, "Un perro murciano"—literally a dog from the province of Murcia—is a play on the title of Buñuel's first film, *Un Chien andalou* [An Andalusian dog], thus bringing a cycle to completion. Cabrera Infante ends his last essay on Buñuel on a positive note, to the effect that Buñuel and his films give us "simplicidad y un discreto encanto que no pasa de moda" [simplicity and a discreet charm that doesn't go out of style], an homage to Buñuel's film *Le charme discret de la bourgeoisie* [The Discreet Charm of the Bourgeoisie] (France, 1972). He closes with a disclaimer that his impressions are not a hostile homage, "sino una celebración del arte de la fuga hacia el arte de Luis Buñuel" [but rather a celebration of Buñuel's art of the flight toward art]. His loyalty remains with Buñuel, and he closes with "Ustedes creen que diría estas cosas de Dalí?" [Do you all think I would say these things about Dalí?] ("Un perro," 48).

The one Buñuel film that came close to being shot in Cuba was *El ángel exterminador*. Despite its renown for stripping away the facade of bourgeois sophistication, Cabrera Infante is pointed in his criticism, intimating that Dalí's grace is lacking in the film. But Cabrera Infante is no longer just an audacious film critic; he is the angel exterminator of language.

Notes

1. *Bohemia* (Havana) 44, 22 (19 October 1952): 23, 24, 127–29; and in *Writes of Passage*, trans. John Brookesmith, Peggy Bowers, and Guillermo Cabrera Infante (London: Faber and Faber, 1993), 84–96.

2. Buñuel, in an interview with G. Caín, "El elefante de Buñuel" [Buñuel's elephant], *Carteles* 38, 21 (26 May 1957): 42; hereafter cited in the text as "Elefante." Translations of materials not yet published in English are by Ardis L. Nelson. Cabrera Infante's writing on Luis Buñuel began in 1955 with a film review of *Robinson Crusoe* (1952), a brief essay that begins with a long quote from Buñuel cited from *Cahiers du Cinema* on what he considers to be the subject of the film: the absence of love or friendship. This review was written originally for *Carteles* 36, 40 (2 October 1955): 42, and is entitled "Una isla llamada Buñuel" in *Un oficio del siglo veinte* (Havana: Ediciones R, 1963), 80 (hereafter cited in the text as *Oficio*), and "An

Island Called Buñuel" in *A Twentieth Century Job,* trans. Kenneth Hall and Guillermo Cabrera Infante (London: Faber and Faber, 1991), 56 (hereafter cited in the text as *Job*). His praise of "this more than excellent adaptation" of the Daniel Defoe novel is rather tongue-in-cheek, exposing his limited knowledge by saying that it "seems to be the only movie agreeable to the senses made by the teratological director of *Un Chien andalou*" (*Job,* 56).

Cabrera Infante also saw *Subida al cielo* [Mexican bus ride] (1952) and *La ilusión viaja en tranvía* [Illusion travels by streetcar] (1954). He next reviewed *Ensayo de un crimen* [The criminal life of Archibaldo de la Cruz] (1955) based on a work by the Mexican playwright Rodolfo Usigli. He considered this film the best of what he had seen of Buñuel so far. For Cabrera Infante *Ensayo de un crimen* is a humorous spoof on a Freudian interpretation of the effects of childhood trauma. He sees the film as an opportunity for Buñuel to showcase some of his surrealistic techniques such as "la sorpresa gratuita" [gratuitous surprise], sadism, and fetishes. This review was written originally for *Carteles* 37, 22 (27 May 1956): 42 and is entitled "Divertimento Macabro" both in *Oficio,* 105–6, and in *Job,* 74–75.

3. Raymond D. Souza, *Guillermo Cabrera Infante: Two Islands, Many Worlds* (Austin: University of Texas Press, 1996), 112.

4. Suzanne Jill Levine, "Wit and Wile with Guillermo Cabrera Infante," *Américas* 47, 4 (1995): 29; hereafter cited in the text as "Wit and Wile."

5. Morse Peckham, *Man's Rage for Chaos: Biology, Behavior, and the Arts* (New York: Schocken Books, 1967). The idea of "interartistical" references in Cabrera Infante's *Exorcismos de esti(l)o* is developed by Rosemary Geisdorfer Feal in her essay "The Duchamp Effect: G. Cabrera Infante and Readymade Art," *Criticism: A Quarterly for Literature and the Arts* 31, 4 (Fall 1989): 402.

6. Inez Hedges has investigated both the surrealists' and Carl Gustav Jung's debt to alchemy in *Languages of Revolt: Dada and Surrealist Literature and Film* (Durham, N.C.: Duke University Press, 1983).

7. André Bréton, *Manifestoes of Surrealism,* trans. Richard Seaver and Helen R. Lane (Ann Arbor: University of Michigan Press, 1969), 297.

8. Freddy Buache, *The Cinema of Luis Buñuel,* trans. Peter Graham, International Film Guide Series (New York: A. S. Barnes and Co., 1973), 9.

9. Kirk J. Schneider in *Horror and the Holy: Wisdom-Teachings of the Monster Tale* (Chicago: Open Court, 1993) argues that "[e]vil, as conceived by classic horror, then, is the inability to *handle* constrictive or expansive endlessness; it is not the endlessness itself" (130).

10. James B. Twitchell, *Dreadful Pleasures: An Anatomy of Modern Horror* (New York: Oxford University Press, 1985).

11. Linda Badley, *Film Horror, and the Body Fantastic,* Contributions to the Study of Popular Culture, no. 48 (Westport, Conn.: Greenwood Press, 1995), 10.

12. Hedges, *Languages of Revolt*, 83.

13. Bréton, *Manifestoes*, 37, 47.

14. *Job,* 279. G. Caín's review of *Vertigo,* originally written 15 November 1959, was entitled "De entre los muertos" (*Oficio,* 364–72) ["In Search of Long Lost Love" (*Job,* 278–84)].

15. Buache, *Cinema*, 9.

16. Luis Buñuel, *My Last Sigh: The Autobiography of Luis Buñuel,* trans. Abigail Israel (New York: Random House, Vintage Books, 1984), 108; hereafter cited in the text as *My Last Sigh.*

17. Guillermo Cabrera Infante, "Un perro murciano" [A Murcian dog], *Cambio 16* 873 (22 August 1988): 46–48; quote is from p. 46.

18. Buache, *Cinema*, 23.

19. "Buñuel al desnudo" [Buñuel in the nude], *El País* (1 August 1983): 23.

20. The scenario for this film was suggested by the unpublished play *Los náufragos* by José Bergamín. Cabrera Infante has suggested that some other considerations may have been the real reason behind Guevara's short-sighted decision. There had been a falling out between Guevara and Manuel Barbachano Ponce, who was to be the producer of this venture, with regard to the Havana branch of Barbachano's magazine *Cine revista* [Film Review]. In addition, Buñuel's political views were considered to be too iconoclastic for the new revolutionary Cuba (Cabrera Infante, telephone interview by the author, 23 August 1997).

21. Guillermo Cabrera Infante, "The Phantom of the Essoldo," 108–43, *London Tales*, ed. Julian Evans (London: Hamish Hamilton, 1983).

22. *El País* (19 March 1978): 34–36.

23. *El País Semanal* (3 December 1978): 1–8.

24. Titus Petronius Niger, also known as the emperor Nero's "arbiter of excellence," was a governor and poet. Guillermo Cabrera Infante, "Lobos, licántropos y manía lupina," *Cambio 16* 829 (19 October 1987): 178–81; hereafter cited in the text as "Lobos."

25. *El Urogallo* 8 (December 1986): 29–32.

26. See Carlos Cuadra's analysis of "the anxiety of influence" between Cabrera Infante and Borges in "The Man Who Knew Too Much" in this volume.

27. While Borges complains of Hyde's having negroid traits in the cinematic versions, Cabrera Infante counters that this characteristic was suggested in the text.

28. Cabrera Infante, "Borges y yo," *El País* (16 June 1986): 34. For a discussion and analysis of this essay, see Cuadra's, "On Borges: The Man Who Knew Too Much."

29. Cabrera Infante's review of *Nazarín* (1959) was written originally for *Carteles* 41, 29 (17 July 1960):26–28 and is entitled "Buñuel, la caridad y el cristo que ríe" (*Oficio,* 412–25) and "Buñuel, Charity and the Christ Who Laughs" (*Job,* 316–18).

Up in Smoke

REGINA JANES

They order, said I, these matters better in France.
—Laurence Sterne, *A Sentimental Journey*

Cigars can be a metaphor, you know.
—Guillermo Cabrera Infante, *Holy Smoke*

In the rainy winter of 1996–1997, readying André Malraux for the Pantheon, the French authorities changed his image for the sake of example and public health. Malraux smoking would henceforth appear *sans* cigarette. The peculiar curve of the fingers, the hunch of back and shoulder, the slant of the head surrendered their meaning to the airbrush of good intentions. A decade earlier, Guillermo Cabrera Infante's *Holy Smoke* (1985) had celebrated tobacco, the cigar, the curl of smoke in the air. Then even the French reformed. Is it Cabrera Infante's *métier* to make us miss something that was bad for us when we had it, whether smoking or youth or Batista's U.S.-saturated Cuba? In the Pyrrhic triumph of imagination over reality we find ourselves permanently impoverished by the absence of something we don't want back.

Holy Smoke was the first book Cabrera Infante wrote in English, without a prior excursion through Spanish. It begins—where else?—at the movies, meandering a little uncertainly, until Frankenstein's monster puffs, a connoisseur: " 'Good! *Good.*' That, even among corpses, is *savoir vivre.*"[1] Through life, through death, through English into French, circling around the manly Havana no longer made in Havana, languages and cultures intersect, collaborate, and disappear. Quintessential Cabrera Infante, *Holy Smoke* gives us the fifth element, neither earth, air, fire, nor water, but smoke. Deliberately weightless, the work nevertheless sums up Cabrera Infante's career and shows more clearly than even the major fictions—though not without their assistance and pressure—where the trajectory of exile has brought him.

Although *Holy Smoke* has not received a great deal of critical attention, the attention it has received has been astute and valuable. Ardis L. Nelson addresses the problem of genre—what kind of book is this?—and locates the work in the tradition of Menippean satire, the olio or stew that contains something of everything for everyone. (As detractors such as John Updike demonstrate, the downside of something for everyone is not enough of one thing for some. Let them read Updike.) Applying Mikhail Bakhtin's analysis of Menippean satire as a dialogic form, Nelson observes the work's oxymoronic construction, its mingling of genres, times, languages, narrative voices, and tones, its replacement by verbal play and impish commentary of character and plot development, its secure position among the "anatomies" of a subject or an obsession.[2] Kenneth Hall, focusing on the figure of the dandy, remarks that *Holy Smoke* shares both its aesthetic and its nostalgia with *Tres tristes tigres* (1967) [*Three Trapped Tigers* (1971)] and *La Habana para un Infante difunto* (1979) [*Infante's Inferno* (1984)].[3] Antonio Prieto Taboada makes an important question of a fact Anglophone readers take for granted—that the book is written in English. What does it mean for Cuba or the Cuban exile community that its principal literary spokesman has shifted not only his citizenship but his language to English?[4]

As such observations suggest, *Holy Smoke* is a *summum* of displacements. A silly English exclamation (holy smoke!) displaces a silly Spanish tongue twister (tres tristes tigres, tree-tired tigers?); a cigar displaces the phallic activity of *La Habana para un Infante difunto* (a woman is only a woman, but a good cigar is a smoke); another Cuba burns, another Havana disappears into memory. Cabrera Infante has described the book as an "autobiography written in smoke."[5] Since for Cabrera Infante autobiography is always the displaced cultural history of Havana in the 1950s and 1960s, Havana is now a cigar. In the cigar, his Havana has become portable and gone into exile. The shift to English is also a product of exile. If the ratio of English to Spanish inverts *Tres tristes tigres,* the movement into English is neither permanent nor stable. The last words and the initial—at least ostensible—inspiration of the book are French. In a third language the text spins away from the political and cultural opposition posited by the contention between English and Spanish to take up a momentary finality in French, in literature. The last words of the text are those of a French poem, but they do not last as last words.

The final fade-out on Stéphane Mallarmé lasts only until the credits begin. Contrary to bibliographic convention, Cabrera Infante's acknowledgments do not come at the beginning, tucked on a verso in very small print, the way acknowledgments and permissions in a book always appear. Instead, they are inserted at the end, after the final scene, and run forever, like credits in a modern movie. Then the lights go up, but not before the publisher has promised to insert corrections "in the next edition of this volume" (329). Unlike the "ya no se puede mas" [can't go no further] that ends *Tres tristes tigres,* this book achieves the bookish equivalent of a movie's "función continua," the "continuous showing" of *La Habana para un Infante difunto.*[6] A new edition promises an afterlife of repetition with variation: play it again, Sam. So if *Holy Smoke* begins at the movies and ends in a poem, it displaces its literary acknowledgments to make itself end more like a movie. Yet what makes it most like a movie is a promise that can be made only in a book. Thus the text slips back and forth, like its punning, in its playfulness, sometimes fuming, never quite exploding. These cigars are to be enjoyed. Meanwhile, interpretation is the project of finding shapes in the smoke rings—very like a camel (Camel?), very like a whale.

Critics, reviewers, and jacket blurbs alike tell us that *Holy Smoke* is about tobacco, or the weed, or the cigar. Among his predecessors, Cabrera Infante cites J. M. Barrie's *My Lady Nicotine* and Compton Mackenzie's *Sublime Tobacco.* Although Cabrera Infante shares a subject and a passion with those works, his title signals a difference. There is no tobacco, no cigar, no weed, no substantial object, in Cabrera Infante's title. The only noun is "smoke," a product of combustion, created by the consumption, the burning, the destruction of the beloved substance that others name—tobacco, nicotine, the weed, the cigar. Yet even smoke is not there as a substance. Instead, an ambiguous exclamation, a silly imprecation, a casual euphemism, a meaningless oxymoron, a form of words presides airily over the more substantial body of the text. From time to time, the phrase descends to punctuate the text, appearing in the dialogue of this movie or the mouth of that star. Separated from the visual and auditory experience that defines the medium, a movie evoked in writing is by definition absent in substance. Insubstantiality is all.

Nevertheless, *Holy Smoke* is about tobacco, the weed, the cigar, the cigarette, snuff, the chew; its history, manufacture, and manipulation in politics, texts, movies, photographs, dinners, anecdotes, economics, memory, and psychoanalysis, as sign, symbol, and index. There is also an occasional whiff of grass. Looking for shapes in the smoke and between the Cabreran puns turns up the rise and fall of smoking in the first part and an anthology of writing about tobacco in the second. In the first part, two cultures meet: the almost indigenous, misnamed Indian with his plant-with-many-names and the intrusive European. From that encounter a third develops, the tobacco culture of Cuba. Often moving into his most tender style (a clear, transparent, pun-free zone), Cabrera Infante describes the transport of tobacco, the sizes, shapes, and names of cigars, the craft of cigar making, the metaphysics of the *vitola,* and the dispersal of the industry, its owners, and its craftsmen by the Cuban revolution. The Spanish words for brands, colors, procedures, craftsmen, tools litter the text and then vanish. An image of barely smoked, wasted, plundered cigars, of a mark and type that no longer exists, focuses political disillusion in an anecdote of Fidel. Happier cigars go to the movies, but they cannot remain there.

The first section of the book ends with smoking under attack from the "Smokeless" in France, Spain, Italy, and the past (Mark Twain rebuked on a paddle wheeler). If sundry unsympathetic authorities, from conquistadores to "my father who at age 84 doesn't smoke yet" combine against the serenity of the smoker, imaginary reversals are still possible. So the son, who does smoke, makes Columbus plead for permission *not* to smoke. In that world of human chimneys, smoking is normative, and not smoking is not. The imaginary world of the past is the world of this book, and after Columbus's weaseling plea the text stretches into an anthology of writing about smoking, others' imagined worlds, and others' pasts.

Holy Smoke resembles Cabrera Infante's major fictions in its surface procedures, its linguistic texture, its insistent playfulness. As to its classification as fiction or nonfiction, it demands, as Menippean satire always has, the category "other." Since cigars displace characters and movie plots and snippets of reading replace authorial inventions or personal memories, "nonfiction" seems apt enough. The cigars are never allowed to talk in their own voices; they never take over their own fable. Much of the pleasure of the book derives from instruction, even if the form the information takes does not engender confidence. Pocketing up Cabrera Infante's material to resell elsewhere might produce a burn in the pocket and the cheek. Calling the work "nonfiction" seems to have the writer's endorsement—or does it? As Cabrera Infante observes in the same interview in which he described *Holy Smoke* as an autobiography, "I don't think my works are fiction. What is fiction is the way I write them." So *Holy Smoke* must be both fiction and nonfiction. The sentences cancel each other out, and they are both true. Consider again the assertion, with its terrible pathos, that *Holy Smoke* is "an autobiography written in smoke." The desperate, universal sadness of that phrase turns over into quite another thing when one registers the ludicrous consequence.

If *Holy Smoke* is an autobiography written in smoke, then Cabrera Infante is a cigar. That *has* to be a fiction, surely? He can burn out (horrid prospect for a writer), and he hates "Tautological illogical Gigi" because she thinks he's ugly ("an ugly black cigar is love!"), doesn't love him, and crushes his wrapper. He fumes a lot, but when he explodes, he looks silly and rarely does any real harm. He may dream of harboring a missile but only in paranoid spy fiction (87). The principal crime is cigar abuse, which may be serious (and then the cigar is Cuba, not Cabrera, as in the anecdote of Fidel and the plundered and wasted cigars) or seriocomic. "[I]n any war movie cigars are never lit. Cigar-smokers live longer in wartime but cigars suffer a lot" (210). The point is that the identification is made, is possible, is certain, and, having become irresistible, immediately becomes ridiculous. Now and then a trace of something more serious—exile, loss, death—opens up a rift in the text; then the text at once closes up and moves on.

That pattern or habitual manner critics have struggled over in the major fictions, ever since *Tres tristes tigres.* Is the work merely playful (hence trivial, in the common-garden view), or does it have a subversive intention, a revolutionary consciousness, an antiauthoritarian thrust (hence a value that merits sustained critical attention)? Or is it merely "a high culture commodity posing with a popular mask," "a pitiful evasion of reality" deficient in "any truly revolutionary consciousness"? Does the standard critical practice relative to Cabrera Infante make sense: first celebrating the text's "playfulness and irreducibility" and then proceeding gravely, without noticing the contradiction, to posit "serious intention and a coherent (if alternative) structure?" These views, ably canvassed by Philip Swanson, reveal the deficiency of literary theory relative both to politics and to comedy, even as the quarrels instance (or, to enter properly into the spirit of such discourses, *instantiate*) new levels of critico-comical absurdity.[7] To insert *Holy Smoke* into such debates would seem, on the face of it, more ludicrous than the debates themselves, but today's absurdity is tomorrow's serious position.

As to the political, no writing is more antiauthoritarian than Cabrera Infante's, and no consciousness is less revolutionary. The two terms are, indeed, contradictions in terms. As the tone of those who chide others for their futile, puny masquerades suggests, revolutionary consciousness is monologic, monolithic, didactic, and programmatic. Its monologism distressed Bakhtin enough to invent the term, and it drove Cabrera Infante from Cuba. Contrariwise, the antiauthoritarian continuously invites the reader to participate in and to extend the verbal games, ploys, and shifts that the text produces. The only authority it claims is in the reader's gift, attention. In its way the antiauthoritarian thrust—or gibe—is didactic (it teaches a way of being and behaving), but it also represents itself as isolated, caught in a commercial web, responsive to economic forces beyond its control, but determined to assert a liminal freedom, conscious of its limits, not dismayed by them. There is no embarrassment in *Holy Smoke* over the fact that cigar making and tobacco growing are industries.

As to the comic or playful, the difficulty it presents derives from the same absence of single-mindedness that is objected to in the political stance. Comedy is the most complex of literary activities, seriousness the least. Seriousness simplifies and elevates, taking us, at its best, out of ourselves. Revolutionaries, after all, imagine better worlds than most of us live in. (Like George Bernard Shaw's heaven, their imagined worlds may be better than any we want to live in.) The comic contradicts, multiplying selves that we would rather not be. As comedy comes closer to the serious issues we want simplified, it complicates our relationship to them, becoming funnier and more painful. If comedy irritates the surfaces, it is not entirely deficient in the experience or projection of depth. When comedy entertains pathos, it suggests in its ludic energy the *vanitas* at the heart of whirl.

Among the moments in *Holy Smoke* that sum up the project of the book is one that defines the liminal position of exile. If Pretorius among the corpses brackets the first section, the image of a writer smoking brackets the second. The first writer smoking is our author, presenting himself as vestibule, the place of entry to the collection he is about to offer his readers. That collection will end with the second image of a writer smoking, Mallarmé, and that too will be a summation. The tone is elegiac, and the speaker's situation reminds us that the exile has no place. Having no place, he has, like the dandy, no responsibilities but rests for the moment in between:

> My idea of happiness is to sit alone in the lobby of any old hotel after a late dinner, when the lights go out at the entrance and only the desk and the doorman are visible from my comfortable armchair. I

> then smoke my long black cigar in peace, in the dark: once a primeval bonfire in a clear of the forest, now a civilized ember glowing in the night like a beacon to the soul. An elegy is my choice smoke and I, the worst Tibullus, become thus a vestibule. (*Holy Smoke,* 242)

The point of this space, of course, is that one cannot stay there. The Cuban shaman and his community of peaceful smokers are long gone, replaced by civilized isolation. The communal cigar has become the solitary smoke of retired civility, and that smoke has become an elegy, a poem, a web of words. Tibullus, the Roman elegist [c. 48–19 B.C.], preferred love and loss in retirement to war or politics. Choosing the past, love, and art, the poet is a conduit for the elegiac meditation that goes through him to others. Art, like smoke, comes in and goes out, it does not remain, it cannot settle. The rueful absurdity of that hopeless pun, as "the worst Tibullus [becomes] thus a vestibule," makes the sentence circle back on itself, in rings, coming to rest in impermanence.

The ember glowing in the night reappears in Mallarmé's "clair baiser de feu" [clear kiss of fire], from the poem that closes Cabrera Infante's text. Choosing Mallarmé to end his text is a gesture that insists on the elegiac and denies the absurdity that the Cabreran text also insists upon. In *Holy Smoke* the pathos and the comedy are in both the smoke and the butt. Mallarmé's poem, for the sake of the smoke, advises leaving out the butt.

As Kenneth Hall points out, the title given to Mallarmé's untitled "Toute l'âme résumée" repeats the parody of Maurice Ravel's "Pavane pour une Infante defunte" [Pavane for a dead Infanta] which becomes *La Habana para un Infante difunto* [Havana for a dead Infante]. In *Holy Smoke* the phrase becomes "Le Havane pour un instant parfum." This third version (the third light on a match, which may or may not be lethal) may be rendered variously, as "Havana for a pressing perfume," "Havana for an insistent scent," or, the syntax mallarméanized, "Havana for an instant, perfume." Cabrera Infante's French has the advantage of presenting both the progressive, adjectival pressure of "pressing, insistent" and the nominal stasis that echoes the author's last name, "instant, infante." The repetition, with variation, of the joke suggests once again that the burning cigar replaces the burning Infante of *Infante's Inferno.* That recognition in turn has the consequence that one text replaces another.

Mallarmé's poem celebrates smoke rings as poetry and the poet's soul, summed up in a breath.[8] That soul lodges all the past, mingling living and reading, writing and experience. When the cigar or the poet burns, he produces the only part of him that has any value—smoke, literature. What he leaves behind, stub, ash, body, biography, is as undesirable and disposable as any other dead thing. In the autobiographical identification between poet and cigar, the poet is simultaneously everything—the *sine qua non*—and nothing—the base reality from which something (poetry) emerges. That something is utterly distinct from its origins and alien to them, another thing altogether.

By choosing Mallarmé to end his own book, Cabrera Infante folds himself as writer over into someone else's literature "Abolis en autres ronds" [Lost in other rounds].[9] Since he has already given over the last hundred pages of his book to other writers writing on tobacco, the gesture seems both justified and apt. The collector, the reader, and the writer merge. But Cabrera Infante's account, or aesthetic, differs at a crucial point from Mallarmé's, even as it endorses it. Cabrera Infante's text is inspired, he tells us, by a broken bicycle wheel turned by Marcel Duchamp's ludicrous pose into Cartier Bresson's art and Cabrera Infante's motive.

At the center of the book, Cabrera Infante describes a photo of Duchamp by Bresson. Duchamp stands by a worn-out bicycle and holds aloft a cigar stub "just like the Statue of Liberty," also of French design, a gift to America. William Shawn had commissioned the piece that became *Holy Smoke* for the *New Yorker,* but Cabrera Infante prefers to represent himself resisting the reiterated temptation of Cass Canfield, his American editor, to write a book on cigars. Adamant as Adam, the obviously always already fallen Cabrera Infante insists that cigars are only for enjoying, but then he found inspiration, a motive, in the rings. "Things are in smoke, art is in the rings. The wheel of a bicycle can be a ring too. The book, I thought, could be for Duchamp and the rings would then be considered Marcel waves, but he would remain aloof, aloft. Just like the rings. Hello, halo" (*Holy Smoke*, 164). The wheel, broken, reduced, rests on the represented ground but mounts through the image of the ring to Marcel waves. The figure of Duchamp is then detached from the feminized image, and the recapitulation of ascent continues—aloof, aloft. "Rings" brings us back to smoke, and then it's easy—the ring that rises above Marcel waves is, hello, a halo, the original holy smoke.

The pivot is the chiasmus that turns over into parallelism, and back again: "Things are in smoke, art is in the rings." For Mallarmé, the figure is a chiasmus: art is smoke, rings are things. Broken bicycle wheels, at any rate, are things that belong in William Butler Yeats's rag-and-bone shop. Like cigar butts, they are perhaps too precise. For Cabrera Infante, the figure is also a parallelism: if there are smoke rings, then art is in things, even broken bicycle wheels.

If *Holy Smoke* is the first book Cabrera Infante wrote in English, it is also the first book he ended in French. As he tells it, the making of *Holy Smoke* has American commercial motivations but French artistic inspiration, three times over. Nor could he have made his placement and use of Mallarmé's French more conspicuous: the last words, the title of the last section, an anticipation in the introduction to the last section. The effect is to flee from the dominant language of the text to still another language. Liminality is reasserted, and English is in turn displaced. The language of the text exiles itself from itself and takes up residence in still another place. Ordinarily, obligations and responsibilities work against the sense of liminality. They settle us and make us feel as though we belong—and that perhaps is the real problem with exile. The exile has no duties to others determined by his relationships to a larger community, to those duties that traditionally settle one down. Cabrera Infante has no responsibility to English, though he takes—and gives—much pleasure in it. Instead, he suggests through his own practice the relationship of language to language, shifting codes, changing habits, moving hotels, and returning to the source, words, your wandering writing.

Notes

1. G. Cabrera Infante, *Holy Smoke* (New York: Harper and Row, 1985), 2.

2. Ardis L. Nelson, "*Holy Smoke:* The Anatomy of a Vice," *World Literature Today* 61, 4 (1987): 590–93.

3. Kenneth E. Hall, "Dandyism and *Holy Smoke,*" *Hispanófila* 111 (1994): 73–82.

4. Antonio Prieto Taboada, "Idioma y ciudadania literaria en *Holy Smoke* de Guillermo Cabrera Infante," *Revista Iberoamericana* 57, 154 (1991): 257–64. He also rightly insists that the book is bilingual; its jokes often depend on its English being read with a Spanish accent, a feature Anglophone readers may miss.

5. "Ingenio y Trucos con Guillermo Cabrera Infante," interview with Suzanne Jill Levine, trans. Carlos Tripodi, *Americas* 47, 4 (July–August 1995): 29.

6. *Tres tristes tigres* (Barcelona: Editorial Seix Barral, 1967), 451; *Three Trapped Tigers,* trans. Donald Gardiner and Suzanne Jill Levine with Guillermo Cabrera Infante (New York: Harper and Row, 1971), 487. *La Habana para un Infante difunto* (Barcelona: Editorial Seix Barral, 1979), 689. In *Infante's Inferno,* trans.

Suzanne Jill Levine, with Guillermo Cabrera Infante (New York: Harper and Row, 1984), "continuous showing" is reversed, for "Movies must have an end," 392.

7. Philip Swanson, *The New Novel in Latin America: Politics and Popular Culture after the Boom* (New York: Manchester University Press, 1995), 44, 46, 51, 53.

8. From Stéphane Mallarmé, *Poems,* trans. Roger Fry, commentary Charles Mauron (New York: Oxford University Press, 1937), 231–33. Fry's translation may be helpful:

All the soul indrawn
When slowly we exhale it
In many rounds of smoke
Lost in other rounds

Proves that some cigar
Burns skilfully how-so-little
Its ash withdraws itself
From the clear kiss of fire

So the choir of songs
Flies it to your lip
Exclude if you begin
The real as being base

Its too sharp sense will overscrawl
Your vague literature.

9. The text in *Holy Smoke* includes an extraneous "d" viz. "Abolis en d'autres ronds." While the French might want to say "des autres ronds," it can't do so without spoiling the meter. Cabrera Infante makes one interesting—and significant—change in Mallarmé's text: Mallarmé's second line "Quand lente nous l'expirons" [When slowly we exhale it], Cabrera Infante changes to "nous l'aspirons" [we inhale it], a livelier rendering.

Mea Cuba: The "Proust-Valía" of History

NEDDA G. DE ANHALT

La historia no es lo que hemos hecho o hacemos sino lo que hemos dejado que los otros hagan con nosotros. Desde hace más de tres siglos nuestra manera de vivir la historia es sufrirla.

[History is not what we have done or do, but what we have allowed others to do to us. For more than three centuries our way to live history is to suffer it.]

—Octavio Paz, *Puertas al Campo* [Doors to the field]

Guillermo Cabrera Infante, a master of language, is Cuba's Marcel Proust; Mnemosyne, the goddess of memory, is his muse, as he writes in *Mea Cuba*.[1] Through poetic imagination Cabrera Infante evokes time past, present, and future. Like so many Cubans, Cabrera Infante has suffered oppression and exile. He describes Cuban political history as "la madre de la infamia . . . una puta que dormía en el lecho de Procusto" (*Mea Cuba* [1992], 308) ["the mother of infamy . . . a whore who slept on Procrustes' bed" (*Mea Cuba* [1994], 272).] History is not his passion, it is his obsession.[2]

Cabrera Infante's critical attitude has made him *malgre'lui,* a historian of his time. Although he is not known as a historian, he has stood up against history. He has interpreted, translated, and written it. *Mea Cuba* is Cabrera Infante's chronicle of political events under Fidel Castro's communism, from 1959 to the 1990s, and a doorway to his prophetic predictions. As a sad trapped tiger, he has watched his country break and crumble before his eyes. *Mea Cuba* is part of Cuba's history and has made history, not in the manner of Robert Graves but akin to Arthur Koestler: Cabrera Infante represents the heroic figure of the lonely rider whose conscience demands perpetual spiritual rebellion against tyranny.[3]

In 1992, the publication of *Mea Cuba* in Spain was greeted enthusiastically, and in a few months the edition was sold out. With such an auspicious beginning, one might have expected a reprint and a flurry of awards, but the Spanish publishing house did not reprint *Mea Cuba.* Cabrera Infante's followers were astounded that the hand of censorship and repression from Havana continued to have such a long, forceful reach.[4] *Mea Cuba* is not only a great literary monument to the modern essay but a remarkable tour de force of memory allied to humor and the magical style that is perhaps Cabrera Infante's greatest gift. This book is important because Cabrera Infante, like Proust, reveals truth through the essential relationship between time and language.

The body of Cabrera Infante's work can be seen as a gigantic *madeleine* that encompasses the modern history of his beloved Cuba. Cabrera Infante has had a long love affair with Cuban slang and dialect and has managed to reinvent a native Cuban language. He faithfully captured and enlivened the language of everyman in his masterpiece *Tres tristes tigres* (1967) [*Three Trapped Tigers* (1971)]. In *Así en la paz como en la guerra* (1960) [*Writes of Passage* (1993)] he tried to make sense of the violence and cruelty that permeate Cuba's history. In *O* (1975) he claimed his right to fragment a chronology that is keenly observant of contemporary manners, songs, characters, and the trivia of Havana and London through the prism of time. In *La Habana para un Infante difunto* (1979) [*Infante's Inferno* (1984)] he shared with his readers the rapture of every smell and taste in Havana's streets, bars, nightclubs, and movie houses. He found his vocation in Havana, his Jerusalem of Gold, and an image of eternity. In *Vista del amanecer en el trópico* (1974) [*View of Dawn in the Tropics* (1978)] he fictionalized Cuban history in moving poetic prose impassioned with sea breezes. In *Exorcismos de esti(l)o* (1976) [Style exorcisms] he recaptured his love of freedom in spectacular concrete poems. In *Arcadia todas las noches* (1978) [Arcadia every night] he reminds us of the privileged time we spend watching films by the movie directors we admire, where we escape into other worlds. In *Holy Smoke* (1985) he mythified a Cuban invention, the cigar. In *Un oficio del siglo veinte* (1963) [*A Twentieth Century Job* (1991)] he reminds us that criticism in any country is inextricably bound with freedom of expression. And in his prose piece *Delito por bailar el chachachá* (1995) [Crime for dancing the chachacha] he captured the vital associative chain between melody and rhythm.

Mea Cuba is a collection of essays with a dystopian vision that has worked itself into many fields and has challenged Cuban political thought. Like other Hispanic writers, Cabrera Infante is prodded by the ghost of the poet, teacher, journalist, essayist, diplomat, soldier, and Cuban patriot José Martí (1853–1895). Both Cabrera Infante and Martí have left us with fragments of "master" literature; both have also proven themselves to be writers first, and writers of political essays second; and both are imbued with the desire to see Cuba free from tyranny. However, the effect of their writing could not be more different.[5] Martí's texts are architecturally akin to sermons, solemn and vibrant with patriotism and emotion, while Cabrera Infante's writing is witty and erudite, dense and abbreviated, and always in the service of an artistic aim.[6]

Cabrera Infante's influence on linguistics is as important as his achievement as a writer; his writing stands as a total release from the bondage of gravity, solemnity, and inhibition. It is baffling and exhilarating. *Mea Cuba* resounds with satire and irony. Puns crowd each other with disciplined accuracy. His ingenuity places him in the company of writers such as Anatole France, Jonathan Swift, and George Orwell, whose respective works include *L'Ile des Pingouins* (1908) [*The Island of Penguins*], *Gulliver's Travels* (1854), and *Nineteen Eighty-Four* (1949).[7]

France's humorous brand of skepticism and prophetic bent are similar to Cabrera Infante's. France tells the story of amoral and inhuman penguins, clerical-soldiers greedy for power and ready to kill any dragon or to accuse any innocent man in order to keep their privileges. They blindly follow a religion, inspired by a virgin who in reality is a prostitute. They are always chanting patriotic hymns and repeating mottoes they do not believe. Like humans, the penguins are ready to burn at the stake anyone who does not step in line. Does this ring a bell? Of course, Anatole France's Island of Alca could be a copy of Castro's Cuba.

Swift is closer to Cabrera Infante in his special brand of satire. Before Swift wrote *Gulliver's Travels*, and while he was the dean of Saint Patrick's Cathedral in Dublin, he was already known in England as a political and satirical writer. Close to two hundred years ago on the floating island of Lipide, Swift spoke of two moons orbiting around Mars, but who believed him? Before writing his masterpiece *Tres tristes tigres*, Cabrera Infante was the "dean" of the literary scene as director of *Lunes*, the cultural supplement to a revolutionary magazine/newspaper in Castro's Cuba. In exile, Cabrera Infante assumed the role of a Cassandra who alerted the world to the repressive surveillance of Fidel Castro's police, the G2. This police force, coincidentally, bears the same name as that of Batista's own repressive forces. In *Mea Cuba* Cabrera Infante warns that Cuba had taken on the characteristics of Swift's "Laputa." Homosexuals were tortured in the name of "rehabilitation," a "double-think" technique of the party in the UMAPs.[8] He also warns of the dangers of totalitarianism. In Nazi Germany Joseph Goebbels labeled the Jews "bacteria." Cubans that run away into exile are classified by Castrian terminology as "gusanos" [worms]. In this "age of assassins," who believed Cabrera Infante? It was 193 years before Swift was vindicated. For Cabrera Infante it will not be that long.

The title *Mea Cuba* is a double entendre. The author is both poisoned with a sense of guilt and, at the same time, has the possessiveness of a lover: Mea Culpa, Mea Cuba [My Fault, My Cuba]. Cabrera Infante shares a collective guilt with all Cubans. It is understandable, since Castro, like Hitler, could not have created chaos and destruction by himself. That is why guilt covers the bovine portion of the Cuban population that sided with the tyrant, as well as scholars and intellectuals who looked the other way when Castro made his grab for power. For Cabrera Infante, guilt will always be alive as the reminder of this collective crime.

Cabrera Infante, like the French novelist Albert Camus, knew early privation and rejected the optimism of Christianity.[9] He sees Cubans as if they were an unhappy Sisyphus condemned not to push the stone of Castro's regime but to hold the stone with all its weight. In *Mea Cuba,* Cabrera Infante—paraphrasing Anthony Burgess—stands like Homer breathing fire through his mortiferous puns: "la castroenteritis," "la castradura que dura," and "la espera estoica"[10] He warns us that Castro's regime has converted Cuba into an Orwellian world with public and private Kafkaesque nightmares. Cabrera Infante, unlike so many English writers, is neither a utopian as was H. G. Wells nor a candid traveler like Edna O'Brien.[11] This Homer is a sort of Roquentin who sees the results of a dogmatic revolution and is overwhelmed by its absurdity.[12] He goes into exile and embraces freedom.

The essays in *Mea Cuba* are well orchestrated and could be heard as an opera containing memorable arias such as: "Lorca hace llover en La Habana" (*Mea Cuba* [1992], 108–20) ["Lorca the Rainmaker Visits Havana" (*Mea Cuba* [1994], 87–96)]; "Yo acuso en el Wilson Center" (*Mea Cuba* [1992], 254–65) ["J'Accuse at the Woodrow Wilson Center" (*Mea Cuba* [1994], 231–38)]; "Voces cubanas, voces lejanas" (*Mea Cuba* [1992], 473–76) ["Hearing (Distant) Voices" (*Mea Cuba* [1994], 480–82)]; and "El ave del Paraíso Perdido" (*Mea Cuba* [1992], 481–84) ["The Bird of Paradise Lost" (*Mea Cuba* [1994], 489–91)]; among others. The overture, or opening movement, touches on nearly every major theme and symbol of the *Mea Cuba* essays and thrusts the reader into the Cuban political arena: "Aviso" (*Mea Cuba* [1992], 15) ["Notice" (*Mea Cuba* [1994], xii)]; "Génesis/Exodo" (*Mea Cuba* [1992], 16) ["Genesis/Exodus" (*Mea Cuba* [1994], 1)]; and "Naufragio con un amanecer al fondo" (*Mea Cuba* [1992], 17–19) ["Shipwreck with a Sunrise in the Background" (*Mea Cuba* [1994], 3–5)]. With each interlude the writer's tone intensifies in a crescendo, and the sound and fury of the puns wind their way into our minds and hearts. Certain melodies or themes create a devastating discord: the struggle between tyranny and freedom, Havana and Cuban literary figures recovered, spiritual and physical signs of exile. The tempo of the essays is treated by the author in different measures, playing the binary against the ternary. From a "Vivace," "Presto," and "Allegretto" in "La respuesta" (*Mea Cuba* [1992], 23–32) ["Answers and Questions" (*Mea Cuba* [1994], 11–19)], the speed moves to an "Andantino," to be followed by an "Andante" in "Vidas para leerlas" (*Mea Cuba* [1992], 315–405) ["Parallax Lives" (*Mea Cuba* [1994], 329–416)], that leads to "Vida única" (*Mea Cuba* [1992], 406–35) ["Live Lives" (*Mea Cuba* [1994], 417–44)] in a "Larghetto," and finally ends in the delicacies of tone required for a great finale with an unexpected "Adagio."

The essays in *Mea Cuba* are "reactive." Cabrera Infante left Cuba in 1965 on a flight to Belgium, where he had been serving as cultural attaché.

After he not only rejected the directrix of a castrating revolution but dared to openly criticize it as well, he himself was attacked by servants of the Cuban regime from all over the world. The first pages of *Mea Cuba* were written as a defense to these cunning articles. They comprise, as Alastair Reid aptly explained, miscellaneous letters, articles, conferences, memories, portraits, and essays.[13] Yet the touching issue in them is the sensibility of a writer infused with nostalgia and the hope that, through telling the world his story, he can reestablish the credibility of his country and his beloved city, Havana. Cabrera Infante offers, at the same time, an "identity card" of Cuban history. This knowledge frees the reader from the "official" history in order to discover and become an accomplice to the real history of Cuba.

Cabrera Infante, like Proust, is obsessed with truth and time. Mnemosyne, the muse of memory and Cabrera Infante's muse, represents his imagination and a form of his rebellious attitude toward history. The truth about the past has to be preserved at all costs. When Combray and Balbec, the beloved cities of Proust's narrator in *Remembrance of Things Past,* appear from memory, they are seen from multiple vantage points: when he was young, when he was 20, and what he felt standing before a landscape. Havana also rises between past, present, and future in an original time as close to eternity as the memory of Cabrera Infante's narrator in *Mea Cuba*.[14] The essence of this city is so rich that the Havana of his youth, the Havana he saw in ruins at the time of his mother's death in 1965, and the Havana he longs for are permeated with the same qualities, although seen under very different circumstances.

History is supposedly written by the conquerors, and is not easily fathomed. Cabrera Infante expressed his vision of the Cuban regime that changes its embroidery each night: "se escribe y reescribe siempre: la tela en que Penélope borda la imagen de un Ulises constante, inconstante" (*Mea Cuba* [1992], 225) ["the eternal writing and rewriting the cloth of history on which a revisionist Penelope weaves the image of her constant (by night), inconstant (by day) Ulysses the crafty" (*Mea Cuba* [1994], 281)]. One of the gloomiest aspects of Cuban history is that after 38 years of tyranny, a great deal of truth has been crushed by silence, manipulation, and propaganda. The author of *Mea Cuba* knows about these dangers and wants to set the record straight. He clings tenaciously to dates, names, events, and his right to judge and condemn.

Overture

Before the curtain rises in *Mea Cuba,* we hear a muted trumpet announcing two pivotal dates: Sunday, 28 October 1492, marking Columbus's discovery of Cuba in "Génesis," and 3 October 1965, when Cabrera Infante left Cuba for good in "Exodo" (*Mea Cuba* [1992], 16) ["Exodus" (*Mea Cuba* [1994], 1)]. This second date prepares the overture for a story about a "Paradise" converted into a tropical communist "Inferno."[15]

The curtain rises and Cabrera Infante explains the paradox of his life as the son of Communist Party founders in Cuba, growing up with the party's contradictions and inconsistencies and becoming a writer who is neither a politician nor a political writer but who chose to become the latter for ethical reasons. Cuba is, metaphorically, a drifting ship full of trapped rats trying to run away, with hysterical images of Fidel Castro and Adolf Hitler screaming, "This ship will not sink." In "A propósito" (*Mea Cuba* [1992], 20–22) ["By the way" (*Mea Cuba* [1994], 6–8)], Cabrera Infante relates an incident in 1985 after a trip to Barcelona. Upon his return to London, he had trouble getting into his apartment, which had been ransacked, although nothing had been taken.[16] A Scotland Yard detective identifies

Cabrera Infante as an exile from Castro's Cuba. The detective informs him that he was indeed lucky; exiled Eastern European writers had been robbed of their manuscripts and even murdered, as in the case of Gregory Markov. Markov, an exiled writer, verbally attacked the ruling communist family in Bulgaria and was killed with a poison-tipped umbrella in London. The narrator graciously invites his uninvited guests to read *Mea Cuba.*

Act One

A great many things are revealed rather quickly in this untitled first act—hidden scandals, secrets, and public memories. The situations, characters, and historical events are presented in a straightforward fashion where nothing is superfluous; nevertheless, the reader is provided occasional guidance. There are many issues and layers associated with the tyrannical power that had confiscated democracy in Cuba. The reader must know all and, like a Caruso, the author obliges with the full splendor of his voice. This is no mean task. Each act calls for an incessant but varied approach with reinforcement of words and melodies. There are 27 scenes, each one rising to a higher pitch. The prodigious vigor of Cabrera Infante's most ferocious prose is reserved for Castro, the major villain of this story. He uses language to corrode and denigrate the despotic power that has not only persecuted the author but has also expropriated the psyche of the Cuban people.

Disguised as an actor, Cabrera Infante confesses that for his task he has chosen the most difficult genre: comedy. His mottoes are from Martí, "About the tyrant say everything, say even more," and from Shakespeare's Bottom in the second scene of the first act in *A Midsummer-Night's Dream,* "Yet my chief humor is for a tyrant."[17] He mocks and makes great fun of the tyrant, exactly as Proust did with Charlus, Bloch, Madame Verdurin, Norpois, and so many of his other characters. Descartes said: "Cogito ergo sum" ["I think, therefore, I am"]. For Proust and Cabrera Infante this might translate: I ridicule, therefore, I am. For Cabrera Infante alone, the phrase might be: Loquor ergo sum [I talk, therefore, I am].

An author's talent for parody is his secret weapon. In "La respuesta de Cabrera Infante" (*Mea Cuba* [1992], 23–32) ["Answers and Questions" (*Mea Cuba* [1994], 11–19)] an explanation is offered for the exile's choice. A country, Cabrera Infante says, is not only geography, it is history. And in Cuba, "La geografía era la misma, estaba viva, pero la Historia había muerto" (*Mea Cuba* [1992], 26) ["Geography was alive, but history had died" (*Mea Cuba* [1994], 14)]. In "La peliculita culpable" (*Mea Cuba* [1992], 61–62) ["P.M. Means Post Mortem" (*Mea Cuba* [1994], 52–54)], the case of the short film *P.M.* is rested, the "Cuban Revolution" is efficiently dismantled, and its surreality is proclaimed.[18] The revolutionary dream of "educational achievement" and "balanced diet" fail when certain books are forbidden, the press is repressed, and human rights are violated. The famous case of Heberto Padilla is exposed in great detail. Frightening statistics from 1964 are offered: more than 2,000,000 Cubans are obliged to belong to the CDR, which means they are spies. Since then more than 1,500,000 have fled the country, leaving an experiential void that has yet to be filled.[19]

For a brief moment Cabrera Infante steps back and lets a silent chorus of "official" absentee writers be humiliated by a UNEAC document announcing the 1968 expulsion of Cabrera Infante and pianist Ivette Hernández, both considered to be "traitors to the revolutionary cause."[20] The other document, explaining Julio Cortázar's opinion on the Padilla case, is a masterpiece of impure political naivete, or pure political cynicism, if you like. The author accepts the poet Ismail Hikmet's wise advice, "Travel. Be a presence with your absence," and shares fascinating anecdotes and gossip—a "Who's Who" in the Cuban artistic panorama. An encounter with Franco's police meant: *"Goodbye Madrid!—Hello London?"* (*Mea Cuba* [1992], 108; *Mea Cuba* [1994], 450).

In "Lorca hace llover en La Habana" (*Mea Cuba* [1992], 108–20) ["Lorca the Rainmaker Visits Havana" (*Mea Cuba* [1994], 87–96)], Cabrera Infante poeticizes the visit of the Spanish poet Federico García Lorca to Havana in 1930.[21] His prose intermingles imagery from a photograph of García Lorca taken by Walker Evans, which shows a well-dressed dandy in an elegant white suit; descriptions of Havana from Ernest Hemingway's novel *To Have and Have Not* (1937), which he wrote in Cuba; descriptions of the surreal beauty of Havana written by traveler Joseph Hergesheimer; Jorge Luis Borges's impressions of Havana, taken from the *Encyclopedia Britannica*; and references to the city found in popular songs and nostalgia.[22] He ends the essay with a description of the scene at a banquet in Havana held in honor of García Lorca and interrupted by a sudden torrential rainstorm. Lorca, fascinated by the spectacle, stood up and, in respectful silence, paid tribute to nature. This "solo singing" will hold a place of honor for many readers as a Proustian trip: Havana lost, Havana regained.[23]

In "La Habana para los fieles difunta" (*Mea Cuba* [1992], 120–25) ["Havana Lost and Found: A Dead City—or the City of the Dead?" (*Mea Cuba* [1994], 100–105)], the image of the city, as inconstant as the sea that surrounds it, has changed radically. It is the same Havana but transformed into a ghost of itself, a painted whore ready to greet tourists. Havana is a temptress and a tormented city. Can its essential integrity ever be recovered? In "El martirio de Martí" (*Mea Cuba* [1992], 126–31) ["The Martyrdom of Martí" (*Mea Cuba* [1994], 109–13)], the mythical figure José Martí, his exile and death, are expressed in triumphant prose. Martí, like Cabrera Infante, spent more time in exile than he spent in Cuba, but this exile allowed him to become one of the finest writers of the nineteenth-century, just as Cabrera Infante's exile has allowed him to become one of the finest writers of this century. Cabrera Infante explains exile not as a historical or geographical situation but as an emotional one. He defines exile as "una tierra que el escritor lleva siempre consigo" (*Mea Cuba* [1992], 127) ["a land that the writer carries with him always" (*Mea Cuba* [1994], 110)]. "¿Quién mató a Calvert Casey?" (*Mea Cuba* [1992], 131–56) ["Who Killed Calvert Casey?" (*Mea Cuba* [1994], 114–37)] is about the life and times of Calvert Casey, the remarkable Cuban writer who committed suicide in Rome in 1972. It is also a "J'Accuse" to a number of infamous tourists who, having received confidences from Cubans, did not keep their secrets, placing the lives of Cuban citizens in danger.[24]

"Entre la historia y la nada" (*Mea Cuba* [1992], 157–89) ["Between History and Nothingness" (*Mea Cuba* [1994], 138–72)] is an inventory of Cuban suicides. Except for Sweden, Cuba has the highest suicide rate in the world. Castro's Cuba is also one of the few countries in the world where executions by firing squad are performed on teenage boys, some as young as 16 years of age. In "El prisionero político desconocido" (*Mea Cuba* [1992], 215–19) ["The Unknown Political Prisoner" (*Mea Cuba* [1994], 196–200)], Cabrera Infante recalls the 1703 image of the "Man in the Iron Mask" to demonstrate that totalitarian policies mean total war against political prisoners. In "Prisioneros de la Isla del Diablo" (*Mea Cuba* [1992], 220–24) ["Prisoners of Devil's Island" (*Mea Cuba* [1994], 201–5)], Cabrera Infante makes a comparison between two islands converted into political prisons and two victims of a corrupt system. Alfred Dreyfus was the victim of conspiratorial military forces, and Gustavo Arcos was the victim of Fidel Castro.[25] Cabrera Infante uses the image of "new blankets" in Cuban jails, as well as those in Nazi extermination camps, as a metaphor for an obscene vision in which

Red Cross volunteers in Europe and political tourists in Cuba give glowing reports of conditions under the respective tyrannies to the "outside world." Instead of an alarmed awakening, as in *The Golden Cockerel*, and an urgent warning: "Open your eyes and beware!," the visitors parrot: "Cocorico!" ["Everything is fine and dandy!"] in order to protect the despicable Dondon kings.[26]

"Un retrato familiar" (*Mea Cuba* [1992], 224–30) ["Portrait of an Aging Tyro" (*Mea Cuba* [1994], 281–90)] refers to Carlos Franqui's extraordinary autobiographical-historic book *Retrato de familia con Fidel* (1981) [A family portrait with Fidel].[27] The portrait has a forceful "yang-like" description of Castro and reads like the cut of an ax. "Nuestro prohombre en La Habana" (*Mea Cuba* [1992], 233–38) ["Notable Men in Havana" (*Mea Cuba* [1994], 210–15)] is a personal criticism of Nobel laureate Gabriel García Márquez, who succumbed to the fascination of totalitarian figures such as Fidel Castro and General Torrijos.[28] This essay is an indictment of the fickleness and unpredictability of countries with democratic traditions, such as the contradictory practices of the United States, which treats its friends as enemies and invites citizens of enemy countries to give lectures and hold positions at universities.

The artists Jacques Louis David, a cynical French court painter, and Walker Evans, the American photographer who produced unforgettable images of Havana, provide the opportunity for an enjoyable discussion about clichés.[29] One such meaningless expression for Cabrera Infante is "Latin America," a term coined by Michel Chevalier, one of Napoléon III's bureaucrats in nineteenth-century France.[30] The historical and social realities of the so-called "Latin American" countries do not coincide with artificial divisions; so for him there is only North, South, and Central America and Mexico.[31]

Cabrera Infante's pièce de résistance, "Yo acuso en el Wilson Center" (*Mea Cuba* [1992], 254–65) ["J'Accuse at the Woodrow Wilson Center" (*Mea Cuba* [1994], 231–38)], is not a thriller but rather a choker that might confuse someone trying to follow the story. Cabrera Infante is purposely obscure and deprives his readers of some important connecting threads. When Emile Zola wrote his famous letter to President Félix Faure in defense of Dreyfus, which was published in *L'Aurore* on 13 January 1898, the French novelist and intellectual engaged the reader with a prolonged detour for several pages and cinched his argument at the conclusion of his letter with a series of forcefully dramatic statements. Cabrera Infante has successfully improved upon this recipe for writing with unabashed frankness and passion. He meanders through a complex maze, moving in and out of gloomy passageways, onto twisted paths that lead to dangerous, overhanging cliffs before finally delivering the coup de grâce in his Cuban "I accuse."

In "El nacimiento de una noción" (*Mea Cuba* [1992], 292–304) ["Hey Cuba, Hecuba?" (*Mea Cuba* [1994], 247–59)], Cabrera Infante submits that this is not the Age of Aquarius for Cubans but rather the Age of Exile. The narrator, as a cinematographic D. W. Griffith, heralds the disquieting and improbable news. No one would have dreamed that for more than a century and a half, the island nation of Cuba has produced more exiles in America than any other country. A hundred years ago, when the Cuban people fought for their independence from Spanish rule, many great men and women went into exile abroad, including the poets José María Heredia, José Martí, Juan Clemente Zenea, Gertrudis Gómez de Avellaneda, and the novelist Cirilo Villaverde. Others have opted for a so-called "exile on the *inside*," as in the cases of contemporary writers Julián del Casal, José Lezama Lima, and Virgilio Piñera.[32]

"¿Ha muerto el socialismo?" (*Mea Cuba* [1992], 304–7) ["Has Socialism Died?" (*Mea Cuba* [1994], 269–71)] is the author's personal response to a questionnaire and an eloquent analysis of ethical attitudes. The first act closes at a critical moment with "¿Qué cosa es la historia, pues?" (*Mea Cuba* [1992], 307–13) ["What is History, pues?" (*Mea Cuba* [1994], 272–77)] when the narrator, as director, presents the dramatis personae, and offers a summary of the subject backed up by a choral performance by the likes of Herodotus, Thucydides, and Plutarch.

The compass of Act One keeps up with the laughing/crying pace of "Vesti la giubba" [Put on the clown costume].[33] The narrator, as an "allegro agitato ed appassionato Pagliaccio" [happy, agitated, and impassioned clown], laughs for the love that has been destroyed and mourns the ruination of his city, jeering at the tyrant and his cowardly and treacherous accomplices, while crying with anguish for the thousands of men, women, and children who have drowned in the ocean while trying to escape from this "Paradise." As the show must go on, the need for laughter becomes the dim hope that sustains this Pagliaccio in the face of an apparently desperate present and future.

ACT TWO: VIDAS PARA LEERLAS [PARALLAX LIVES]

The paronomasia or pun of this title is that it can also be read as "Vidas paralelas" [parallel lives]. In this section of the book Cabrera

Infante is like Orpheus descending into hell in search of an intellectual and artistic elite in order to save Cuba from oblivion. When he looks back, the Euridices spring to life. A riot of color erupts across the stage as a cinematographer, a ballerina, and writers such as Lino Novás Calvo, Néstor Almendros, Enrique Labrador Ruiz, Gastón Baquero, José Lezama Lima, Reinaldo Arenas, Virgilio Piñera, Lydia Cabrera, and Alejo Carpentier form the cast. Unlike Lot's wife, they are not turned into pillars of salt, although Cabrera Infante makes no bones about liberally seasoning his gossip and anecdotes with plenty of salt. This is not the first time that he has paid tribute to great Cuban artistic figures. In *Tres tristes tigres* a chapter is devoted to remarkable parodies of literary styles.[34] It remains one of the glories of the book. *Cosi fan tutte*? Not at all. This punster is a monster that enjoys mimicry, ever ready to unmask minor villains. If Proust enjoyed looking at portraits of famous artists, making funny comparisons with living persons, Cabrera Infante has made famous his verbal portraits. Carpentier's depiction is a good example of how to receive Tosca's kiss. In "Carpentier, cubano a la canona" (*Mea Cuba* [1992], 370–88) [Alejo Carpentier, a Shotgun Cuban (*Mea Cuba* [1994], 383–99)], the writer comes across as a "Castrato" courier who delivers his master's orders with virtuosity. Also a "four-letter" word reveals that Carpentier's French accent is faked when he forgets himself and swears in perfect Spanish. The scene shifts to a metro ride that confirms that the central character in this portrait truly lies like a prince. In the end, is this rake punished? Or *la commediae finita*? By no means.

ACT THREE: VIDA ÚNICA

The reader will unavoidably fall under the magic spell of Cabrera Infante's incredible capacity to sustain an even chord in order to capture time, memory, and nostalgia. The aim of this triumvirate is to project the sad, highly poetic and almost mystical air of the never-never land called "Exile." The results show the tragedy of exile in a series of impressionistic essays that includes a farewell to the Cuban world champion chess player Capablanca and a satirical piece that fulfills Orson Welles's, George Orwell's, and Aldous Huxley's fantasies by depicting the Cuban exile community as being totally invisible to some scholars and intellectuals.

The conclusion of *Mea Cuba* is not a victory symphony, as in *Julius Caesar*, but rather reaches the ethereal heights of tender joy in

"El ave del paraíso perdido" (*Mea Cuba* [1992], 481–84) ["The Bird of Paradise Lost" (*Mea Cuba* [1994], 489–91)], a love scene in which Cabrera Infante tries to relate to another author's soul.[35] Blessed be the blue bird of nostalgic happiness because, with its exiles, it will be able to recover time lost. Memory will be free to wander and Cuba, an infinitely more powerful entity, reappears like some magical experience.

This great finale could not be more Proustian. If *Mea Cuba* had ended with the essay "El exilio invisible" (*Mea Cuba* [1992], 477–81) ["The Invisible Exile" (*Mea Cuba* [1994], 483–88)], it could not have been more devastating. Instead, an unexpected turn is taken in the form of a glorious flashback. Cabrera Infante was looking for truth, and he has found it; if he was looking for truth through the essence of time, he has discovered the value of time past. The trip is over. Was an unexpected turn taken after all? No. When he cannot go back to the promised land he prays "Next Year in Jerusalem!"—a miracle might occur. How could he put a limit on an unlimited emotion? The ending of *Mea Cuba* is not an ending at all. It is a beginning. For Cabrera Infante, the only way to resurrect Havana is through time, memory, and writing, and this is exactly what he has done in *Mea Cuba.* As long as he longs, he will remember, and as long as he keeps writing about Cuba, the book of life will be an open one, a limbo without an end but with both a Genesis and an Exodus.

Encore

The influence of Proust on the work of Cuban writers has been profound. Despite the fact that Proust and Cabrera Infante had very different backgrounds, both came from homes in which their parents were sensitive to culture and their mothers gave them a sense of direction.

Marcel Proust was born in Auteuil into the French bourgeoisie. At home, he was surrounded by servants and members of his family, including his father Adrien Achilles Proust, a Catholic medical doctor, his Jewish intellectual mother, Jeanne Weil, and his younger brother Robert. The young Proust adored the provincial rustic life of Illiers, where his father's family had once owned a small grocery store.

Cabrera Infante was born in Gibara in the province of Oriente, where he had a poor but happy childhood. His parents, Zoila Infante Castro and Guillermo Cabrera López, were communist intellectuals.

In 1942, the then adolescent Cabrera Infante, along with his parents and younger brother Sabá, moved to Havana. Cabrera Infante fell in love with the urban charms of the city of Havana, which would later become an inspiration for his writing.

As an adult, Proust led an active social life. He found a kind of political salvation by defending Captain Alfred Dreyfus and Colonel Georges-Marie Picquart during the years of the Dreyfus affair.[36] The collapse of France's moral values, coupled with Proust's poor health, reinforced his already pessimistic outlook on life. Near the end of his life, with only his housekeeper Celeste Albaret to help him, Proust secluded himself in his room and worked to prove that time lost could be recovered through writing. His desire to live in seclusion was to fulfill the obsession to finish his novel *A la recherche du temps perdu* (1913–1927) [*Remembrance of Things Past*] and because of this obsession, he remained happily ignorant of world events.

Cabrera Infante, along with his wife Miriam Gómez and his two daughters from a previous marriage, isolated himself in his London apartment in order to finish his work. His London apartment became his haven, or, as he said later on when he looked back to this period in his life: "If your country does not exist anymore, what do you say? My only country is this flat."[37] Although he may have lived like a hermit, Cabrera Infante, unlike Proust, was always well informed about world affairs. What is most admirable besides his gift of writing with humor and vivacity is the courage and honesty with which he attacks human rights violations and political repression in Cuba.

Proust did not abandon the real world for an imaginary one. It is true that if he had not visited aristocratic homes, he would not have been able to recreate their ambiance and personality. But he did not use a historical event like the Dreyfus affair to create a literary fiction as did Roger du Gard with *Jean Barois* (1913).[38] Proust took the opposite approach and went from the imaginary to the real. Cabrera Infante departs from reality toward the imaginary. The fact that Cabrera Infante's parents were founders of the Communist Party in their hometown and that the author took an active part in Castro's revolution made it possible for Cabrera Infante to recreate his experiences in Cuba with imagination and with an exceptional facility for detail.

Proust mocked the aristocracy. Cabrera Infante mocks the horrors and corruption of Cuba's ruling revolutionary elite. For Proust and Cabrera Infante, only artistic creation through the act of writing could bring personal salvation. Both authors have a highly individualized writing style and each has a most civilized wit. Both are vengeful and aggressive and enjoy ferocious ridicule. Both love digressions and surprise endings, and both are "visual" writers who adore music. Proust was a devoted student of painting and the natural world, while Cabrera Infante is a dedicated student of film and human nature. Both authors are thinkers who are usually seen as writers rather than philosophers. Both writers use language in unexpected ways and both are considered to be pivotal literary figures within their countries.[39]

One of the most striking similarities between Proust and Cabrera Infante is the way in which each writer is able to recreate his remembrances of childhood. For both men, the past intrudes on the present in the form of sensory experience told from the perspective of the adult reenacting, or reliving it. Each author recognizes and reveals that, through art, the past can be reconstructed and that the experiences of our youth can be revisited. For Cabrera Infante and Proust, art is the only path to salvation and the only remedy to fight the ravages of time. In essence, each man has only the past to write about because he truly leaves the past *De Profundis.*[40] In *A la recherche du temps perdu,* Proust intertwines the artistry of Ulster the painter, Bergotte the writer, and Vinteuil the musician in order to give pleasure through their memories of time past. An image or fragrance, anything that could bring back the remembered scent of an old church or a city, was the perfect answer to Proust's dreams and wishes. Cabrera Infante has devoted most of his considerable skills to evoking, in a similar way, the essence of his beloved city of Havana. Exile tests his skills of imagination and his time of solitude is populated with thoughts and remembrances of Cuba that become more alive as they enter the realm of fiction. The city of Havana is presented as a projection of cinematic planes with varying structural tonalities. Is Havana a Balbec that the narrator remembers as a sacred place? For Cabrera Infante, Havana is not only a lost city but one beautified and magnified in legendary proportions through language.

Cabrera Infante's memory is like a garden full of ecstatic poetry for his country. It is the kind of revolutionary poetry that will cancel any discord between history and an idea. Proust transformed the denial of his mother's kiss into literature, while Cabrera Infante converts the denial of official history into capital "Proust-valía."[41] When Cabrera Infante writes, he attempts to revisit the experiences of his childhood, experiences that he believes will never betray him.

Postscript for the Curious

The prelude of "El ave del paraíso perdido," the famous sequence of essays on exile in which Cabrera Infante uses sudden "flashbacks," is one of his finest creations. The finale of the book is gentle and yet powerful and effective enough to convey, in essence, the message for the entire book.

In exile we tend to rescue or invent our own reality. This reality is recognized in a writer's imagination because his dreams and visions are waiting for him. Nostalgia is the most precious treasure an exile can possess. It is ours alone, yet at the same time, it unites our personal memories with those of others. Memory goes back to our conscience and, as Octavio Paz says, once we have conscience, we are free to make a choice. Cabrera Infante takes an unorthodox course, as he shares a cathartic literary experience through a sort of communion with another writer. In 1962 Cabrera Infante found a book in a bookstore in the old section of Havana that had been recommended by Borges. It was *Allá lejos y hace tiempo* (1938) [*Far Away and Long Ago* (1918)] by William Henry Hudson, the English writer who was born to American parents in Argentina and who became destitute and died in London.[42]

For Cabrera Infante, reading this book by Hudson was like sharing destiny. A book written by an exiled writer, any writer, is a book of exodus, and as Cabrera Infante remembers Hudson's book, his memory merges with Hudson's. It is the unity of sharing similar feelings and understanding the same ideas. As he reads Hudson's words, he sees a bird singing on the patio. "¿Es por casualidad un pájaro de Argentina?" (*Mea Cuba* [1992], 483) ["Is it by chance a bird from Argentina?"] Hudson asked his wife (*Mea Cuba* [1994], 491). No, it comes from childhood and past dreams and any exile can listen to its humming. The main difference between Proust's and Cabrera Infante's approaches is that Cabrera Infante's narrator does not reject his dreams and he embraces his past naturally. Proust's narrator rejects many of the things in which he believed after discovering that they were false.

In *Mea Cuba,* one book is finished when another book is recovered. Images and words become one when Cabrera Infante travels a road similar to the one followed by Hudson, suffering similar heartaches and deprivations. The metaphor of seeing exile as a recovered book and traveling along a path with someone else through time and space is a beautiful spiritual adventure. Cabrera Infante has displayed great insight into the absurd nature of the history of an exile. He sees Cuba as the metaphor of a paradox: "Cuba es un paraíso del que huimos tratando de regresar" (*Mea Cuba* [1992], 475) ["Cuba is a paradise from which we flee by trying to return" (*Mea Cuba* [1994], 481).

History is full of surprises and can be a nightmare. As Paz said, "La historia, por sí misma, no tiene sentido: es un escenario transitado sólo por fantasmas sucesivos. La historia es inhumana . . . porque su único personaje es una entidad abstracta: la humanidad" [History in itself has no meaning: it is a stage crossed only by ghosts, one after the other. History is inhuman . . . because its only character is an abstraction: humanity].[43] But history can also be a meeting place where, by revisiting the past, one can make amends and free the spirit. History does not necessarily have to end in chaos. In spite of Cuba's history of violence, treason, and greed for power and the great sadness and loss for the Cuban people, a human being can achieve a sort of identity and reconciliation. Recovering the past creates a transfiguration of his beloved island and that is the true significance of the book. It is based on two important premises: I remember, therefore I exist, and I am responsible, therefore I am free.

If anyone wants to know what it was like to live on the island during those Castrian years, it is to *Mea Cuba* they must go. *Mea Cuba* may be an immense cantata that depicts the passion and death of Castro's communism. Or it may be an opera rich in disappointment with an unusually optimistic ending that must be heard. *Mea Cuba,* Cabrera Infante's masterpiece, is the evocation of a terrible era, an invocation of beloved voices, an accusation of a corrupt regime, a defense of human values, and a meditation on the significance of exile. Guillermo Cabrera Infante's testimony is an act of freedom.

Notes

1. Marcel Proust (1871–1922) was one of the greatest French novelists of the twentieth century, author of *Les plaisirs et le jours* (1896), *A la recherche du temps perdu* [*Remembrance of Things Past*] (1913–1927, seven volumes), and *Jean Santeuil* (1952, three volumes). The second volume of *A la recherche du temps perdu, A l'ombre des jeunes filles en fleurs,* received the Prix Goncourt in 1920. Guillermo Cabrera Infante, *Mea Cuba* (Barcelona: Plaza and Janés, 1992); *Mea Cuba,* trans. Kenneth Hall and Guillermo Cabrera Infante (New York: Farrar, Straus, Giroux, 1994); hereafter cited in the text.

2. Procrustes was a burglar who tied travelers to his bed and made them fit; if their legs were too short, he stretched them, if they were too long he cut them off. Procrustes has been used as a symbol of tyranny and enforced order. Cabrera Infante enhances this symbolism by depicting History as a whore in his bed.

3. Robert Graves (1895–1996) was an English poet and historian. The author of several volumes of poetry and critical essays, he is well-known for his serial adaptation of "I, Claudius" (1934).

Arthur Koestler (1905–1983) was born in Budapest, Hungary, and fought in the Spanish Civil War. He initially embraced Marxist ideals, which he later rejected. He is best known for the novel *Darkness at Noon* (1941), which criticized the Stalinist purges in Moscow.

4. The Mexico City presentation of *Mea Cuba* supports this supposition. The 26 May 1993 event at the Cultural Center in San Angel was delayed by bomb threats, which required that police search the auditorium. Although many frightened people left, the place was packed. The presenters were Enrique Krauze, Carlos Monsivais, Alejandro Rossi, José de la Colina, and myself. I was the first to read a paper. No sooner had I finished than I was publicly insulted by the Castrian "macho squad" in the audience. Krauze, in sotto voce, requested that I not reply. Rossi replied saying that he felt personally insulted that a colleague, and the only woman on the panel, had suffered this aggression. When a telephone line direct to London was opened to the public for discussion, Cabrera Infante was also verbally attacked by the same squad. In Mexico City the aggression continued for days in other forms: phone calls to my home and derogatory articles in newspapers, such as *La jornada.* Only José de la Colina came to my defense one week later in *Novedades.*

5. The comparison of these writers can be found in the essay "*Mea Cuba*" by Nedda G. de Anhalt, published in the Mexican literary magazine *unomásuno* 818 (5 June 1993): 5.

6. I am not implying that José Martí was without humor. His play "Amor con amor se paga" proves that he had humor. But his essays, though they give free reign to his passions, are serious.

7. Jonathan Swift (1667–1745), born in Dublin, educated in Ireland, and the author of *Tale of a Tub* and *Gulliver's Travels,* must have had some knowledge of the Spanish language. Naming the land Laputa (the whore) indicates that he did. Unfortunately, many Cubans have taken to prostitution as a way of survival with the blessing of Fidel Castro, who has publicly acknowledged in his speeches the "culture of our women prostitutes." "They do it for pleasure, not for necessity." It goes without saying that this collapse of values is a consequence of the communist regime's failure and not the so-called "blockade," which is really an "embargo" that does not prevent the regime from receiving goods from other countries.

George Orwell (1903–1950) was born in India. His real name was Eric Blair. He fought in the Spanish Civil War and wrote *Homage to Catalonia, Burmese Days, A Clergyman's Daughter, The Road to Wigan Pier, Coming Up for Air, Keep the Aspidistra Flying,* and the masterpieces *Animal Farm* and *Nineteen Eighty-Four.*

8. UMAP (Unidad Militar de Ayuda a la Producción) [Military Unit for the Aid of Production] was the Orwellian euphemism used by Castro's regime to name concentration camps throughout Cuba during the 1970s where homosexuals and other dissidents—religious and political—were detained.

9. Other famous Cuban writers, such as Eugenio Florit, Gastón Baquero, Justo Rodríguez Santos, José Lezama Lima, and Enrique Labrador Ruiz embraced Christianity. Lorenzo García Vega is a follower of Buddhism.

10. Often, the greater the writer, the more difficult the translation. Joyce is one example. Cabrera Infante is another. These ingenious puns can be literally translated: "Castroenteritis" [a sickness] (*Mea Cuba* [1992], 231; *Mea Cuba* [1994], 279); "castradura que dura" [castration that lasts] (*Mea Cuba* [1992], 265; omitted in *Mea Cuba* [1994]). But the author makes a brilliant double meaning with "dura"

that at the same time is "hard" and "lasting." "Espera estoica" [stoic wait] (*Mea Cuba* [1992], 468; *Mea Cuba* [1994], 470), in Spanish plays on a similar sound of the Russian "Perestroika."

11. Herbert George Wells (1866–1946) was a British pioneer and science-fiction novelist, best known for his novels *The Time Machine, The Island of Dr. Moreau,* and *The Invisible Man.* Edna O'Brien is a contemporary British novelist.

12. Roquentin is the main character in the novel *La Nausée* (1938), written by Jean Paul Sartre, winner of the 1964 Nobel Prize in literature.

13. Alastair Reid (b.1926), Scottish poet and author of *Weathering, Passwords, Whereabouts, Supposing, To Lighten My House, I Will Tell You of a Town, Borges: A Reader* (in collaboration with Emir Rodríguez Monegal), and *An Alastair Reid Reader: Selected Prose and Poetry,* in his article "Talking Cuba," *New Yorker Review* (2 February 1995): 14–16.

14. The idea of the author converted into a pedantic and cosmopolitan narrator is not to fool anyone but to enhance the author's critical dissection. Proust's narrator, for example, identified with Jewish Swann but maintained a distance from the Dreyfus affair, even though Proust was known to call himself the first "Dreyfusard." Cabrera Infante's narrator is close to the author's ideas and feelings and is a sort of conscience.

15. In *Tres tristes tigres* Cabrera Infante used a similar idea as a way of introduction with the master of ceremonies at the Tropicana nightclub. The MC presents guests who will be the characters in the story. Guillermo Cabrera Infante, *Tres tristes tigres* (Barcelona: Editorial Seix Barral, 1967); *Three Trapped Tigers,* trans. Donald Gardner and Suzanne Jill Levine with Guillermo Cabrera Infante (New York: Harper and Row, 1971).

16. Reinaldo Arenas in an interview "Aquel mar una vez más" [That sea once more] referred to a similar incident that happened to him in his New York apartment. His window was left open and things were misplaced, although nothing was taken. He explained that the purpose of such actions was to create paranoia and a sense of persecution (Nedda G. de Anhalt, *Rojo y naranja sobre rojo* [Mexico: Editorial Vuelta, 1991], 144).

17. José Martí in *Versos sencillos,* vol. 12, no. 38, of *Gran Enciclopedia Martiana,* 15 vols. (Florida: Editorial Martiana, 1978), 51. The verses are "Del tirano? / Del tirano / Di todo, di más!;y clava / Con furia de mano esclava / Sobre su oprobio al tirano." William Shakespeare, *A Midsummer-Night's Dream* (Boston: Roberts Brothers, 1870), 11.

18. *P.M.* is a brief film in the style of free cinema produced by Sabá Cabrera, Cabrera Infante's brother, and Orlando Jiménez Leal that examines nightlife in Havana. It was the first work of art to suffer censorship and political judgment and was labeled counterrevolutionary. Later Jiménez Leal was the film director who, in collaboration with Néstor Almendros, directed *Conducta impropia* [Improper Conduct], a film that won the Human Rights Prize in Strasbourg in 1984.

19. CDR stands for Comité de Defensa de la Revolución [Committee for the Revolution's Defense], to be read "committee of spies."

20. UNEAC stands for Unión Nacional de Escritores y Artistas Cubanos [National Cuban Union of Writers and Artists].

21. Federico García Lorca (1898–1936) was a Spanish poet and playwright and the author of the *Romancero gitano* (1928) and the plays *Yerma, Doña Rosita la soltera,* and *La casa de Bernarda Alba.*

22. Walker Evans (1903–1975) was a famous North American photographer who, during the 1930s, traveled to Cuba to photograph the island. In 1934 the Museum of Modern Art in New York held an exhibition that showcased Evans's photographs.

23. In "Lorca hace llover en La Habana" I found a remarkable coincidence with a verse of the Cuban poet Gastón Baquero (Banes, Oriente 1918–Madrid, 1997) in his "Carta en el agua perdida" (*Poesía completa* [Salamanca: Fundación Central Hispano, 1995], 258–61), dedicated to García Lorca, in which Baquero says: "¡Un monumento de aguas quisiera levantarte!" [A water monument I would like to bestow upon you!]. That is exactly what Cabrera Infante has done in his essay "Lorca the Rainmaker Visits Havana." The spiritual approach of both writers is touching, especially since this poem of Baquero was unpublished until 1995.

24. "J'Accuse" was a most memorable defense of the French-Jewish Captain Alfred Dreyfus written by the French intellectual Emile Zola (1840–1902), author of 20 volumes known as *Rougon-Macquart*.

25. Gustavo Arcos accompanied Fidel Castro in the same car during the Moncada Barracks assault in which he received wounds to his legs. He became the Cuban ambassador in Belgium in 1959 but was soon recalled by Castro to Havana, where he was accused, without any proof, of being a part of a conspiracy he knew nothing about. In 1982, he was sentenced to 14 years in prison, and his brother Sebastián was sentenced to 11 years in prison. For Cabrera Infante, Arcos is a "punished" hero.

26. *The Golden Cockerel* or *Le Coq D'or* or *Zolotoy Pyetushok* is a Russian opera in three acts by Nikolay Andreyevich Rimsky-Korsakov (1844–1908), first performed in 1909. It is based on a fairy tale by Aleksandr Sergeyevich Pushkin (1799–1837), who had heard the story from his nurse. In Rimsky-Korsakov's fairy-tale land, King Dondon sits on his magnificent throne, but his army is no good and soldiers can be seen sleeping at their posts. An astrologer gives the king a golden cockerel that will be quiet when all is well but will crow when there is danger.

27 Carlos Franqui, *Retrato de familia con Fidel* (Barcelona: Editorial Seix Barral, 1981).

28. Cabrera Infante is not the only author to publicly criticize and question García Márquez's support of the Castro dictatorship. Another Cuban author and poet, Reinaldo Arenas (Holguín 1943–New York 1990) in *Necesidad de libertad* [Need for Freedom] (México: Kosmos, 1986), 65–69, shares Cabrera Infante's attitude, calling García Márquez a "vedette of communism" (67).

29. Jacques Louis David (1748–1825) was a French court painter during the reign of Louis XVI who, for Cabrera Infante, symbolizes the artist as the opportunistic cynic. With Danton, Robespierre, and Saint Just, David exalted terror but was not decapitated as were the others. Cabrera Infante is obviously referring to the double standard that exists among many Cubans who had once worked for Batista and who now occupy important positions within the Castro regime. These same collaborators will certainly find a position within a new regime once Castro is no longer in power.

30. "Guillermo Cabrera Infante: Interview with Armando Álvarez Bravo," *El Nuevo Herald* (9 October 1991): 1D, 4D.

31. G. de Anhalt, *Rojo y naranja sobre rojo*, 228.

32. José María Heredia (Santiago de Cuba 1803–Mexico 1839) was the author of many famous poems, including "Niágara," "En el Teocalli" [In the Cholula

Teocalli], and "Himno al desterrado" [Hymn to the Exiled]. José Martí (1853–1895) was a Cuban spiritual leader and author of *Ismaelillo, Versos sencillos* [Simple verses], *Lucía Jerez, Amor con amor se paga* [Love with love is paid], and countless volumes of essays. Juan Clemente Zenea (Bayamo 1832–Havana 1871) was an outstanding poet and author of "Fidelia," "A una golondrina" [To a swallow], "Las sombras" [The shadows], and "En días de esclavitud" [Slavery days]. Even though this poet had a Spanish safe-conduct from the minister of Spain in the United States, he was executed by firing squad by the Spaniards in Cuba.

Gertrudis Gómez de Avellaneda (Camagüey 1824–Madrid 1873) became a literary precocity when at age six she created her first verses in honor of her father's death. She is the author of many beautiful poems, but "Al partir" [When you leave] is the most famous. She also wrote the novels *Sab* (1841) and *Guatimozin* (1846) and the plays *Leoncia* (1841), *Alfonso Munio* (1844), and *Baltasar* (1858), among others. Cirilo Villaverde (Pinar del Río 1812–New York 1894) created *Cecilia Valdés* (1882), the first great Cuban novel of the nineteenth century. Julian del Casal (Havana 1863–Havana 1893) was an outstanding poet and author of *Hojas al viento* [Leaves in the wind] (1880) and *Nieve* [Snow] (1890).

José Lezama Lima (1910–1976) at the age of 21 wrote a remarkable poem entitled "La muerte de Narciso" [The death of Narcissus]. As a leading cultural figure in Cuba, he founded several important literary magazines, including *Verbum, Espuela de plata, Nadie parecía,* and *Orígenes.* His books of poetry include: *Enemigo rumor* [Enemy's rumor] (1941), *La fijeza* [The fix] (1949), and *Dador* [Giver] (1960). He also wrote several collections of essays, including *La expresión americana* [The American expression] (1957), *Tratados en La Habana* [Treaties in Havana] (1958), and *La cantidad hechizada* [The bewitched quantity] (1970), but his masterpiece is the novel *Paradiso* (1966). Lezama Lima lived the last years of his life in Cuba in seclusion and literary oblivion imposed by Castro's cultural regime. Lezama Lima and Piñera are important Cuban writers and Cabrera Infante wrote an essay about them entitled "Tema del héroe y la heroína" (*Mea Cuba* [1992], 317–48) ["Two Wrote Together" (*Mea Cuba* [1994], 331–60)]. Virgilio Piñera (Cárdenas 1912–Havana 1979), creator of the "Theater of the Absurd" before Ionesco, was the author of several books of poetry, including *Las furias* [The furies] (1941), *La isla en peso* [The island in all its weight] (1943), *La carne de René* [The flesh of René] (1952), *Pequeñas maniobras* [Small maneuvers] (1963), and *Presiones y diamantes* [Pressures and diamonds] (1967); and numerous plays including "Falsa alarma" [False alarm] (1948). Because he was a homosexual, he suffered persecution. He was arrested in 1960 at his beach home in Guanabo, and his apartment was sealed.

33. "Vesti la giubba" is the famous aria sung by the tenor Canio in the first act of Ruggiero Leoncavallo's opera *Pagliacci* (1892).

34. Cabrera Infante, *Tres tristes tigres* [*Three Trapped Tigers*]. The section of the book is entitled "La muerte de Trotsky referida por varios escritores cubanos, años despues—o antes" (225–58) ["The death of Trotsky as described by various Cuban writers, several years after the event—or before," (235–78)].

35. *Julius Caesar* is an opera in three acts by George Frederick Handel, first performed in London in 1724.

36. In 1884 Captain Alfred Dreyfus was unjustly accused of treason to France. The case against Dreyfus was based on a piece of handwriting called *Bordereau* that was actually written by Esterhazy, the true spy. Dreyfus was imprisoned under the most inhuman conditions on Devil's Island. The false documents that the military presented in a "Secret Dossier" during both processes in order to "reinforce"

Dreyfus's guilt highlight a paradox: France, the birth nation of freedom, equality, and fraternity was guilty of turning this French-Jewish officer into a martyr of injustice.

37. Guillermo Cabrera Infante, "InFidelity with a Cuban Exile: Interview with Christian Tyler," *Financial Times* (London) (19 November 1994).

38. Roger Martin du Gard (1881–1958) was the French author of *Les Thibault,* the story of a French family destroyed by the First World War (1914–1918) and *Jean Barois,* the great novel that recreates the events surrounding the Dreyfus affair and the experiences of the protagonist and his friends, the young French founders of a magazine. The novel, written in 1913, shows the point of view of a generation that saw its great hopes and expectations overshadowed by national and world events.

39. Other similarities between Proust and Cabrera Infante do not concern this work. This essay tries to establish only general tendencies and influences.

40. *De Profundis* is the title of a novel by Oscar Wilde (1856–1900) and it is used for its literary significance [very profound].

41. The pun "Proust-valía" is Cabrera Infante's in *Mea Cuba*. The author transforms the Marxist economic term of "plus-valia," which appears in *Das Kapital* and refers to the difference between the value of a finished product and the salary of a worker, to an onomatopoetic "Proust-valía." "Esa ojeada al pasado es lo que un marxista llamaría la Proust valía" (*Mea Cuba* [1992], 310). This play on words is lost in the English translation: "That slow glance at the past is what we could call Proust's sight" (*Mea Cuba* [1994], 274).

42. William Henry Hudson (Quilmes, Argentina 1841–London 1922) was an author and naturalist who wrote on his personal experiences in bird watching and nature study in the remote regions of South America. His best-known novels are *Green Mansions* (1904) and *The Purple Land* (1885). Along with his autobiography, *Far Away and Long Ago*, they are vivid accounts of life in Argentina. *Far Away and Long Ago* (New York: E.P. Dutton and Co., 1918) and *Allá lejos y hace tiempo: relatos de mi infancia*, trans. Fernando Pozzo and Celia Rodríguez de Pozzo (Buenos Aires: Casa Jacobo Peuser, 1938).

43. Octavio Paz, *Puertas al campo* [*Doors to the field*] (1966; reprint, Barcelona: Editorial Seix Barral, 1972), 47.

Selected Bibliography

RICHARD D. CACCHIONE WITH ARDIS L. NELSON

First Editions of Guillermo Cabrera Infante's Books

Así en la paz como en la guerra. Havana: Ediciones R, 1960.
Un oficio del siglo veinte. [G. Caín, pseud.]. Havana: Ediciones R, 1963.
Tres tristes tigres. Barcelona: Editorial Seix Barral, 1967.
Vista del amanecer en el trópico. Barcelona: Editorial Seix Barral, 1974.
O. Barcelona: Editorial Seix Barral, 1975.
Exorcismos de esti(l)o. Barcelona: Editorial Seix Barral, 1976.
Arcadia todas las noches. Barcelona: Editorial Seix Barral, 1978.
La Habana para un Infante difunto. Barcelona: Editorial Seix Barral, 1979.
Holy Smoke. New York: Harper and Row, 1985.
Mea Cuba. Barcelona: Plaza and Janés, 1992.
Delito por bailar el chachachá. Madrid: Alfaguara, 1995.
Ella cantaba boleros. Madrid: Alfaguara, 1996.
Mi música extremada. Ed. Rosa M. Pereda. Madrid: Editorial Espasa Calpe, 1996.
Cine o sardina. Madrid: Alfaguara, 1997.
Cervantes, mi contemporáneo. Madrid: Alfaguara, 1998.
Todo está hecho con espejos. Madrid: Alfaguara, 1999.
La ventana pineal. Madrid: Alfaguara, 1999.

Selected Essays Written by Guillermo Cabrera Infante

Guillermo Cabrera Infante's essays have appeared in almost 100 journals, magazines, and newspapers in at least 17 countries. Several of his essays have been published more than once, usually first in a journal and subsequently in one of his books or in another periodical. Whenever possible we have listed the first known appearance of his essays. Film reviews and essays included in Cabrera Infante's published collections of essays, such as *Un oficio del siglo veinte, O, Exorcismos de esti(l)o, Mea Cuba, Mi música extremada, Cine o sardina,* and *La ventana pineal* are not necessarily included here.

"El actor como político y el político como actor." *Vuelta* (México) 57 (August 1981): 14–17.

"Actores y electores." *Claves* (Madrid) 12 (May 1991): 2–8.

"Adiós al amigo con la cámera: en la muerte de Néstor Almendros." *El Pais* (Madrid) (6 March 1992):30.

"After the Fuck." Trans. Susan [*sic*] Jill Levine and the author. *Salmagundi* (Saratoga Springs, N.Y.) 82–83 (Spring–Summer 1989): 185–221.

"Aguas de recuerdo." *Bohemia* 2, 21 (13 June 1948): 20–21, 64–66.

" 'Alejandro Nevsky', 'el destino de un hombre' y 20 años de realismo socialista." [G. Caín, pseud.] *Carteles* (Havana) 41, 22 (29 May 1960):42–44.

"¿Alguien ha visto los ojos de Cary Grant?" *Diario 16* (Madrid) (22 July 1984): VI–VII. Section: Cine.

"Alice in Wondercontinent." *Review: Latin American Literature and Arts* (New York) 47 (Fall 1993): 14–15.

"Alicia, en el continente de las Maravillas." *El País* (Madrid) (23 September 1988): 15.

"Alicia resucitada a través del espejo." *El País* (Madrid) (23 October 1977): VIII. Section: Arte y Pensamiento.

"Alrededor de Octavio Paz." *El Nuevo Herald* (Miami) (31 March 1994): 13A.

"An American Myth (a fragment)." *Review* 76 (New York) 17 (Spring 1976): 54–63.

"El american tranquilo." *El País* (14 August 1982):17.

"El amor que (no) se atreve a decir su nombre." *Vuelta* (México) 2, 13 (December 1977): 49–50.

"Antonio Ortega vuelve a Asturias," *Los Cuadernos del Norte* (Oviedo) 6, 30 (March–April 1985): 62–65. Section: Los Cuadernos de Asturias.

"Apocalypse in Wonderland." Trans. Donald Gardner and Suzanne Jill Levine. *Mundus Artium* (Athens, Ohio) 3, 3 (Summer 1970): 98–105.

"Ardua ad ashtray." Review of *The Ultimate Pipe Book,* by Richard Carleton Hacker. *Daily Telegraph* (London) (31 December 1988).

"El arte breve y Vincente Minnelli feliz de." In *Arcadia todas las noches,* 159–84. Barcelona: Editorial Seix Barral, 1978.

"El arte (en parte) de Bonifacio." *Bonifacio* (Madrid) (1995): 1–4. Brochure for Galería Antonio Machón.

"At Tranquilina's Knee." Trans. Ann Wright. Review of *The Fragrance of Guava: Plinio Apuleyo Mendoza in conversation with Gabriel García Márquez. London Review of Books* 5, 10 (2–15 June 1983): 18–19.

"Auge, decadencia y auge del club inglés." Icosaedros series. *El País Semanal* (Madrid) (12 November 1978): 31.

"El ave del paraíso perdido." *Linden Lane Magazine* 1, 1 (January–March 1982): 7.

"Ave félix." *El País Semanal* (Madrid) (7 December 1980): 4–6.

"El Ave Fénix en el Paraíso." *Ideas '92* (Coral Gables) 10 (Spring 1992): 1–10.

"¡Ave Marías!" *El País* (Madrid) (27 July 1998): 9–10.

"El bacilo de Hitchcock." *Consenso* (New Kensington, Pa.) 1, 1 (May 1977): 19–35.

"Bad Babs." In *Diablesas y Diosas (14 perversas para 14 autores),* ed. Joaquín Romaguera i Ramió and Eduardo Suárez, 9–15. Barcelona: Editorial Laertes, 1990.

"Bajo el volcán o la vida vista desde el fondo de una botella de mescal." *Los Cuadernos del Norte* (Oviedo) 2, 6 (March–April 1981): 60–65. Section: Los Cuadernos de Literatura.

"Ballet de Cuba." *Lunes de Revolución* (Havana) 53 (4 April 1960): 2–5.

"Barbara en el recuerdo." *Cambio 16* (Madrid) 953 (26 February 1990): 108–9.

"Bath no sólo quiere decir baño." *El País* (Madrid) (21 September 1988): 13.
"Beldad y mentira de Marilyn Monroe." *El País* (Madrid) (9 August 1982): 18.
"La belleza de la bomba." [Jonás Castro, pseud.] *Carteles* (Havana) 37, 32 (5 August 1956): 58–60.
"Bienvenida lady salsa." *Diario 16* (Madrid) 184 (8 July 1984): 1–2. Suplemento Cultural.
"The Biggest Splash." *FMR International* (New York) 52 (October 1991): 17–24.
"The Bishop of Hippo. . . ." *Daily Telegraph* (London) (24 November 1990).
"Bites from the Bearded Crocodile." *London Review of Books* 3, 10 (4–17 June 1981): 3–8.
"Blonde on Blonde: A Love Letter to Melanie Griffith." *American Film* 13, 5 (March 1988): 48–52.
"Boleros son." *Claves* (Madrid) 18 (December 1991): 54–58. Section: Folklore.
"Borges y yo." *El País* (Madrid) (16 June 1986): 34.
"La breve vida feliz de François Truffaut." *Diario 16* (Madrid) (25 October 1984): 3–4.
"Brief Encounters in Havana." *World Literature Today* 61, 4 (Autumn 1987): 519–25.
"El brillante Brian de Palma." *Hombre de Mundo* (Panama) (December 1978): 22–23.
"Brubrú." *El País* (Madrid) (22 September 1988): 15.
"Buñuel al desnudo." *El País* (Madrid) (1 August 1983): 23.
"Buñuel, la caridad y el cristo que ríe." [G. Caín, pseud.] Review of *Nazarín*. *Carteles* (Havana) 41, 29 (17 July 1960): 26–28.
"By Myself." Preface to *Guillermo Cabrera Infante and the Cinema,* by Kenneth E. Hall, xiii–xxi. Hispanic Monographs. Newark, Del.: Juan de la Cuesta, 1989.
"Caín by Himself. Guillermo Cabrera Infante: Man of Three Islands." *Review: Latin American Literature and Arts* (New York) 28 (January–April 1981): 8–11.
"La calumnia que no queda." *El Nuevo Herald* (Miami) (20 April 1994): 11A.
"Capa hijo de Caissa." *Cambio 16* (Madrid) 897 (6 February 1989): 110–17.
"Carta de Cabrera Infante a Umberto Valverde." *El Espectador* (Bogota) (24 January 1982): 7. Section: Magazín dominical.
"Cartas son cartas." Icosaedros series. *El País Semanal* (Madrid) (29 May 1977): 17.
"La castroenteritis." *Diario 16* (Madrid) (7 March 1990): 27.
"(C)ave Attemptor! A Chronology of GCI (After Laurence Sterne's)." *Review 72* (New York) 4/5 (Winter 71/Spring 72): 4–9.
"La caza del facsímil." *Cambio 16* (Madrid) 583 (31 January 1983): 86–87.
"Una cenicienta del siglo XX: La vida de Audrey Hepburn." [G. Caín, pseud.] *Carteles* (Havana) 35, 50 (12 December 1954): 61–63, 102–3.
"Censor Obseso, Obsceno: *Tres tristes tigres* acosados, cazados por la Censura." *Nueva Sociedad* (San José, Costa Rica) 100 (March–April 1989): 216–22.
"El censor como obsexo." *Espiral/Revista* (Madrid) 6 (1979): 167–84 Issue: Erotismos.
"The Censorship of the Scythe." Review of *Federico García Lorca: A Life,* by Ian Gibson. *Guardian* (Manchester) (30 June 1989): 26.
"Centenario en el espejo." *Mundo Nuevo* (Paris) 13 (July 1967): 62–66.
"La ceremonia del té." Icosaedros series. *El País Semanal* (Madrid) (25 September 1977): 12–13.
"Chaplin resucitado." *Cambio 16* (Madrid) 588 (7 March 1983): 104–6.
"Christmas Carroll." *El Independiente* (Madrid) (4 July 1987): 27.
"Cine censura: ¡lo prohibido!" *Carteles* (Havana) 38, 3 (20 January 1957): 44–45

"Cine en Nueva York." *Carteles* (Havana) 36, 41 (9 October 1955): 42–45.

"City in search of its identity." Review of *Barcelona: A Thousand Years of the City's Past*, by Felipe Fernández-Armesto. *Sunday Telegraph* (London) (28 April 1991): xi.

"La comedia (musicale) e finita!" *El Nuevo Día* (Puerto Rico) (13 November 1983): 12–16. Section: Domingo.

"Cómo hacer actuar a una trinchera y morir para contarlo." *Hombre de Mundo* (Panama) (January 1979): 22–25.

"La confundida lengua del poeta." *Primera Plana* (Buenos Aires) 7, 316 (14–20 January 1969): 64–65.

"Corín Tellado: visita ¿o misión cumplida?" *El País* (Madrid) (23 August 1981): 6–7. Section: Libros.

"Corneado por Monty Python o la vida de Brian." Review of Monty Python's *La Vida de Brian,* directed by Terry Jones. *Los Cuadernos del Norte* (Oviedo) 1, 4 (October/November/December 1980): 38–40. Section: Los Cuadernos de Cine.

"Cuando Emir estaba vivo." *Diario 16* (Madrid) (19 October 1986): IV–V. Suplemento semanal: Culturas.

"*Los 400 golpes,* el 'Premio André Bazin' y la miseria de los festivales." [G. Caín, pseud.] *Revolución* (Havana) 332 (4 January 1960): 24.

"Cuba y sus sones." *Vuelta* (México) 7, 75 (February 1975): 39–43.

"Los cubanos bailan en el cine." [G. Caín, pseud.] Review of *Cuba baila. Carteles* (Havana) 41, 14 (3 April 1960): 42–44.

"Cuba's Shadow." *Film Comment* (New York) 21, 3 (May–June 1985): 43–45.

"Cuerpos Divinos (fragmentos)." *El Paseante* (Madrid) 26 (1996): 6–11.

"Cuervos y marcianos." *Clarín* (Buenos Aires) (12 July 1998): 7. Suplemento: Cultura y Nación.

"¡Dance, disco, dance!" Icosaedros series. *El País Semanal* (Madrid) (28 January 1979): 21.

"Danzas y diosas del musical." *El País* (Madrid) (4 July 1981): 5. Section: Artes.

"De entre los muertos." *Cambio 16* (Madrid) 644 (2 April 1984): 117.

"De mortuis." *El País* (Madrid) (28 April 1987): 11–12.

"Dead Dandy." Icosaedros series. *El País Semanal* (Madrid) (30 July 1978): 9.

"The Death of Virgilio." Introduction to *Cold Tales,* by Virgilio Piñero, ix–xiv. Hygiene, Colo.: Eridanos Press, 1988.

"Delito por bailar el chachachá." *Mundo Nuevo* (Paris) 25 (July 1968): 59–71.

"Del sentimiento cómico de la vida." *La Nación* (Buenos Aires) (30 July 1995): 1–2. Section 7: Cultura.

"¿Derecho de copia o delito de copia? Un mal de imprenta que atacó ya al Quijote—y todavía dura." *Vuelta* (México) 14, 161 (April 1990): 31–34.

"Desde el Swinging London." *Mundo Nuevo* (Paris) 14 (August 1967): 45–46, 48, 50, 52–53.

"El detective que canta." *Cambio 16* (Madrid) 793 (9 February 1987): 86–88, 90.

"El diablo y Margaret te." *El País* (Madrid) (25–26 December 1990): 11–12.

"Un día como otro cualquiera." *Lunes de Revolución* (Havana) 100 (27 March 1961): 9–12.

"Un día inolvidable." *Lunes de Revolución* (Havana) Extra Issue (7 March 1960): 13–14.

"El día que murió Jesús." *Lunes de Revolución* (Havana) Special Issue (30 April 1960): 29–30.

"Un diario que dura más de cien años." Prologue to *Diarios/José Martí*, by José Martí, 7–22. Barcelona: Galaxia Gutenberg, Círculo de Lectores, 1997.

"Días callados en Cliché." *Cambio 16* (Madrid) 911 (15 May 1989): 130–31, 133.

"Diccionario del Angel." *Babelia*, Supplement of *El País* (Madrid) (25 January 1997): 11.

"La doble caída de Jacobo Arbenz: Una entrevista con Luis Cardoza y Aragón por Guillermo Cabrera Infante." *Lunes de Revolución* (Havana) 22 (17 August 1959): 21–22.

"El don de las niñas." *El País* (Madrid) (16 February 1986): 15. Section: Domingo.

"Dos museos belgas." *Guadalimar: Revista Mensual de las Bellas Artes* 1, 8 (10 December 1975): 50.

"The dust of Madrid." Review of *Fortunata and Jacinta*, by Benito Pérez Galdós, trans. Agnes Moncy Guillón. *Observer* (London) (1 February 1987): 31. Section: Review.

"El Edén tiene siempre dos Evas." *El País* (Madrid) (3 July 1986): 1, 6–7. Section: Libros.

"El elefante de Buñuel." *Carteles* (Havana) 38, 21 (26 May 1957): 42–45.

"Ella cantaba boleros." *Lunes de Revolución* (Havana) 128 (23 October 1961): 8–10.

"Ellos vivieron en Kensington." Icosaedros series. *El País Semanal* (Madrid) (21 August 1977): 9, 26.

"En busca del amor ganado." Icosaedros series. *El País Semanal* (Madrid) (8 January 1978): 14–15.

"En espera del Piñera total." *El País* (Madrid) (26 December 1983): 3. Section: Libros.

"En los límites de la locura." *El País* (Madrid) (12 December 1996): 3. Supplement: Los límites del cuerpo humano.

"En serie, pero 'sui géneris.' " *El País* (Madrid) (28 May 1983): 6. Section: Artes.

"Encuentros y recuerdos con José Lezama Lima." *Vuelta* (México) 1, 3 (February 1977): 46–48.

"English Profanities." Trans. Peggy Boyers. In *Lives on the Line: The Testimony of Contemporary Latin American Authors*, ed. Doris Meyer, 59–71. Berkeley: University of California Press, 1988.

"Entre la historia y la nada (Notas sobre una ideología del suicidio)." *Escandalar* (Elmhurst, N.Y.) 5, 1–2 (January–June 1982): 68–83.

"Entrevista a Silvana Pampanini." [G. Caín, pseud.] *Revolución* (Havana) 2, 81 (11 March 1959): 1, 16.

"Epilogue for Late(nt) Readers." *Review 72* (New York) 4–5 (Winter 1971/Spring 1972): 23–32.

"Eppur si muove? o el hundimiento del Swinging London." *Primera Plana* (Buenos Aires) 6, 290 (16–22 July 1968): 37–38, 40–43, 45–46, 48–50.

"El escritor y la aspereza." *Vuelta* (México) 8, 86 (January 1984): 51–52.

"Los escritores versus USA." *Lunes de Revolución* (Havana) 55 (18 April 1960): 3–10.

"El español no es una lengua muerta." *El País* (Madrid) (23 January1987): 11–12.

"Espías con salsa inglesa." Icosaedros series. *El País* (Madrid) (12 February 1978): 5.

"Et in Arcadia." *El País* (Madrid) (20 September 1988): 13.

"Una Eva que llevaba consigo el paraíso." *Cambio 16* (Madrid) 950 (5 February 1990): 126–28.

"An exile's indictment." *Sunday Telegraph* (London) (4 March 1990): 17.

"El exilio invisible." *Vuelta* (México) 7, 81 (August 1983): 47–49.

"Exorcising A Sty(le)." Trans. Suzanne Jill Levine. *Review 74* (New York) 12 (Fall 1974): 61–62.

"*Exorcismos de esti(l)o* (Fragmentos)." *Papeles de Son Armadans,* year 19, vol. 72, no. 214 (Palma de Mallorca) (January 1974): 87–94.

"Fábulas rasas." *Papeles de Son Armadans,* year 21, vol. 80, no. 239 (Palma de Mallorca) (February 1976): 159–66. Section: Plazuela del Conde Lucanor.

"Farewell to a Man with the Camera." *Review: Latin American Literature and Arts* (New York) 46 (Fall 1992): 26–28.

"La felicidad es un ardor renuente (historia de un mito)." *El País* (Madrid) (5 October 1987): 11.

"Une femme qui se noie." Trans. Albert Bensoussan. *La Nouvelle Revue Française* 528 (January 1997): 57–68.

"El Fenómeno Punk." *El Universal* (Caracas) (7 August 1977): 1–29.

"Festibalada." *Festival* (San Sebastián) 31st ed. (19 September 1983): 3.

"La ficción es el crimen que paga Poe." *Los Cuadernos del Norte* (Oviedo) 4, 19 (May–June 1983): 2–7. Section: Novela criminal.

"El fin como principio." *Espiral/Revista* (Madrid) 2 (1977): 225–29.

"El final feliz de Vincente Minnelli." *Hombre de Mundo* (Panama) 3, 11 (November 1978) 3, 11: 32–33.

"Flann O'Brien, el Otro Irlandés." *El Universal* (Caracas) (9 March 1980): 4–1, 4–4. Section: Culturales.

"Flann O'Brien un Escritor (casi) Desconocido." *El Universal* (Caracas) (2 March 1980): 4–1, 4–2. Section: Culturales.

"Flann O'Brien: un sólo escritor y muchos nombres." *Espiral/Revista* (Madrid) 3 (1977): 175–218.

"Formal de Hyde." *El Urogallo* (Madrid) 8 (December 1986): 29–32.

"La fortaleza en el fuerte." [G. Caín, pseud.] *Revolución* (Havana) 2, 315 (12 December 1959): 1, 16.

"¡Fortunio Bonanova!" *GQ* (Madrid) 7 (December 1995–January 1996): 170.

"Las fotos del cine." *Hombre de Mundo* (Panama) 4, 4 (April 1979): 22–24.

"García Márquez à La Havane." *Esprit* (Paris) 10 (October 1983): 149–52.

"Un genio nada frequente." *El País* (Madrid) (10 August 1986): 9–10.

"Gershwin 'Swings.' " *Babelia*, Supplement of *El Pais* (Madrid) (19 September 1998): 4–5.

"Gloria in excelsis dea." *Cambio 16* (Madrid) 595 (25 April 1983): 162–63.

"Goodbye Charlie." *Diario 16* (Madrid) (29 April 1989): iv–v.

"El gran Cukor." *El Nuevo Día* (Puerto Rico) (3 July 1983): 16–20. Section: Domingo.

"Greene's easy pieces." Review of *Mornings in the Dark,* ed. David Parkinson. *Spectator* (London) (22 January 1994): 31–32.

"Guantanamerías." *El País* (Madrid) (11 April 1993): 11–12.

"Un guión para la locura." *Cambio 16* (Madrid) 672 (15–22 October 1984): 126–28.

"El halcón maltés." *Babelia*, Supplement of *El Pais* (Madrid) (26 September 1992): 8–9.

"¿Ha muerto el socialismo?" *Cambio 16* (Madrid) 939 (27 November 1989): 103.

"Happily accepting the spell of baseball in Cuba." *Miami Herald* (7 March 1987): 15. Section: Sports Special.

"Hasta el último gentleman." Icosaedros series. *El País Semanal* (Madrid) (2 July 1978): 6–7.

"Havana and Have None." Review of *Ernest Hemingway Rediscovered,* by Norberto Fuentes. *Daily Telegraph* (London) (8 April 1989).

"Hawks quiere decir halcón." In *Arcadia todas las noches,* 85–126. Barcelona: Editorial Seix Barral, 1978.

"The Heart of Havana." Review of *Walker Evans: Havana 1933*. *Independent Magazine* (London) 65 (2 December 1989): 76–80.

"Hemingway y Cuba y la Revolución." *Lunes de Revolución* (Havana) 118 (14 August 1961): 16–19.
"La herida inmoral." *Lunes de Revolución* (Havana) Final Issue (6 November 1961): 3–4.
"El héroe castigado (Vidas de un héroe III)." *Diario 16* (Madrid) (3 October 1984): 3–4.
"El héroe premiado (Vidas de un héroe II)." *Diario 16* (Madrid) (2 October 1984): 3–4.
"El héroe renuente (Vidas de un héroe I)." *Diario 16* (Madrid) (1 October 1984): 3–4.
"Historia de dos zapatos." *GQ* (Madrid) 6 (October–November 1995): 170.
"Historia de un bastón." *La Gaceta de Cuba* (Havana) 4, 43 (March–April 1965).
"Hitchcock ¡hitch, hitch, hurrah!" *Diario 16* (Madrid) (20 May 1984): VI–VII. Suplemento semanal: Culturas.
"Hitchhiker." *El Nuevo Día* (Puerto Rico) (27 August 1989): 17–21. Section: Domingo.
"Hoax." *Babelia*, Supplement of *El País* (Madrid) (18 July 1998): 17.
"Hollywood a la moral." [G. Caín, pseud.] *Carteles* (Havana) 35, 38 (19 September 1954): 39.
"Holmes sweet Holmes." *El País* (Madrid) (11 January 1987): 25.
"El hombre que quería ser William Holden." *El País* (Madrid) (4 December 1981): 11.
"Un hombre llamado Navaja." *El Nuevo Día* (Puerto Rico) (30 September 1984): 4–7.
"Homosexuales históricos." Icosaedros series. *El País Semanal* (Madrid) (24 July 1977): 19.
"Horizontes de grandeza." [G. Caín, pseud.] Review of *The Big Country*. *Revolución* (Havana) 2, 70 (26 February 1959): 12.
"Hoy cumpleaños Lolita." *El Nuevo Día* (Puerto Rico) (20 February 1983): 15–16.
"Humo en la boca." *El País Semanal* (Madrid) (9 March 1997): 57–60, 62–63.
"Icosaedros." *El País Semanal* (Madrid) (17 April 1977): 19.
"Imágenes de La Habana en la mirada del caminante." *Cambio 16* (Madrid) 943 (25 December 1989): 178–80.
" 'Imago Mundi' * " *El País* (Madrid) (11 June 1993): 13–14.
"In a pampas of dreams." *Guardian* (Manchester) (25 July 1990): 39.
"In search of Esmeralda." Review of *Aphorisms*, by Georg Christoph Lichtenberg. *Daily Telegraph* (London) (11 August 1990).
"In the lap of the gods." Review of *Judy Garland*, by David Shipman. *Spectator* (London) 269, 8580/8581 (19/26 December 1992): 69.
"In the midst of a tropical *mañana*." Review of *Walker Evans: Havana 1933*, with essay by Gilles Mora. *Daily Telegraph* (London) (17 December 1989).
"Include Me Out." In *Requiem for the "Boom"—Premature: A Symposium*, eds. Rose S. Minc and Marilyn R. Frankenthaler, 9–20. Montclair, NJ: Montclair State College, 1980.
"Indiana Jones y Compañía en el Templo del Mal." *El Universal* (Caracas) (22 July 1984): 4–1, 4–2. Section: Culturales.
"Infante's Inferno." Review of *Legacies: Selected Poems*, by Heberto Padilla, trans. Alastair Reid and Andrew Hurley. *London Review of Books* 4, 21 (18 November–1 December 1982): 20–22.
"Una inocente pornógrafa." *Mundo Nuevo* (Paris) 16 (October 1967): 79–86.

"El interminable reinado soviético en el ajedrez." *Cambio 16* (Madrid) 768 (18 August 1986): 90–91.

"Invasión de los colores vivos." *El País* (Madrid) (25 November 1986): 13–14.

"The Invisible Exile." In *Literature in Exile,* by John Glad, 34–40. Durham: Duke University Press, 1990.

"James Mason: Los juegos prohibidos de un villano inteligente." *Diario 16* (Madrid) (29 July 1984): IX. Suplemento cultural: Disidencias.

"El jazz en el cine." [G. Caín, pseud.] *Revolución* (Havana) 2, 88 (19 March 1959): 12.

"Joe Losey, americano." *Cambio 16* (Madrid) 657 (2 July 1984): 124–25, 127.

"John Huston y la filosofía del fracaso." In *Arcadia todas las noches*, 127–58. Barcelona: Editorial Seix Barral, 1978.

"José Miguel Rodríguez, ángel 'naïf' de la pintura con 'popgrama.'" *El País* (Madrid) (15 December 1979): 2. Section: Artes.

"Juego de los espías: realidad y ficción." *El País Semanal* (Madrid) (19 February 1978): 5.

"Julio Iglesias visto por Cabrera Infante." *El Tiempo* (Bogotá) (20 January 1985): 15–16. Supplement: Lecturas Dominicales.

"K. va al cine." *El País* (Madrid) (3 July 1983): 8–9. Supplement: 1883–1983: Centenario del nacimiento de Kafka.

"La lengua de la revolución." *Realidad* (Rome) 1, 1 (November–December 1963): 99–104.

"La letra con sangre." *Lunes de Revolución* (Havana) 104–5 (May 1961): 28–30.

"La letra con sangre entra: La configuración de la moderna mitología del vampiro." *Babelia*, Supplement of *El Pais* (Madrid) (6 February 1993): 11, 14.

"A life after The End." *Sunday Telegraph* (London) (5 August 1990): xiii.

"Listas." *El País Semanal* (Madrid) (11 September 1988): 11–16.

"Lives of a Hero." Trans. Peggy Boyers. *Salmagundi* (Saratoga Springs, N.Y.) 67 (Summer 1985): 13–33.

"Lo que este libro debe al censor." Prologue to *Tres tristes tigres,* ix–xiii. Caracas: Biblioteca Ayacucho, 1990.

"Loas a Lolita." *Vuelta* (México) 7, 76 (March 1983): 52–54.

"Lobos, licántropos y manía lupina." *Cambio 16* (Madrid) 829 (19 October 1987): 178–81.

"Londres, un paseo al pasado." *El País* (Madrid) (2 November 1986): 23–24. Section: Domingo.

"Lorca hace llover en La Habana." *Cuadernos Hispanoamericanos* (Madrid) 433–34 (July–August 1986): 241–48.

"La luna nona de Lino Novás." *Vuelta* (México) 7, 80 (July 1983): 42–43.

"La Lupe cantaba: Con el diablo en el cuerpo Y un ángel en la voz." *Diario 16* (Madrid) (30 January 1993): I–III. Suplemento semanal: Culturas.

"Lydia Cabrera." *Independent* (London) (18 November 1991): 21.

"The Lynch Mob." *El Paseante* (Madrid) 17 (1990): 117–21.

"Manet, el moderno." *El Nuevo Día* (Puerto Rico) (15 May 1983): 12–13, 15–16. Section: Domingo.

"La marcha de los hombres." *Lunes de Revolución* (Havana) 89 (4 January 1961): 39–41.

"Marilyn Monroe: renace una estrella." *Vuelta* (México) 12, 133–34 (December 1987–January 1988): 71–73.

"Martí y el exilio." *Claves* (Madrid) 52 (May 1995): 48–50, 52–54.

"Más sobre el suicidio en Cuba." *Vuelta* (México) 7, 79 (June 1983): 50–51.

"Mehr Lichtenberg en el 250 Aniversario del Feliz Nacimiento del Autor Alemán." *Vuelta* (México) 16, 190 (September 1992): 47–48.

"Lo mejor de Londres." *Gente Viajes* (Madrid) 5 (September 1988):34–44.

"Meta-End." *Latin American Literary Review* (Pittsburgh) 8, 16 (Spring–Summer 1980): 88–95.

"Meta-final." *Alacrán Azul* (Miami) 1, 1 (1970): 18–22.

"El 'metro' de Budapest." *El País* (Madrid) (9 May 1986): 58.

"Mi personaje inolvidable." *Escandalar* (Elmhurst, N.Y.) 2, 3 (July–September 1979): 8–24.

"Mi querido censor." *La Nación* (Buenos Aires) (25 September 1988): 1–2. Section: Letras, 4A.

"Un Miami de vicio." *El País Semanal* (Madrid) 472 (27 April 1986): 24–26.

"Un milagro fabricado: Joseph von Sternberg diseñó el mito de Marlene Dietrich." *Babelia,* Supplement of *El País* (Madrid) (9 May 1992): 6–7.

"Minotauromaquias." *Plural* (México) 5 (February 1972): 5–8.

"Mira más allá de la muerte." *El País* (Madrid) (11 November 1978): 25.

"Miriam Gómez va de compras." *El Nuevo Día* (Puerto Rico) (6 November 1988): 6–11.

"Mis mejores lecturas." *Diario 16* (Madrid) (20 April 1989): I–II. Section: Libros.

"El misterio de Anton Checov." *Lunes de Revolución* (Havana) 91 (16 January 1961): 16–17.

"Mis tres encuentros con un pintor." *Lunes de Revolución* (Havana) 123 (18 September 1961): 31–32.

"Mitomanía: Las barbas de Castro iniciaron una época de canción protesta y falda corta." *Babelia,* Supplement of *El País* (Madrid) (1 May 1993): 6–7.

"Mordidas del caimán barbudo." *Quimera* (Barcelona) 39–40 (July–August 1984): 66–82.

"More haunted than hunted." Review of *The Chase,* by Alejo Carpentier, trans. Alfred Mac Adam. *Sunday Review,* Supplement of *Independent on Sunday* (London) (18 March 1990): 19.

"Morritz Ravelli's Left Foot Piano Concerto." Trans. Edith Grossman. *Nimrod* (Tulsa) 26, 2 (Spring/Summer 1983): 59–61. Special issue: Latin American Voices II: After the Boom.

"¡Mucho Marlowe!" *El País* (Madrid) (2 October 1986): 1, 4. Section: Libros.

"La muerte del showman." *Carteles* (Havana) 39, 14 (6 April 1958): 30–31, 114.

"La muerte de un actor." *Carteles* (Havana) 36, 42 (16 October 1955): 44–45, 107.

"La muerte viene hacia el delator." *Mundo Nuevo* (Paris) 11 (May 1967): 36–37.

"Una mujer con talento mundano." *El País* (Madrid) (20 August 1981): 19. Section: La Cultura.

"Mujeres que ruedan." *La Nación* (Buenos Aires) (13 June 1993): 1. Section 7: Cultura.

"Música debajo de una campana de cristal." *El País* (Madrid) (15 December 1986): 11–12.

"La música viene de ninguna parte." *Hombre de Mundo* (Panama) (March 1979): 22–24.

"My Dinners with Borges." In *The Borges Tradition,* ed. Norman Thomas di Giovanni, 15–34. London: Constable and Company Limited, in association with the Anglo-Argentine Society, 1995.

"Nadie pregunta por el ballet inglés." *El País Semanal* (Madrid) (4 December 1977): 23.

"Neon High Noon." *FMR* International, English language ed. (New York) 43 (April 1990): 21–40.

"Néstor Almendros, un Oscar que habla español." *El País* (Madrid) (12 April 1979): 32.
"Ñico Saquito y el sentimiento paródico." *GQ* (Madrid) 4 (June–July 1995): 154.
"Nicolás Guillén: Poet and Partisan." *Review: Latin American Literature and Arts* (New York) 42 (January–June 1990): 31–33.
"No más fotos de Jesse." *El País* (Madrid) (23 March 1986): 10. Section: Domingo.
"¡No se tire!" [Jonás Castro, pseud.] *Carteles* (Havana) 35, 26 (27 June 1954): 16–18.
"No sólo de miedo vive el hombre." *El País* (Madrid) (14 August 1979): 40.
"No, yo no soy Humbert Humbert." *Vuelta* (México) 11, 130 (September 1987): 49–51.
"Una novela feliz." *Destino* (Barcelona) 38, 1. 998 (16–22 January 1976): 22–24.
"Nuestra música (moderna) es agria, pero . . ." *Carteles* (Havana) 39, 1 (5 January 1958): 48–50, 87–88.
"Nuestro prohombre en La Habana." *El País* (Madrid) (3 February 1983): 9–10.
"Offenbach, Bach de los bulevares." *El País* (Madrid) (16 August 1980): 7. Section: Artes.
"Oh Bahia." Trans. Alfred Mac Adam. *Review: Latin American Literature and Arts* (New York) 47 (Fall 1993): 16–19.
"Oh, Hooly-oh." *El País* (Madrid) (8 August 1983): 19.
"Orígenes (Cronología a la manera de Laurence Sterne)." In *Guillermo Cabrera Infante,* ed. Juan Ríos, 5–18. Madrid: Espiral/Editorial Fundamentos, 1974.
"Orson Welles, un genio demasiado frecuente." In *Arcadia todas las noches,* 9–58. Barcelona: Editorial Seix Barral, 1978.
"La otra cara de caracortada." *Diario 16* (Madrid) (1 April 1984): VI–VII. Suplemento semanal: Culturas.
"Otro inocente pornografo." *Mundo Nuevo* (Paris) 20 (February 1968): 51–54.
"Paisajes con Goytisolo al frente." *Quimera* (Barcelona) 27 (January 1983): 56–59.
"Paquito d'Rivera, un cubano que nació para el jazz." *El País* (Madrid) (12 December 1981): 5. Section: Artes.
"Paris vu par Guillermo Cabrera Infante." *Le Point* (Paris) 877 (10 July 1989): 75.
"Pauline's perilous pen." *Boston Sunday Globe* (17 November 1985): B27–28.
"Pax cubana." *Vuelta* (México) 18, 215 (October 1994): 55–57.
"Pepito Grillo en el vientre de la ballena." *Los Cuadernos del Norte* (Oviedo) 4, 21 (September–October 1983), 52–61. Section: Los Cuadernos de Cine.
"Peregrinaje: Hacia la Revolución." *Lunes de Revolución* (Havana) 70 (2 August 1960): 37–39.
"Un perro murciano." *Cambio 16* (Madrid) 873 (22 August 1988): 46–48.
"The Peruvian Candidate." *Guardian* (Manchester) (4 April 1990): 46.
"Piñera's Virgil." *Review: Latin American Literature and Arts* (New York) 35 (July–December 1985): 19.
"Pintura sobre ruedas." *El País* (Madrid) (21 May 1978): 24–26.
"La plus que lente." *Plural* (México) 8, 5 (February 1976): 6–9.
"Un poeta de vuelo popular." *Vuelta* (México) 14, 160 (March 1990): 45–47.
"Un poeta pervertido." Icosaedros series. *El País Semanal* (Madrid) (17 September 1978): 19.
"Un poeta popular." *Diario 16* (Madrid) (4 November 1989): VI. Suplemento semanal: Culturas.
"Polvo enamorado." *Cambio 16* (Madrid) 942 (18 December 1989): 97.
"Por el camino de West." *El País* (Madrid) (29 November 1980): 8. Section: Artes.
"Por quién doblan las películas." *Cambio 16* (Madrid) 861 (30 May 1988): 142–48.
"Por siempre Rita." *El País* (Madrid) (16 May 1987): 29.

"Portentos, magias y maravillas de la tecnología." *Cambio 16* (Madrid) 881 (17 October 1988): 190–91.
"Portrait of a Tyrant as an Aging Tyro." Forward to *Family Portrait with Fidel: A Memoir,* by Carlos Franqui, vii–xix. First American Edition. New York: Random House, 1984.
"A Portrait of Ardis Reading my Books." Preface to *Cabrera Infante in the Menippean Tradition*, by Ardis L. Nelson, xiii–xx. Hispanic Monographs. Newark, Del.: Juan de la Cuesta, 1983.
"Predicciones y predilecciones." *Cambio 16* (Madrid) 593 (11 April 1983): 98–99.
"El presentador presentado." *Vuelta* (México) 4, 38 (January 1980): 10–11.
"El prisionero político desconocido." *El País* (Madrid) (31 August 1986): 11–12.
"Prisioneros de la isla del Diablo." *El País* (Madrid) (9 August 1988): 7–8.
"Prólogo al prólogo." Preface to *La Fiesta Innombrable*, eds. Nedda G. de Anhalt et al, 7–8. Mexico: Ediciones El Tucan de Virginia, 1992.
"Puro humo." *Diario 16* (Madrid) (8 September 1985): III–VI. Suplemento semanal: Culturas.
"Puro humor." *GQ* (Madrid) 5 (August–September 1995): 138.
"¿Qué cosa es la historia, pues?" *El País* (Madrid) (26 November 1991): 13–14.
"¿Qué hay en un nombre?" *El País* (Madrid) (31 December 1986): 11.
"¿Qué le pasó a Harry d'Arrast, el genio vasco de la comedia americana?" *Cambio 16* (Madrid) 801 (6 April 1987): 150–51, 153.
"¿Quién es Ciro Bianchi y por qué está diciendo esas cosas de mí?" *Vuelta* (México) 18, 217 (December 1994): 59–64.
"¿Quién está cansado de Londres?" *El País* (Madrid) (1 June 1987): 13–14.
"¿Quién inventó esa cosa loca?" *Babelia*, Supplement of *El País* (Madrid) (30 August 1997): 4–5.
"¿Quién mató a Calvert Casey?" *Quimera* (Barcelona) 26 (December 1982): 42–53.
"Ravaging roaches." Review of *Driving through Cuba: an East-West Journey,* by Carlo Gébler. *Daily Telegraph* (London) (23 July 1988): VIII.
"Recuento fílmico de 1953." [G. Caín, pseud.] *Carteles* (Havana) 35, 3 (17 January 1954): 93–96.
"Un recuerdo infantil de Stevenson." *El País Semanal* (Madrid) (6 November 1983): 3.
"Remington Visits With Edison." *American Film* 11, 4 (New York) (January–February 1986): 14, 52–53.
"Renace una estrella." *Cambio 16* (Madrid) 818 (3 August 1987): 88–91.
"Repeticiones de amor del arte del ajedrez." *Cambio 16* (Madrid) 767 (11 August 1986): 90–93.
"¿Réquiem por Pablo?" *Lunes de Revolución* (Havana) 42 (11 January 1959): 2.
"La resurrección de los 'Teds.'" Icosaedros series. *El País Semanal* (Madrid) (9 October 1977): 20.
"El retiro." *El País* (Madrid) (7 March 1987): 9.
"Un retrato." *El País* (Madrid) (26 August 1979): IV–V. Section: Arte y Pensamiento.
"Un retrato de Jesse." *El Miami Herald* (26 March 1986): 17.
"Retrato del artista comisario." *El País* (Madrid) (24 January 1988): 13.
"Retrato del artista como coleccionista: en la muerte de John Kobal." *El País* (Madrid) (31 October 1991): 38.
"Retrato del artista ya maduro." *Cambio 16* (Madrid) 667 (10 September 1984): 74–75.
"Un retrato familiar." *Revista de la Universidad de México* (México) Nueva Época. 37, 6 (October 1981): 2–6.

"Las revelaciones epistolares de James Joyce." *El País* (Madrid) (20 November 1977): III. Section: Arte y Pensamiento.
"Un rey absolutamente necesario." *El País* (Madrid) (27 April 1986): 6. Section: Domingo.
"The Riddle of Arenas." Review of *The Assault*, by Reinaldo Arenas. *Spectator* (London) 274, 8705 (13 May 1995): 38–39.
"The Rock and the Moon Pope." *Miami Herald. Tropic Travel: A Special Issue* (6 October 1985): 34–37, 41.
"Rompiendo la barrera del ruido." In *Guillermo Cabrera Infante*, ed. Rosa M. Pereda, 249–56. Escritores de todos los tiempos 3. Madrid: EDAF, 1978.
"Rosa Eslavida en el año 2000." *Visión* (Mexico) (15 November 1975): 72, 75.
"A Rumba Dance on a Grave." Trans. Alfred Mac Adam. *Review: Latin American Literature and Arts* (New York) 48 (Spring 1994): 90–91.
"Saliendo volando de Río de Janeiro." *El País* (Madrid) (19 September 1988): 13.
"Salsa para una ensalada." In *Literatures in Transition: The Many Voices of the Caribbean Area,* ed. Rose S. Minc, 21–36. Gaithersburg, Md.: Hispamérica, Montclair State College, 1982.
"Un saludo a todos menos uno." *Linden Lane Magazine* (Princeton) 1, 2 (April–June 1982): 5.
"Sartre, una entrevista entre recuerdos." *Carteles* (Havana) 41, 12 (20 March 1960): 36–37, 80.
"Scenario: O de la novela al cine sin pasar por la pantalla." *Revista de Occidente* (Madrid) 40 (September 1984): 7–19.
"Los secundarios." *Movies* (New York) 1, 2 (August 1983): 34–38.
"Seseribo." *Casa de las Américas* (Havana) 5, 32 (September–October 1965): 43–59.
"Sherlock Holmes contra Conan Doyle." Icosaedros series. *El País Semanal* (Madrid) (24 September 1978): 28.
"Si te dicen que cayeron: Minnelli y Cary Grant." *Cambio 16* (Madrid) 789 (12 January 1987): 62–64.
"Sic semper Gloria." *Festival* (San Sebastián) 30th ed. (23 September 1982): 3.
" 'Sic transit' Gloria Grahame." *El País* (Madrid) (17 October 1981): 4. Section: Artes.
"Sing a song of sin." Review of *My Life,* by Marlene Dietrich, trans. Salvator Attanasio. *Weekend Telegraph* (London) (29 April 1989), xiv.
"Slot City." *FMR* Italian ed. (Milan) 79 (2 March 1990): 21–40.
"Sobre una tumba una rumba." *El País* (Madrid) (12 June 1993): 33.
"Una sola unión contra todas las amenazas." *Lunes de Revolución* (Havana) 90 (9 January 1961): 2–3.
"Las sombras me encontraban insomne." *Diario 16* (Madrid) (3 May 1987): III. Suplemento semanal: Culturas.
"Una sonatina letal." *El País Semanal* (Madrid) (22 February 1998): 10.
"Lo splash più grande." *FMR* Italian ed. (Milan) 9, 88 (1991): 5–12.
"*Star Trek,* película para el 80." *El País Semanal* (Madrid) (13 January 1980): 24–27.
"Surtido de libros." *El Nuevo Herald* (Miami) (19 March 1994): 13A.
"Talent of 2WO Cities." *Review: Latin American Literature and Arts* (New York) 35 (July–December 1985): 17–18.
"Tall failures in an outpost of progress." Review of *Death in Chile,* by Tony Gould. *Guardian* (Manchester) (6 August 1992): 24.
"The Taming of the Shrewd." Review of *Kissing Kate* by Barbara Leaming. *Spectator* 275, 8720 (London) (26 August 1995): 27–28.

"El Tennessee desemboca en La Habana." [G. Caín, pseud.] *Revolución* (Havana) 2, 106 (9 April 1959): 2.

"Texts/con/Texts." Trans. Gregory Kolovakos. *Review* 76 (New York) 19 (Winter 1976): 72.

"Thomson's Gazette and cats." Reviews of *A Biographical Dictionary of Film,* 3rd ed., by David Thomson; and *The MacMillan International Film Encyclopedia,* 2nd ed., by Ephriam Katz. *Spectator* (London) (31 December 1994): 26–27.

"To Kill a Foreign Name." *World Literature Today* 61, 4 (Autumn 1987): 531–34.

"To the heart of the dark." Review of *The Storyteller,* by Mario Vargas Llosa. *Sunday Telegraph* (London) (8 April 1990).

"Todo está escrito con espejos." *Vuelta* (México) 1, 6 (May 1977): 7–8.

"Todos cantaban boleros." *Babelia*, Supplement of *El País* (Madrid) (22 March 1997): 4–5.

"Tórtolos en Torcello." *GQ* (Madrid) 10 (June–July 1996): 130.

"Tras vestidos." *GQ* (Madrid) 8 (February–March 1996): 130.

"Tres en uno." Introduction to *Delito por bailar el chachachá*, 9–10. Madrid: Alfaguara, 1995.

"Tres eran (son) tres." *27 Setmana Internacional de Cinema de Barcelona* (17–23 June 1985): 16–17.

"*Tres tristes tigres.*" *Mundo Nuevo* (Paris) 11 (May 1967): 28–36.

"Las tribulaciones del alumno yentl." *Diario 16* (Madrid) (15 April 1984): VI–VII. Suplemento semanal: Culturas.

"La última traición de Manuel Puig." *El País* (Madrid) (24 July 1990): 22–23.

"Und was ist mit meinen Kuba?" *NZZ Folio* (Zurich) 2 (February 1992): 46–51.

"Unida como otro cualquiera." *Lunes de Revolución* (Havana) 100 (27 March 1960): 9–12.

"The Unknown Political Prisoner." In *Soho Square III,* ed. and trans. Alberto Manguel, 112–15. London: Bloomsbury Publishing, 1990.

"Valentino vivo." *Cambio 16* (Madrid) 821 (24 August 1987): 86–87.

"Vampiros, Vampiras y Vampiresas." *Hombre de Mundo* (Panama) (February 1979): 22–25.

"¡Vaya Papaya!" In *¡Vaya Papaya! Ramón Alejandro,* text by Guillermo Cabrera Infante, 3–10. Angers: Le Polygraphe, 1992.

"Vengan bailando." Icosaedros series. *El País Semanal* (Madrid) (4 September 1977): 11.

"La venganza a caballo." *El Nuevo Día* (Puerto Rico) (29 March 1987): 16–18. Section: Domingo.

"Vera efigies de un autor de ficciones." Prologue to *Discontinuidad y ruptura en Guillermo Cabrera Infante,* by Isabel Álvarez-Borland, ix–xii. Gaithersburg, Md.: Ediciones Hispamérica, 1982.

"Verso, anverso, reverso en *Pale Fire.*" *El Pais* (Madrid) (1 May 1986):1–6. Section: Libros.

"Las vértebras de España." *Lunes de Revolución* (Havana) 96 (20 February 1961): 2–3.

"El viajero que no cesa." *El Nuevo Herald* (Miami) (25 April 1994): 13A.

"Vida y muerte de un poeta cortesano." Icosaedros series. *El País Semanal* (Madrid) (15 May 1977) 11, 29.

"Vidas para leerlas." *Vuelta* (México) 4, 41 (April 1980): 4–16.

"El viejo y el mar." *GQ* (Madrid) 9 (April–May 1996): 138.

"Visión de Nueva York: Metrópolis revisitada." *Vanidades Continental* (Miami) 18, 21 (17 October 1978): 84–87.

"Una visita real: La reina en Neuva York." *Carteles* (Havana) 38, 44 (3 November 1957): 38–41.

"¡Viva Berlin! . . . y vive todavía." *Cambio 16* (Madrid) 866 (4 July 1988): 116–17, 119–20.

"Voces cubanas." *Linden Lane Magazine* (Princeton) 9, 4 (October–December 1990): 3.

"La voz de su autómata." *El Nuevo Día* (Puerto Rico) (23 April 1989): 6–11. Section: Domingo.

"La vuelta de Jack el Destripador." *El País* (Madrid) (19 March 1978): 34–36.

"¿Vuelven los 'hippies?' " *El País* (Madrid) (26 June 1986): 11–12.

"Vuelve Drácula." *El País Semanal* (Madrid) (3 December 1978): 1–8.

"Wagner contra Wagner." *Cambio 16* (Madrid) 585 (14 February 1983): 93–95.

"Wallis, la americana que quiso ser reina y casi lo fue." *El País* (Madrid) (7 November 1980): 35.

"Why we are all born either Quixotes or Sanchos." Review of *Cervantes,* by Jean Canavaggio, trans. J. R. Jones. *Sunday Telegraph* (London) (26 August 1990).

"The Women, Little Women, but not The Marrying Kind." Review of *George Cukor: A Double Life,* by Patrick McGilligan. *Spectator* (London) (4 July 1992): 34–35.

"Y de mi Cuba ¿Qué?" *Claves* (Madrid) 22 (May 1992): 24–28.

"¡Y que gane el mejor!" *Diario 16* (Madrid) (9 April 1984): 32–33. Section: Espectáculos.

"Yo también conocí a Samuel Fuller." *Hombre de Mundo* (Panama) (May 1974): 22–24.

"You can always tell." *Fiction* (New York) 6, 3 (15 September 1981): 54–66.

"Un zapatero prodigioso." Cambio 16 (Madrid) 835 (30 November 1987): 182–83.

Index

◆

Contributors

Nedda G. de Anhalt is a writer and critic who was born in Havana, Cuba, and lives in Mexico City. She is the author of two books of interviews with Cuban writers in exile: *Rojo y naranja sobre rojo* (1991) and *Dile que pienso en ella* (1999). Her other publications include *Cine: La gran seducción* (1991), *Allá donde ves la neblina* (1992), and three books of short stories: *El correo del azar* (1984), *El banquete* (1991), and *Cuentos ináuditos* (1991).

Richard D. Cacchione is a bibliographer and poet who resides in New York City. He is currently researching materials on several Cuban and Italian authors, including a major annotated bibliography on Guillermo Cabrera Infante. He has published articles on Lydia Cabrera and Giovanni Batista Amendola and the book *Blanca Varela: Voz fuerte, voz sensible: Bibliografía anotada* (1999).

Carlos Cuadra is assistant professor of Spanish at the Stephen F. Austin University in Nacogdoches, Texas. His area of research is Guillermo Cabrera Infante and twentieth-century Hispanic poetry, especially Félix de Azúa, Virgilio Piñera, and Eduardo Espina.

Kenneth Hall is professor of Spanish at the University of North Dakota. His publications include *Guillermo Cabera Infante and the Cinema* (1989), *John Woo: Painting the True Colors of the Hero* (1999), and articles on Latin American narrative. He has translated *Mea Cuba* (1994), Cabrera Infante's political essays, and *Un oficio del siglo veinte* (1963) [*A Twentieth Century Job (1991)*], Cabrera Infante's film criticism.

Regina Janes is professor of English at Skidmore College and philosophy editor for the *Scriblerian*. She is the author of: *Gabriel García Márquez: Revolutions in Wonderland* (1981) and *On One Hundred Years of Solitude: Modes of Reading* (1991). She has published articles and interviews with contemporary Latin American writers Alejo Carpentier, Guillermo Cabrera Infante, Carlos Fuentes, and Mario Vargas Llosa, and on numerous eighteenth-century subjects.

Suzanne Jill Levine is professor of Latin American literature at the University of California, Santa Barbara. In 1996 she was a Guggenheim Fellow and received the Gregory Kolovakos PEN Award for career achievement as translator of Hispanic literature, including the works of Guillermo Cabrera Infante, Manual Puig, Adolfo Bioy Casares, Severo Sarduy, and José Donoso. She is cotranslator of *The Selected Essays of Jorge Luis Borges* (1999) and she is currently writing a literary biography of Manuel Puig.

William Luis is professor of Spanish at Vanderbilt University, where his teaching and research focus on Latin American, Caribbean, Afro-Hispanic, and U.S. Latino literature. His publications include *Literary Bondage: Slavery in Cuban Narrative* (1990) and *Dance between Two Cultures: Latino Caribbean Literature Written in the United States* (1997). He was a visiting professor at Yale University in 1998.

Lydia Rubio is a Cuban artist who has lived in Miami since 1987. Her paintings of narrative sequences and word-image connections have been widely shown and reviewed. The cover piece of this book, *Barco de Aire (1995)*, is part of the *Written on Water* exhibition, a series of 45 paintings and sculptures inspired by the Cuban boat exodus of 1994. She is represented by Bridgewater Lustberg Gallery in New York.

Raymond D. Souza is professor of Spanish at the University of Kansas and author of five books and 45 articles on Spanish-American literature. His most recent book is *Guillermo Cabrera Infante: Two Islands, Many Worlds* (1996). He has chaired the department of Spanish and Portuguese at the University of Kansas and served as president of the Association of Colombianists from 1987 to 1989.

Justo C. Ulloa and Leonor A. Ulloa are professors of Spanish at Virginia Polytechnic Institute and Radford University, respectively. They have published jointly on José Lezama Lima, Severo Sarduy, Octavio Smith, Samuel Feijóo, and Rodríguez Feo. Justo is editor in chief of *Cuban Literary Studies*, and Leonor is founder and editor of *MIFLC Review*. In 1998 Leonor was named Commonwealth Distinguished Professor.

The Editor

Ardis L. Nelson is professor of Spanish and chair of the department of foreign languages at East Tennessee State University, where she teaches Hispanic cinema and Spanish-American literature. She is the author of *Cabrera Infante in the Menippean Tradition* (1983) and numerous articles on Guillermo Cabrera Infante and Central American writers Carmen Naranjo and Juan Felipe Toruño.